SCENES FOR MANDARINS

Translations from the Asian Classics

SCENES FOR MANDARINS

The Elite Theater of the Ming

Cyril Birch

NEW YORK

Columbia University Press

Columbia University Press

New York   Chichester, West Sussex

Copyright © 1995 Columbia University Press

All rights reserved

Library of Congress Cataloging-in-Publication Data

Birch, Cyril, 1925–

Scenes for mandarins : the elite theater of the Ming / [translated
with commentaries by] Cyril Birch.

p.   cm. — (Translations from the Asian classics)

Includes bibliographical references.

ISBN 0-231-10262-3

1. Chinese drama—Ming dynasty, 1368–1644—History and criticism.
2. China—Social life and customs—960–1644.   I. Title.
II. Series.

PL2386.B57   1995

895.1'24609—dc20   95-3382
                                                        CIP

Casebound editions of Columbia University Press books are printed on
permanent and durable acid-free paper.

Printed in the United States of America

c   10   9   8   7   6   5   4   3   2   1
p   10   9   8   7   6   5   4   3   2   1

For Dorothy,
who has loved to watch these plays,
and for our grandchildren
Alison, Ben, and Michael,
who surely will.

CONTENTS

Illustrations   *xi*

Acknowledgments   *xiii*

INTRODUCTION
To the Reader as Fellow Mandarin   1

THE WHITE RABBIT AND THE NEGLECTED WIFE
The *White Rabbit* Plays   21

Two Icons of Xi Shi, Legendary Beauty: 61

XI SHI AS INNOCENCE
Liang Chenyu's *The Girl Washing Silk*   63

XI SHI AS EXPERIENCE
Shan Ben's *The Plantain Kerchief*   107

THE PLIGHT OF THE AMOROUS GHOST
Tang Xianzu's *The Peony Pavilion*   141

A QUIZ FOR-LOVE
Wu Bing's *The Green Peony*   183

BIGAMY UNABASHED
Ruan Dacheng's *The Swallow Letter*   219

Notes   *249*

Suggested Readings   *255*

ILLUSTRATIONS

The White Rabbit: The cruel Sister-in-law beats Tertia.   20–21

The Girl Washing Silk: Xi Shi dances.   62

The Girl Washing Silk: Xi Shi dances before the Queen of Yue.   86–87

The Girl Washing Silk: Xi Shi and her maidens gather lotus.   96–97

The Plantain Kerchief: Frailty and Long Xiang quarrel on their
wedding night.   106–107

The Plantain Kerchief: Frailty and Long Xiang are spied on by Frailty's
mother and maid.   126–127

The Peony Pavilion: Bridal Du, in spirit form, arrives at the gate of Liu
Mengmei's studio.   140

The Green Peony: Gu Can and Liu Wuliu wait while Che Shanggong
makes his excuses before the examiner Shen Zhong.   182

The Swallow Letter: The parents-in-law of Huo Duliang urge him to make
peace with his two wives, and Governor Jia arrives bearing the imperial
proclamation of investiture for all—the classic comic grand finale.   218

ACKNOWLEDGMENTS

Any misinterpretations in this book are my own. For what I have correctly understood I am indebted to many people, too many to name individually, but including:

- colleagues at Berkeley and across the country, and the students who took part in my seminars;
- drama specialists in Taiwan, and in Beijing, Shanghai and other Chinese cities;
- the actors and musicians both professional and amateur whose dedication has preserved and fostered the high traditions of the Chinese theater.

The notes at the end are mostly references that will make clear what I have borrowed from the work of other scholars. In general I have kept notes to a minimum, preferring to incorporate explanatory material in introductions and commentaries and within the texts of my translations themselves.

I am grateful to the Woodrow Wilson International Center for Scholars and to the Institute of Chinese Studies, Chinese University of Hong Kong, for research opportunities and support; and to Jennifer Crewe and Joan McQuary of Columbia University Press for their enthusiastic and skillful assistance.

The illustrations, from contemporary woodblock prints, are reproduced courtesy of the East Asian Library, Berkeley, to whose invaluable help over the years I am deeply indebted; and of the Palace Museum, Taipei; the Classics Press, Yangzhou; and the Hsueh-sheng and Ming-wen Book Companies, Taipei.

The *White Rabbit* chapter was previously published in *Chinese Literature: Essays in honor of James I. Crump* (Ann Arbor, Mich.: Center for Chinese Studies, 1993). Some of the material in the *Peony Pavilion* chapter appeared in *Interpreting Culture Through Translation: A Festschrift for D. C. Lau* (Hong Kong: Chinese University Press, 1991). The translated scenes from *The Swallow Letter* appeared in *Renditions*, no. 40 (Autumn 1993).

SCENES FOR MANDARINS

Introduction

Four hundred years ago few foreigners visited the ancient city of Suzhou on the Grand Canal, or the "southern capital," Nanjing, or the other cities of the lower Yangzi valley. Even fewer would ever have received an invitation to a social gathering in the private residence of a mandarin. But in order to explain the nature and purpose of this book I am asking you to imagine your way into exactly this very improbable situation.

Today is the birthday of our friend the provincial governor, and you and I are to join a small group of our fellow mandarins to help him celebrate. The premises of his official yamen will be quieter than usual—no court session today, no milling throng of petitioners, no troops to review, no executions scheduled, no tax accounts to audit, no traveling inspector to entertain. But there will be plenty of activity in the spacious recesses of his private quarters. He will want his gardens to look their best, the paths swept and the bamboos and blooming tree-peonies displayed to perfection on this already sultry late spring day. The banquet will be choice—his cook has a subtle touch with our local lake fish—and we shall be cool enough because it will be served in the new open-sided hall he has added for summer use. And there will be a play.

I have seen the new hall already. More like a large pavilion, quite spacious, and a graceful addition to the general lines of the residence, with its crimson pillars and lightly curving gray-tiled eaves. The playhouse gives the effect of an extension of the hall on a smaller scale. It too is open-sided, but marked off by a low balustrade. The raised stage will give us a good view of the players as we sit at table in the main body of the hall, comfortably ensconced on large porcelain stools—nothing so grateful on a humid afternoon as the cool of porcelain through one's silk gown.

It will all be very intimate: half a dozen actors of the governor's household troupe, a trio of musicians in accompaniment, flute, lute, and wooden clappers at the side of the stage. However, since you, my friend, like myself, are from a foreign country, I have had the forethought to write this introduction to explain what I have learned about the background to the kind of performance that will be given today. And since, unlike myself, you have not had the good fortune to be taught the Chinese language, I have translated into English a few of the scenes from which today's selection is likely to be made. It is not entirely a representative selection. Our friend the governor has a preference for light domestic comedy, with plenty of wit in the dialogue and some good poetry in the arias. But some of the scenes are actually masterpieces of our time at the turn of the seventeenth century, this time which in years to come will surely be known as a golden age of the drama in China.

The difficulty with what this book tries to do is not the suggesting of ambience, the describing of music or costume or balletic grace of movement—from a few hints now and again, your imagination will fill in all this rich and necessary background. The question will be, what is this all about? What is bothering these elegant young people, who is this terrifying monarch, where did this bumbling buffoon come from, what is the situation here? This, we know, is poetic drama, lyrical opera—can cold printed English give us the clue to its verbal beauties? It is comedy, we are told—what are they saying that's so amusing?

I try to answer these questions by translating scenes from some half a dozen plays of the late Ming repertoire. At various points the translation will need to be accompanied by commentary to interpret allusions or to explain certain peculiarities of cultural background. To make sense, the isolated scene will need to be placed in the context of the play it represents, but the scene itself, and not the play as a whole, will be our primary focus.

I have two reasons for this concentration on individual scenes. They were the building blocks of which the plays were composed; and more often than not they were performed as separate pieces. The audience would know enough about the story to understand what was happening in this particular scene, at this particular point of the action. The more literate among the playgoers would quite likely have read the texts: if not of whole plays, then a handful of highlight scenes, and if not whole scenes, then at least a selection of arias. Anthologies of popular scenes and handbooks of model arias (*qupu*), with titles like "New Pipes from Jade Valley" or "Rare Notes Plucked from Brocade," were compiled and published with increasing frequency from the middle of the Ming period onward. In the twentieth century many of these have been tracked down in libraries across the world and photographically reproduced, most notably in the monumental *Shanben xiqu congkan* series, over a hundred volumes all told, edited under the direction of Wang Ch'iu-kuei and published in Taipei beginning in 1984.

Moreover, even mandarins and their families at New Years or other times of holiday would not necessarily have either the time or the inclination to give up the couple of days that would be required to sit through an entire play from start to finish. In this respect the drama of the late Ming mandarins was quite distinct from earlier forms of Chinese theater. The *zaju*, or "variety show," of the preceding Yuan dynasty, for example, when the Chinese drama for the first time reached the heights of excellence, was of the normal sort of length to be performed in a single evening. It had a structure of four acts, each built around a song-set of ten or so arias.

The Ming *chuanqi* play (the word translates as "romance") was a different matter entirely. It could run to forty or fifty scenes or more, and although the lengths varied considerably it was possible for an individual major scene to be as substantial as an entire act of a Yuan *zaju*. Plays of the *chuanqi* romance kind told stories taken from old legend, from history, from existing tale or ballad, or from the author's imagination. But whatever the source, the action of the play was likely to be fairly complicated. It could involve a score or more of personages, and no matter what the theme, at the center of every play there invariably stood a couple of lovers, who in most cases would be the principal singers, the stars of the performance.

By convention the *chuanqi* play, the Ming dramatic romance, opens with a prologue in which a minor character sings a brief résumé of the events to be dramatized. The action begins only in scene 2, when the first important character of the play now appears. He is the young hero, the juvenile lead as he would be known in English repertory theater. He introduces himself directly to the audience, and in arias and monologue describes his situation in life, his aspirations and fears. In scene 3 the heroine follows suit, probably in the company of her parents. Most probably she has not yet met the hero. Each subsequent scene takes the action one step further. It presents one, two, or a small number of characters in a specific location. Since no sets are used this may be a garden, a boudoir, a jail cell, a mountain-top, heaven or hell or the bottom of the sea—or any place imaginable, and the people on stage can change locations any time they wish by merely promenading in a circle and announcing where they have now arrived.

A scene can be quite short, it can even consist of dialogue (or monologue) alone without any singing, providing simply a means of narrative transition from one event to another. If the hero is a young scholar headed for the ranks of officialdom, for example, and must leave his pursuit of the heroine to go to the capital to sit for state examination, there will be a scene of leave-taking, then a transitional scene in which the hero describes the rigors and pleasures of the road, then in due course (after perhaps some attention to other characters in the interim) an examination scene. Many more scenes will intervene before the results are announced and celebration fills the stage (since naturally our hero will have passed, high on the list of successful candidates). Major scenes involve the principal characters in action central to the plot. Other scenes can be comic, martial, lyrical, or mixed, and at some point (and usually at the end of the play as well) there will be an occasion for a grand scene, in which a large cast of actors, gorgeously costumed in court or other ceremonial robes, celebrates reunion, climactic development, or a grand finale to the action.

I should explain at this point that I am using the word "actors" as a convenient generic without reference to gender. Both sexes performed before the mandarins. Women have, it is true, been officially banned from the stage at various times in the long history of China. This was the case notably around the turn of the present century, when the art of the female impersonator probably reached its final apogee. But even though bans might protect the morals of audiences in the public theaters of the crowded cities, none could in any case have had much effect within the confines of a mandarin's own private quarters. He was free to foster whatever histrionic talents he could discover among his own servants, male or female, infant or adult. If he could afford it, he could follow the lead of Qian Dai (1541–1622), who in his early forties retired from his post as censor, built a villa modeled on that of the great Tang poet Wang Wei, and there kept a troupe of actresses to perform his favorite plays—*The West Chamber, The Lute,* and the plays of Tang Xianzu.[1] Otherwise he might import troupes from outside, and these could be male, female, or mixed—they might well include the notorious *guanji* or "officially registered entertainers," whose obligation it was to serve whenever required at official functions. And acting ability was only a part of the performer's appeal. There is a hint of other forms of exploitation in a diary entry by Zhang Dai (1597–?1684), whose memoirs are thick with references to plays he has seen. Zhang was an unabashed hedonist who composed his own epitaph, describing himself as "a devotee of the study, of pretty slave-girls and lovely boys, of fine dishes, noble steeds, colorful lanterns, fireworks, acting troupes, music; a tea-maniac and an orange-fanatic, a bookworm and a poetry-demon."

Ruan Dacheng, author of the play *The Swallow Letter,* from which the last of our translated scenes is selected, was only one of numerous mandarins who not only enjoyed the drama and contributed to its literature but themselves kept troupes of actors within their own households. They would choose their servants ("slaves" is not too strong a term, given the facts of purchase and the absence of legal rights) for the promise they showed of personal beauty and quality of voice. The mandarins would even participate in their training as actors, since they themselves, with their womenfolk, were the models and arbiters of dignified deportment and cultivated taste. Zhang Dai describes how Ruan Dacheng, directing his household actors in plays of his own composition, would explain the significance of every stage movement, every piece of clowning, every glance and gesture.

I have already mentioned that the stage for our play will be equipped with neither sets nor curtains. The audience knows the scene has ended when the actors leave their red carpet to retire behind a screen. A new actor appears, and the audience awaits his or her first aria which (at least in the early scenes) will most likely describe a new venue—garden or ruined temple or roadside inn or whatever—in concise concrete images that recall the lyric tradition of the great ages of poetry, the dynasties of Tang and Song. The language is refined, the melodies strictly prescribed, the movements of the actors under exquisite control, and yet the whole occasion is so intimate that the mandarin and his friends, for whose eyes and ears it has all been devised, can feel themselves involved in a way hard to imagine for a devotee of grand opera.

I once spent some time in an office decorated with a poster advertising the great Metropolitan Opera of New York. The poster showed an imagined cutaway view of the Met in mid-performance. A packed audience of thousands, tier upon tier from stalls to balcony, peering over the heads of a large orchestra toward a stage peopled with costumed courtiers and clerics. These colorful personages distribute themselves neatly in groups around a set that incorporates a Ruritanian embassy staircase, a gothic chapel, arches, and spires. The poster's vantage-point is in mid-air outside and behind the opera house, so that thanks to the cutaways we can see the entire elaborate machinery from which depend the elements of the set, the curtains, flats, backdrops, and so on. Behind the onstage set, invisible to the audience, ready for the following night's production, is an entire sailing-ship, perhaps waiting for Tristan and Isolde to languish melodiously on its sloping deck. A Nile barge is off to one side, in danger of denting its prow against a Montmartre tenement building. Various other sets and flats are being constructed and painted in the cavernous basements. We can peek into numerous closets and cubbyholes, all the way up the gargantuan building, gaining glimpses of plumbing fixtures and typists, wardrobe assistants and coffee machines, and everywhere, little knots of people in ceaseless prosecution of the activity of this theater that is a city in itself.

As my eyes roamed over this poster I would find it irresistible to recall what would face my mandarins. Perhaps a garden pavilion, rising a foot or two above the waters of a small artificial lake. Just room enough on its carpeted floor for two or three actors to move (slowly, gracefully) upstage and down, while flautist and pipa player squeeze themselves into the background. In an open-fronted lodge across a few feet of water a select audience of a dozen or so sit at their ease as the sinuous melodies wind through the summer afternoon. Or perhaps it is evening, and dishes are being served by the light of oil-lamps and candles in the reception hall of the Prefect's residence. The guests' tables are so arranged as to provide the best possible view of the actors as they emerge from behind screens to perform their play on the few square yards of carpeted floor.

IMPERIAL AND PUBLIC THEATERS

Of course I am deliberately exaggerating the contrast—there were other ways to watch theater in China, more crowded and sweaty by far. Historians of the drama have described the Ming period as a time when the entire nation was mad about the theater. The news that a play was being put on could attract an audience anywhere in China, at any level of society, in any convenient location from village temple to city tea shop to emperor's private apartments. Plays about heroes, saints, deserted wives, or separated lovers spoke to millions, so vividly and so persistently that a succession of emperors from the founder of the dynasty onward issued decrees in attempts to regulate what was being performed. It is doubtful that these had much effect, beyond getting a few actor-managers in trouble for obscenity, or for endangering public safety by packing too big a crowd into too small a space, or for the lèse-majesté of impersonating, in the face of prohibition, an actual emperor on stage.

Not that the imperial family itself had anything against theatricals. On the contrary, one imperial prince, Zhu Youdun, was an accomplished playwright, author of the still-extant *Perfumed Sachet (Xiangnangyuan)* and some thirty other pieces.[2] Another, Zhu Quan, was an authority on theatrical history and the requirements of performance. Some of the emperors themselves were avid fans of the theater. At least one, Xizong, is recorded as having himself taken part in a court entertainment, playing the role of the founding emperor of an earlier dynasty, the Song. Through most of its three centuries of existence the Ming court maintained companies of hundreds of actors capable of presenting operas of different musical styles from the various regions of the country. And when actors palled, puppets could always provide a novelty. *The History of the Ming Palace* describes an unlikely kind of stage:

> A rectangular wooden tank three feet deep, ten feet long, and several feet in width, waterproofed with a tin lining and filled two-thirds full with water. This rested on benches and was backed by silk screens. . . . Live fish, shrimps, crabs, periwinkles, frogs, and eels played in the water and among the duckweed and water lilies floating on its surface.

Small bamboo rafts supported wooden puppets that stood as much as two feet tall, "barbarian kings, immortals, generals and their troops, figures male and female." Drums beat and music played as the puppeteers from behind the screens paraded and battled their charges, and a master of ceremonies directed the proceedings with a gong, describing the action and furnishing dialogue.[3]

Intriguing as it sounds, this particular puppet entertainment was evidently a small-scale affair, perhaps for the amusement of a few of the royal children. At the other end of the scale were lavish spectacles involving whole troupes of performers on stages equipped with trapdoors and other mechanical devices to bring immortals down from the sky or demons up from hell. One such extravaganza was mounted, during the Qing dynasty, as a birthday celebration for the Qianlong emperor (reigned 1736–1796), at his summer palace in Jehol. The stage rose three stories high and accommodated live camels and horses. These came in useful, since the performances—which continued through ten days—involved episodes from such fictional fantasies as *The Journey to the West (Xiyouji)*, the epic narrative of the Tang dynasty monk who conquered deserts and demons to bring the holy sutras from India to China. There was literally a cast of thousands: a god on entering would be preceded by a series of processions, each of several score of youths identical in height. Upon the climactic appearance of the Maitreya Buddha himself, thousands of extras in no less than nine tiers attended him.[4]

And at the other end of the *social* scale from the imperial court was the village. It was here that one might come nearest to the roots of drama, whose first practitioners in China as elsewhere were not so much entertainers as religious celebrants. Any village of more than a handful of huts had its altar to the god of the soil, and a place of any size might have a temple dedicated to the Dragon King, or to any one of hundreds of Daoist divinities, with perhaps an imposing Buddhist monastery in the vicinity as well.

Festivals throughout the year would see one or other of these shrines exploding with firecrackers to ward off evil spirits, and putting on whatever finery it could muster to encourage the advent of prosperity. Most conspicuous among the celebrations would be the play, performed by the young men of the village, or by whatever strolling troupe the local community could afford to invite. A modern anthropologist evokes for us the scene at a Hong Kong temple festival of recent years. The typical village of late Ming times may have been a good deal less prosperous, but the excitement of the play was surely no less:

> At the temple festivals, which take place annually (or biennially) on the so-called birthday of the god to whom the temple is dedicated, the performances have a specifically religious rationale: they are given for the delectation of the god himself, a kind of birthday present. Usually a temporary mat-shed is erected, facing the main entrance of the temple and about a hundred yards away from it. The image of the god may be brought out, or moved forward, so that he / she can have a better view. The playhouse comprises a stage raised about five feet above ground level, with greenrooms behind, and a huge roof—reminiscent of the Big Top at a circus—stretching across most of the space between the stage and the temple. . . .
>
> At such times a village is literally transformed. . . . A normal population of between three and four hundred, occupying a dozen houses and up to thirty boats, swelled to something over eight thousand with at least five hundred boats. The single drab street along the shore of a fairly remote small island was suddenly filled with lively, colorful, noisy, smelly (incense and the smoke of firecrackers) processions, hawkers and peddlers of several kinds, street performances by lion dancers, and an enormous proliferation of dubiously legal, wildly exciting forms of public gambling. Three teahouses appeared overnight, providing at very reasonable prices food of a kind normally available only in town. All this, and the organization, preparation, and expense involved, are what a villager has in mind when he invites you to visit him "when we next do plays."[5]

Stage and deity, in fact, have a two-way association. The temple, home of the god or goddess, takes care to provide a place for a stage, either permanent or makeshift: every temple, in this sense, is also a theater. Conversely, every theater is a temple. No traditional green room, however modest, will be without its shrine, portable in the case of the traveling troupe. No traditional actor goes on stage without an obeisance before this shrine, and no audience expects a performance to begin without the "Heavenly Officer Bestows

Blessing," a short ritual dance by an actor wearing a mask that beams with benevolence.

In China, as in the world of the theater everywhere, inanimate objects can take on associations that are nothing short of sacred. Even a wooden, tassel-hung, stage-prop executioner's sword can be venerated, if it is the sword that has been used to behead Yang Jisheng in the famous scene 16 of *Cry of the Phoenix (Mingfengji)*. Yang Jisheng is a historical figure who led an abortive attempt to overthrow the villainous sixteenth-century Chief Minister Yan Song. *Cry of the Phoenix* portrays Yang as one of those courageous loyal servants of the throne whose willingness to suffer death itself for the truth's sake is one of the glories of Chinese history. In an early scene the sycophantic Zhao Wenhua advises Yang:

> In times like these a man should study the cricket. If it keeps its mouth shut and its tongue well-hidden it can live in peace and be secure wherever it is. If it still insists on opening its mouth it is asking for death.

To which Yang responds:

> What man can avoid death? The cricket singing on an ancient bough at least dies clean and undefiled. The fly trapped in a muddy pit may well keep its mouth shut, but its death is a degradation.

Given lines like these, it is little wonder that Yang enjoys a saintly reputation. His on-stage execution takes place in the usual way: he kneels, close to the exit stage-left, the sword swishes close to his neck, the dead man scurries inconspicuously into the wings, and a "bloody head" (a bundle wrapped in red cloth) is tossed back on to the stage. But when the play is over the sword that has performed the horrid deed is not stored with the company's other props. It is wrapped in red brocade and placed in a special shrine, where incense and candles are burned in homage to the hero's memory.[6]

Our mandarin friends, on the whole, would only infrequently attend either court or village performance. Not the court because none but members of the imperial family—or poor creatures who had been castrated so as to serve it as eunuchs—could be allowed within the private apartments of the palace, where most of the performances took place. Not the village, unless on some rare occasion the magistrate toured his district to observe the keeping of a festival, or perhaps visited some rural spot close to his own home estate during a period of idleness or retirement. The pieces of the popular culture, whether crude rustic skits or the long drawn-out sagas such as those that told the adventures of the Buddhist saint Mulian who visited Hades to rescue his mother, these were not for the scholar-official, the man of cultivated literary tastes (though his womenfolk, cultivated or not, might warmly welcome an outing to see a temple play as a rare escape from confinement within the walls of the mansion).

There would be nothing, except the risk of developing a reputation for frivolity or even licentiousness, to stop the mandarin from paying a visit to the public theaters that had proliferated through the cities of central China in the time we are describing, the sixteenth and seventeenth centuries. But his preference was above all for the form of theater his own class had begun to monopolize, the *chuanqi* romance that was the crowning glory of the so-called southern drama. And for choice, the performance would take place in the elegant and totally private setting of the elite household itself.

THE SCHOLAR PLAYWRIGHT

By the year 1600 the composition of plays had become more popular among men of letters than in any previous age. The primary ingredient of these plays, after all, was lyric verse to be sung as aria, and the mandarins had been used to reading and composing verse from childhood on. It will be worth our while at this point to look in some little detail at the life of the greatest of the Ming dramatists, Tang Xianzu (1550–1616), from whose great tragicomedy *The Peony Pavilion* we offer a sequence of scenes in the later part of this book. Tang was much too brilliant, too close to genius, to serve as representative of the average mandarin of his time, but many features of his life-history make him a figure of particular interest. His "Four Dreams of Linchuan" (his four major plays, of which *The Peony Pavilion* is the masterpiece) are an outstanding achievement of the elite drama of the Ming dynasty, and in his career as a scholar-official, brief as it was, he shared certain types of experience with many gifted members of the mandarin class as a whole.[7]

Linchuan, Tang's family home, was a county town a few miles to the south of the great Lake Poyang in Jiangxi province, on the southwest fringe of that rich and populous region of east-central China known as Jiangnan, "South of the River" (the river in question being of course the Long River, the Yangzijiang). The first requirement for mandarin status was education, and Tang's ancestors for generations past had been holders of the first degree, known as *xiucai*, "Refined Talent." Possession of this degree, which Tang Xianzu himself attained at the precocious age of thirteen, conveyed privileges and obligations: exemption from corporal punishment for minor misdeeds, for example, but also the expectation that one would use one's knowledge in some way that would promote the public welfare. The Tang were local literati of note, with a celebrated family library and a tradition of generous philanthropic contribution to famine relief, public works, and education.

Tang Xianzu's own training, centered as it was upon preparing for the state examinations, necessarily started out from the Confucian classics. In early childhood he was taught by his grandfather. Later his father established a family school, where the boy could study in the company of gifted youngsters from across the county. Of the scholars engaged to teach him, the most distinguished was Luo Rufang (1515–1588), a leading philosopher of the Taizhou school. The fountainhead of the thinking of this school was the great Wang Yangming, Confucian philosopher of the early Ming whose formulations dominated intellectual developments throughout the second half of the dynasty.

In the family school Tang studied the ethical and political doctrines of Confucius, Mencius, and other thinkers of the formative period; the corpus of early Chinese poetry, historical texts, and time-honored writings on an encyclopedic range of subjects from astronomy to zoology; and the shifting interpretations of all these teachings and texts by Confucian scholars down through the centuries, through the great schools of Neo-Confucianism of the Song period, all the way down to the synthesis that was taking shape in late Ming times between Confucian, Buddhist, and Daoist concepts of behavior and of the universe.

Since women were excluded from service in the bureaucracy they were correspondingly less likely to undergo training in Confucian thought. The widespread religious systems of Daoism and Buddhism, on the other hand, were open to them, and it would have been impossible for a child in a Chinese family to escape the influence of these beliefs as passed on through the womenfolk. In Tang Xianzu's case, as no doubt in many others, it was his paternal grandmother who was closest to him, and who was largely responsible for his lifelong receptivity to Daoist and even more to Buddhist values.

But men also had their contribution to these aspects of his mental growth. The notion of the Chinese gentleman as "a Confucian at the office and a Daoist at home" has been around for a very long time, and Tang's own grandfather at one time in his life had become a Daoist recluse. One of Tang's valued friends later in life was the learned Buddhist monk Daguan. In general, the later decades of the Ming dynasty were more than most times an age of syncretism, when "the three teachings became one," and the strands of all three systems of thought interweave throughout Tang Xianzu's life and writings.

A prime requisite for success in the late Ming state examinations was skill in the composition of the "eight-legged essay." The name of this peculiar monster derived from its prescribed structure, most probably from the four sections, each consisting of two parallel paragraphs, that constituted the central section of the essay. The subject of the essay would be a brief classical quotation, often a saying of Confucius or Mencius, something like, for example, "If the people enjoy sufficiency, how could the ruler suffer from insufficiency?"[8]

After introductory sections known as "broaching the topic," "sustaining the topic," and so forth, the writer composes his central "eight legs" as a demonstration of his intimate knowledge of the classical source and his ability to give a lucid exposition of its profound meaning and relevance for all later ages. The total length of the essay would be no more than a few hundred characters, so there was no room for excess verbiage; yet these central paragraphs had to honor a style of strict parallelism, which essentially involved saying everything twice, rather in the manner of the hymnist who exhorts us "veiled in flesh the Godhead see, hail the incarnate Deity"—the identical concept repeated in paraphrased form. Historians of literature have stressed the influence exerted by this highly formal type of composition, not only on Chinese prose and verse, but on such matters as the pairing of scenes in plays and on the internal structure of the dramatic scene itself.

The skill Tang Xianzu developed in the composition of this abstruse form of examination piece eventually won him a ranking among the "eight great essayists" of the dynasty, and it is hardly surprising that he was able to pass the difficult provincial examination at the age of twenty. This achievement made him the first person in the history of his family to hold the degree of Elevated One (*juren*), and qualified him to go on to attempt the examination at the third level, for the title of Advanced Scholar (*jinshi*) and the chance of high-level appointment in either the central bureaucracy or the provinces.

He attempted this examination, which was held in the capital at intervals of three years, in 1571 at the age of twenty-one, and again in 1574. Though he failed on both occasions he was already making a name for himself as scholar and poet, to such effect that the Grand Secretary of the imperial court Zhang Juzheng, who was the most powerful man in the land after the emperor himself, sought to recruit Tang as a study-companion for his own son. Acceptance of this august invitation would surely have led to high placement in the next examination, but Tang declined—and failed again.

His reasons for declining were no doubt complex. For one thing, his old teacher Luo Rufang had fallen foul of Zhang Juzheng in the past and had suffered impeachment as a result. But whatever other factors may have entered into his decision, Tang Xianzu evidently wished to stay clear of what he regarded as a potentially corrupting influence, and for this and other actions of a similar nature he gained a reputation that endured throughout his life as a man of integrity.

Tang did not succeed in the *jinshi* examination until 1583—a year after the death of Zhang Juzheng. It was his fifth attempt and the culmination of years of study in the Imperial Academy in Nanjing. His reward was appointment in the prestigious Ministry of Rites, the organ that administered the vast multiplicity of ritual and ceremonial functions for the bureaucracy and the imperial court. He spent seven years in the Nanjing branch of this ministry, and by the age of forty had risen to the position of Secretary in the Bureau of Sacrifices, holding the sixth of the nine ranks of the mandarinate.

This proved, however, to be the pinnacle of his career in office. In 1591 he submitted a "Memorial on Ministers and Advisers" for the emperor's perusal. It was essentially a protest against the abuse of authority by Shen Shixing, who had succeeded Tang's old nemesis, Zhang Juzheng, as Grand Secretary. In the manner of many such memorials, it was also a plea for the opening up of the "path of speech," for removal of the blocks that Shen and his cronies had placed in the way of honest advisers to the throne. The emperor saw it as a reflection on his own judgment, and responded by acting not against Shen but against the presumptuous memorialist himself. Tang's rank was reduced and he was dispatched to serve as a jail warden in the southernmost province of Guangdong.

Before long Tang was transferred to what proved to be his last appointment, as County Magistrate of Suichang, a poor rural district in the hill country of southern Zhejiang—and a good place to shelve an outspoken critic of the mighty. In five years there he endeared himself to the populace as a humane administrator. He founded the first academy in the history of the county, defended mountain-dwellers against the depredations of tigers, supported poor tenants in the face of abuses by grasping landlords, and in all his actions strove to set a personal example of upright Confucian conduct. Ten years after his departure the people of Suichang erected a temple to honor him.

When Tang Xianzu left Suichang in 1597 he left public office for good, following the example of the great fourth-century poet Tao Qian and a host of later scholar-officials who had quit the world of affairs, either in disgrace or in disgust, to cultivate their gardens and write their poems in the district of their birth. By this time Tang had already written the first two of his five plays. These two, *The Purple Flute (Zixiaoji)* and *The Purple Hairpin (Zichaiji)*, are both based on the same short novella of the Tang period, but the second play represents a total rewriting rather than a mere revision of the first. Tang never in fact completed *The Purple Flute:* by scene 34 he had covered only one-half of the events outlined in his prologue. He himself admitted that this first effort of his would pass muster only as closet drama.

For one reason, he had paid too little attention to the singability of his lyrics. Later still he was to protest the revisions of his arias made by lesser men overly concerned with such matters as pitching front vowels at high points of the melody and back vowels at low: Tang wanted his poetry sung as he wrote it, and announced that if it cracked the throat of every singer in the empire, that was of secondary importance to him. Even so, and despite the fact that scenes from *The Purple Flute* were presented on the public stage and were immediately popular, for his second play Tang wrote *The Purple Hairpin* as an entirely new version of the same basic material.

Evidently Tang Xianzu had to pit his own creative genius against certain bookish conventions that threatened the very life of the *chuanqi* play. Other operatic genres have known these problems: a modern critic writes as follows of the eighteenth-century Italian opera seria:

> A string of great arias does not make a great opera. The finest operas of this period are, one must admit, more than a mere string of arias—but only a little more. The structure of the genre prevented it from being much more than that. There were many complicated rules about which type of aria should follow another—rules more often obeyed than broken: each principal singer had to have a certain number of arias of different types, and less important singers had to have an allotted number, too, placed so as not to take away from the grand effect made by the stars. The classification of aria types was very complicated: it appears to have been an important consideration to librettist and composer, although it is more than a little puzzling today.[9]

In the case of the Ming dynasty *chuanqi* also, many a matter that seems at the time to have been "an important consideration" presents itself to us as "more than a little puzzling today"!

Choice of subject matter was much less of a problem: romantic love is a major theme in all of Tang Xianzu's plays, as indeed in virtually all of Ming drama. The ninth-century novella Tang took as basis for both his first two plays tells the sad tale of the love and betrayal of a courtesan, Huo Xiaoyu, by a young scholar, Li Yi. For Tang the story gives scope for a fine display of feeling, *qing,* the innate goodness and spontaneity of which is the vital essence of all humanity. In order to extol the value and virtue of this love he transfers the fate of the rejected courtesan Huo Xiaoyu into the comic mode, complete with defeat of villainous rival, elimination of young scholar's jealous doubts, and happy ending for the triumphant couple in a celebratory finale.

Tang wrote *The Purple Flute* in the intervals of studying for the Advanced Scholar degree, and *The Purple Hairpin* most probably during his time in the Ministry of Rites in Nanjing. By the time he retired from office in 1597 he had also completed most or all of his masterpiece, *The Peony Pavilion,* whose preface bears the date of the following year. This play is Tang's ultimate paean to love, to the triumph of love over death. The power of his writing in this play makes itself felt very strongly in the scenes of ghostly wooing that comprise our selection below.

But love in the form of sexual passion is only one manifestation of *qing,* feeling, the entire complex of which is Tang's philosophical concern in his plays: joy and sorrow, fear and anger, desire and hate all have their part to play also. Feeling in this extended sense is not only to be celebrated as vital force but also to be balanced against the transitory nature of life itself—the tyranny of time—and the illusory nature of all worldly phenomena. Almost a generation ago C. T. Hsia wrote a penetrating critique of Tang's dramatic oeuvre under the title "Time and the human condition in the plays of T'ang Hsientsu."[10] More recently the young scholar Wei Hua has categorized Tang's overall concern throughout his five plays as a search for the harmonious reconciliation, in the realm of human feeling, of the claims of Confucian ideals against the transcendental values of Daoism and Buddhism.[11] Tang's last two plays, the "dream" plays *Handan Tale (Handanji)* and *Tale of the Southern Bough (Nankeji)*, are both based on old Daoist parables, but in each of these complex dramas Confucian values and Buddhist aspirations are also at work among the numerous characters. As the two scholars I have cited insist, the fundamental unity of thought throughout the five plays is of greater significance than the apparent shift, after Tang's retirement from office, toward withdrawal into the transcendental realm of Buddhist / Daoist thought.

PLAYS AND MUSIC

The mandarin Tang Xianzu was many things—scholar, thinker, major poet, superb dramatist. He was not however a composer of music, even though music was a major element in all traditional Chinese drama and we should be more correct to use the word "operas" rather than "plays" for his works, as for any piece of traditional Chinese theater beyond the level of simple comic sketch. Since few of the playwrights were in their own persons trained composers, their art consisted rather of fitting new lyrics to existing tunes. A common practice had been to recruit the aid of professional musicians to meet a given dramatic situation by selecting the most appropriate tunes from a repertoire of popular songs. Gradually, as the dynasty aged, this repertoire became standardized even though it remained huge, with hundreds of different melodies in as many as nine basic modes. The scrupulous care some of the dramatists devoted to this process of matching words to music is illustrated

by a tale of the fourteenth-century playwright Gao Ming, author of *The Lute*
(*Pipaji*). This play is regarded as the great progenitor of all *chuanqi* romances,
the first play in the long and involved southern mode to win national renown.
(It was also the first Chinese play to be reincarnated as a Broadway musical—
Lute Song of the 1940s with Mary Martin and Yul Brynner.) A major factor in
Gao Ming's success was his close fusion of words and melody: according to
legend, the constant tapping of the playwright's foot as he measured the me-
ters of his lyrics wore through the solid wood of the floor of his room.

The complete text of *The Lute* is available in a good English translation,[12]
and partly for this reason I have not included any scenes from it in my selection. It was certainly tempting to do so, for the play has a depth of seriousness
rare on the Chinese stage, an overlay of tragedy even though the ending re-
unites the mandarin-hero with both his first and second wives. Fundamentally *The Lute* explores a conflict between love and duty: love in the sense of
devotion to wife and (more especially) parents, and duty as defined by service
to the emperor. Cai Bojie leaves home to serve the nation, wins honors in the
capital, and submits to the temptation to become the son-in-law of the Chief
Minister. But while all this is happening, famine strikes the home village
where his first wife, Wuniang, tries in vain to keep his parents alive. Sadly,
heroically, Wuniang begs her way to the capital, to confront her faithless consort and reclaim her position as first lady of his household. The drama ends
with the penitent Cai Bojie leading his two wives to make sacrifices before his
parents' tomb.

Among other things *The Lute* tells us something about social mobility in
imperial China. But part of the price of this seems all too often to have been
the decision of a young careerist to reject his first wife in favor of an advan-
tageous new marriage. The first wife, selected by family agreement, going as
bride in her teens to a man she had never seen, then left behind in his parents'
home while he launches out on the long path to officialdom: this partner
originally chosen for him by his own parents becomes a liability to the ambi-
tious young scholar-official, and her very existence may then be quietly ignored if not openly negated. Enter the dramatist, who as moralist weaves the
public condemnation of the heartless husband into the stuff of his plot. However prevalent this kind of case may or may not have been in reality, it is
certainly true that sympathy for the neglected wife is a most striking feature
of the early southern drama.

The exemplar I have chosen of this so-favored theme is not Wuniang,
"Fifth Sister," of *The Lute* but Sanniang, "Third Sister" (or Tertia as I call her) of
The White Rabbit (Baituji). This is one of the "four great romances" that ruled
the southern stage with *The Lute* in the earliest years of the Ming period. It is
altogether less polished as a literary artifact, but perhaps no less popular as a

play, or rather as a dramatic theme since it has been presented in many versions and by just about every school of local drama, in every dialect, and with every variety of musical setting.

I have chosen to translate two versions of a single scene from *The White Rabbit*. The scene is "The Birth at the Mill," which in common with the entire play has elements both harrowing and grotesque. These elements are more in evidence in the first version I translate, which (though the actual text I used comes from the eighteenth century) derives from an early tradition of the *White Rabbit* plays, a tradition close to the popular theater of early Ming times. The second version, in contrast, bears clear traces of the refining hand of the late-Ming mandarin playwright. The language is softened, sanitized, prettified, the dramatic impact perhaps reduced, but new subtleties are introduced as the text moves from popular stage (first version) to mandarin's study (second version)—as it happens, the first text is taken from a compilation of actors' scripts, the second from an illustrated edition put out for the private reading of the elite purchaser of books.

In the chapter headed "Xi Shi as Innocence" I present scenes from the play *The Girl Washing Silk (Huanshaji)*, that accomplished something of a revolution in the history of Chinese theater. This innovative opera was the result of collaboration between the dramatist Liang Chenyu and the professional composer Wei Liangfu. In Kunshan, near Suzhou, in the middle of the sixteenth century, this gifted musician brought a new sophistication to Chinese opera by developing a style of music that emphasized the refined languor of the flute and the gentle strum of the pipa or the moon guitar (instruments originating in central Asia that somewhat resemble the lute and mandolin respectively). There is an informative description of the new style by a contemporary commentator:

In Nanjing before the Wanli period (1573–1620), nobles, gentry, and wealthy families would entertain by having arias performed by several actors or perhaps many actors, singing in the northern style. For instruments, they used the zither, the lute, the banjo, and wooden clappers. . . . But later there was a change and they began to use southern arias. Singers employed only one small set of clappers or a fan as substitute, perhaps adding a drum or other clappers. Now, people from the Suzhou area have added the flute and moon guitar. . . .

Southern dramas are performed at large feasts. Originally, there were only two main styles, Yiyang and Haiyan. Yiyang uses colloquial language, and literati from the provinces enjoyed watching it. In Haiyan, there was a lot of the official dialect and it was popular in Nanjing and Beijing. . . . And now there is also the Kunshan style. It is clearer and more mellifluous than Haiyan and yet combines both harmony and sudden changes in melody, extending one word for several breaths. The literati have endowed it with their spirit and greatly enjoy it. As for Haiyan and the other styles, they seem to make one want to fall asleep in the daytime; and as for northern drama, it is like blowing on pipes and beating clay pots—people are bored with it and even scoff at it.[13]

A feminine delicacy predominated in this new mode of theater: whether male or female, the players of women's roles in Kunqu, the drama of the Kunshan school, to this day model their walk, their posture, the way they sit down (perching on the very edge of a chair), or open a fan, or raise a teacup, on the frail elegance of the mandarins' womenfolk, with their bound feet, willowy waists, and tightly wrapped bosoms.

The Girl Washing Silk was "southern drama" in every sense of the term, the product of southern sensibility and southern artifice. There are still gardens in Suzhou where tiny, antique pines are so artfully trained over a couple of man-made "mountains," no more than a few feet in elevation, that they can transport the beholder's fancy to the spectacular landscapes of the Yangzi gorges. Or in Japan we can still trace the esthetic imagination, inspired by the example of the Chinese landscape designers, that makes a musical instrument out of a gravel-filled ditch: at Katsura, outside Kyoto, the visitor sheltering from the rain in an airy pavilion literally hears music as the rain drips from the eaves on to the carefully selected, individually positioned, river-polished pebbles beneath.

The Lute, although its structure is characteristic of the southern school of drama, still breathes the thin air of the arid north in its scenes of starving villagers painfully swallowing husks, of Wuniang stumbling along the dusty road to the capital. In direct contrast *The Girl Washing Silk,* two hundred years later, is southern not only in its structure and its new-style music, but in the unmistakable lushness of its setting. The story retells the ancient legend of Xi Shi, the acme of southern beauty. Her era is the sixth century B.C., when rival kingdoms fought for hegemony in the lands south of the Yangzi. Her fabled beauty may be partly responsible for the reputation enjoyed ever after by the women of Suzhou, where the local dialect itself lends a melodious lilt to seductive voices, and complexions blossom in the soft moist air of the "land of fish and rice."

With this first of our two plays about Xi Shi, composed about 1550, we enter a world of characters altogether more complex than the straightforward moral exemplars of *The Lute* or *The White Rabbit.* The way is being prepared for the subtle art of Tang Xianzu, seen at its finest in *The Peony Pavilion.*

But before we take our leave of the intriguing Xi Shi we present a long, in-volved, and hilarious scene from a farcical work, *The Plantain Kerchief,* by the little-known playwright Shan Ben. In this play the figure of Xi Shi, or at least her immortal spirit, is borrowed for the comic effect of contrast between shameless antique seductress and demure young damsel of the playwright's own decorous day.

In *The Peony Pavilion* Tang Xianzu celebrates the triumph of a girl's love over cold reason, lonely seclusion, separation, even death itself. Although I have published separately my complete translation of this play I include here scenes from its central sequence as representative of the crowning achieve-ment of the *chuanqi* romance. An alternative title of *The Peony Pavilion* is *The Soul's Return.* The heroine Bridal Du, after pining and dying for love of the young scholar Liu Mengmei, is granted leave to return to earth in spirit form to complete their predestined match. Fantastic as the theme may be, the pas-sages between the lovers in these scenes still have the power to move us deep-ly. Acted on the modest "red carpet" stage, with graceful sway of silken sleeve to follow the flute's soft melodies, the effect was intense enough to cause tears and even, lamentably, according to certain contemporary accounts, the suicides of young girls who saw their own faces in the mirror of Bridal's toilet-case.

And yet *Peony Pavilion* is not a tragedy but at least a tragicomedy. In the later decades of the Ming, comedy triumphed, and the plays from which I have made the last of my selections are witness to the turn toward the comic that Tang Xianzu's successors made. In *The Green Peony* and *The Swallow Letter* we have classic instances of the kind of high-style domestic comedy for which the *chuanqi* romance was the ideal vehicle.

But since separate and more complete commentaries accompany each of the scenes that follow, it is time for the wooden block to be struck, the flute to play, and the actors to command our attention. . . .

The White Rabbit and the Neglected Wife

The White Rabbit of Chinese folklore wore no watchchain across his ample waistcoat, nor did any "A-li-ssu" tumble into his premises in a dream. But he did serve as guide to certain wonders. He led a huntsman prince to find his long-lost mother, in a set of legends culminating in the *Baituji,* the *Drama of the White Rabbit,* one of the celebrated "Four Great *Chuanqi* Romances" of the southern-style Chinese theater of Mongol and early Ming times.

Of all the characters in the drama, the prince's mother is the one who will most concern us. She is the archetype of a figure who seemed to mesmerize the early "southern-style" dramatists, the figure of the neglected wife, the companion of poverty who is cast off when her man achieves success later in life. In early versions of the *White Rabbit* play this woman, Sanniang or "Tertia" as we will call her, has a fairy-tale quality about her, the Cinderella innocence of a poor village girl. Later, as we shall see, she becomes gentrified, and we will end our exploration of her story by translating the scene of her greatest heartbreak as it was written by a late Ming dramatist, Xie Tianyou.

We begin with a much earlier version of the same scene, a version that retains the folk quality of its origins. It derives from the earliest stage representations of Tertia's story, probably first put on some time in the thirteenth or fourteenth century, even though paradoxically the scene I translate was actually printed in the eighteenth century, a hundred and fifty years after Xie Tianyou's time, in an anthology which is believed faithfully to preserve the

The White Rabbit: The cruel Sister-in-law beats Tertia as she turns the mill.

acting versions of popular scenes. By this date, the reign of the Qianlong Emperor, Xie Tianyou's more elegant rendering of Tertia's story seems to have lost favor. It was the product of a theater for mandarins, and the tastes of the mandarins of the Qianlong era no longer ran to heartrending tales of deserted wives.

Between the folk version and the late Ming elite version of the "Birth at the Mill" scene from the *Drama of the White Rabbit* we can sense something of the evolution of the southern drama over the centuries from the thirteenth to the seventeenth, and we shall devote some of our commentary to tracing details of this process of development, the growth of what we might loosely call the poetic at the expense of melodrama and a good deal of rather grotesque slapstick.

BIRTH AT THE MILL: AN ECHO
OF THE EARLIEST STAGE VERSIONS

As our first version of the "birthing" scene opens, the stage is empty save for a large drum, red-lacquered, with bulging sides in the Chinese style. A bamboo rod projects at waist height, forming a contraption to represent a large, heavy millstone. There is no attempt to conceal its actual identity because halfway through the scene the Ugly Sister-in-law is going to scoff at the gentle wife's frailty by reminding her, in a burlesque of stage convention, that this is not a real millstone she must turn but merely "the big drum from the orchestra backstage."

Ugly Sister-in-law is a clown role, played by a man to emphasize heavy shoulders, big feet, and general ungainliness. The costume is tunic and skirt in fine silk, but in tones of bright pink and green. In this way Sister-in-law's dress can contrast most effectively with the heroine's, without being so garish as to clash and offend the eye. The heroine, Tertia (Sanniang, Third Maid) is the classic *qingyi* or "black gown" role. She is a model of decorum and quiet beauty in long, almost floor-length gown of black or midnight blue bordered in silver over a pure white skirt. Virtuous wife, whose husband's prolonged absence at the wars threatens to turn into permanent desertion, Tertia has chastely bound her head with a dark-blue turban. One further fact is apparent: her gown bulges with the pillows of an advanced pregnancy.

Tertia has turned her painful millstone on the Chinese stage for seven or eight hundred years. She is the heroine of the *White Rabbit* play, *Baituji,* or rather plays, for there are numerous versions. In all of them the scene of Tertia's giving birth at the millstone is climactic. Here is the scene in its most vividly realized form, as acted around Suzhou in the middle of the eighteenth century. The text is from the *White Fur Robe (Zhuibaiqiu)* anthology, a collection of scenes from many old *chuanqi* plays that have been transcribed virtually syllable by syllable from actual stage performances, so that interjections, hesitations, and the clown's adlibbing are all faithfully preserved:

Bearing the Babe

TERTIA (*enters and sings*):

> (*TUNE: PRELUDE*)
> *No clever scheme to lift the frown from my brow;*
> *how to escape such wicked persecutors?*

"Like a wooden fish hung from a beam, beaten without cease; like a mute eating bitter herbs, has a mouth but can't complain." From the moment my husband went away, I resisted the efforts of my brother and sister-in-law to force me to remarry, and now as punishment they have set me to carrying water by day and turning the millstone all night. Ai-yo—yet I make no complaint in the first place against my parents, nor in the second place against my brother and his wife, nor in the third place against my husband.

> (*TUNE: WUGENG ZHUAN*)
> *I blame only my untoward fate*
> *for the cruel treatment I suffer.*
> *Do my late parents know my grief?*
> *Ah brother, sister-in-law,*
> *how you steeled your hearts against me,*
> *driving off Liu Zhiyuan*
> *and setting me to turn the mill!*
> *I call, but Heaven does not answer*
> *Earth does not hear*
> *and how am I to endure?*
> *What should a maid like me have learned*
> *of turning millstones, carrying water?*
> *All this toiling, all for Master Liu!*

But if I stand here idly complaining and my brother and sister-in-law find out, they'll give me another tongue-lashing.

> (*SAME TUNE*)
> *I face the millstone, brows knit in sorrow,*

forced into this drudgery and no help for it.
My father and mother while they lived
cherished me like a flower,
but now they are gone
my brother and his wife torment me.
Father and mother dead,
orphaned and deserted,
how can I endure?
What should a maid like me have learned
of turning millstones, carrying water?
All this toiling, all for Master Liu!

Oh, oh! In my belly one wave of pain after another, it must be tonight I give birth. Suppose I try to turn the millstone, it's so heavy—yet if I don't turn it my brother and sister-in-law will curse and beat me. Enough, enough!

(*SAME TUNE*)
Still I must turn it
(Oh! Oh!)
my shoulder against the stone.
My head swims
belly so sore and aching legs
spirit numbed with weariness
I can hardly move it at all.
Suppose I hang myself here in the mill
won't that mean betraying Liu Zhiyuan?
My thoughts go round
tears flood my cheeks
how can I ease my mind?
May Heaven protect my giving birth
let father and child meet some day face to face
and husband and wife be reunited.

I am so numb with weariness, all I can do is lie down right here on the millstone and take a nap for a moment before I get up and start turning again. Ah millstone, I grieve that you are so hard to move, but when I wake up you will still be there!

SISTER-IN-LAW (*enters and recites*):
Wouldn't behave like an honest woman
had to go marry Master Liu:
now Master Liu is up and away
millstone's the punishment for you!

Eh? Why can't I hear that mill turning? Let's have a look inside there. Ha! Fast asleep there! (*Beats Tertia*) I'll teach you to sleep!

TERTIA: Oh! Oh! Sister-in-law!

SISTER-IN-LAW: Snoozing there while the mill sits idle!

TERTIA: I can't help it, the millstone's too heavy for me to move.

SISTER-IN-LAW: What a feeble young missie you are! I suppose you'd have liked your big brother to buy a nice marble millstone, or alabaster or serpentine? You'd better loosen up a bit, don't go thinking you can always have things your own way. "Too heavy to move":—what a tale! Out of my way, let me show you. You think it's a real millstone? That's just the big drum from the orchestra backstage!

TERTIA: Sister-in-law, please rest yourself.

SISTER-IN-LAW: Rest myself? The field hands will want their noodles for dinner. If they don't get their noodles, you get seventy or eighty strokes with the rod, I promise you! But we haven't any incense burning, let me just light some, then I can say my rosary while I beat your precious stinking hide! Namo Omitofo, stinking precious darling! Namo Omitofo, stinking little whore! (*Exit*)

TERTIA: Oh, sister-in-law! You are a woman too, how can you fail to understand a woman's agony? My belly hurts so, my labor must be starting. But what time is it? Let me open the window to see.

> (*TUNE: SUO NANZHI*)
> Moon and stars still bright,
> must be near the fourth watch
> from out the window sounds of dogs and fowls.
> Brother and sister-in-law so heartless
> forcing me to grind the grain till dawn.
> I long for Liu Zhiyuan
> far off and not a word.
> Here in the millshed
> cold and silent
> only the wind blows icy chill.

Aiyo, Heaven! Pains again in my belly, this must be . . . . Aiyo! Aiyo! This time worse than ever! Mother!

> (*SAME TUNE*)
> Call on Heaven, Heaven does not answer
> (Aiyo-oh!)
> call on Earth, Earth does not hear.
> Pains in my belly, pains everywhere
> how to endure them?

> *Tonight must be my time to give birth*
> *yet not a soul comes by.*
> *(Aiya-ah! Mother!)*
> *Now pray to ancestors to put forth their power from the shades*
> *to secure an easy birth for mother and child!*

(*She gives birth*) Sister-in-law!

SISTER-IN-LAW (*offstage*): What's the matter?

TERTIA: Let me borrow a tub for a moment.

SISTER-IN-LAW (*offstage*): Tub's split and hasn't been mended yet.

TERTIA: Well then, I know, I'll just have to wipe all clean with the clothes I am wearing. Sister-in-law!

SISTER-IN-LAW: (*offstage*): What's the fuss? All this yelling!

TERTIA: Lend me a pair of scissors for a moment.

SISTER-IN-LAW (*offstage*): The lad stole the scissors to trade for candy.

TERTIA: Oh my child, your mother has nothing prepared, not a thread nor a piece of tile, how am I to manage? I know, I'll just have to bite the cord with my teeth, and for this I'll give you the name "Bittencord." Oh, child! True it is:

> green dragon and white tiger form a pair,
> none can be sure of future good or ill.

(*Exit with babe in arms*)   (*Zhuibaiqiu* 3, 152–55, "Yang zi.")

By the middle of the Qing dynasty (the preface to the *White Fur Robe* anthology is dated 1770) companies rarely performed the long southern-style plays in their entirety any more, but made up a repertoire of individual scenes, obviously those of the greatest climactic interest and audience appeal. "Bearing the Babe" is one of six scenes the anthology preserves from *The White Rabbit*. Another is a scene from early in the play, "The Fuss Over the Chicken," which introduces the hero Liu Zhiyuan and contains some happy clowning with a venal monk, always a popular butt of satire: "When officials are incorrupt their assistants grow skinny, but when the spirits perform as requested our temple offerings are good and rich." Other scenes that continued to hold the stage presented the inevitable reunions of husband and wife, mother and son from late in the play. But none was played as commonly as the birth by the millstone, which continues to draw tears from Chinese audiences to this day in local dramas of a dozen different musical styles.

What the very earliest versions of the scene were like we have no way of knowing. But our eighteenth-century company was performing a version very close to the best-known and most complete recension, *The White Rabbit* as contained in the late Ming collection *Sixty Plays* (*Liushizhong qu*), edited by

Mao Jin, who lived from 1599 to 1659. In the century and a half that had elapsed since Mao Jin's day, actors or their managers had abridged some of the arias and expanded the dialogue in the direction of everyday realism. For example, "What watch is it from the gate-tower?" becomes slightly modernized into "I'll just open the window and see what time it is" (from the watchman's signboard, or in the present case simply the color of the night sky). Tertia punctuates her arias with added scraps of monologue describing her labor pains, and the cries of "aiyo" she emits from time to time are not to be found in earlier texts. Ugly Sister-in-law, like most clown roles in these scenes, speaks throughout in Suzhou dialect and is sometimes close to unintelligible to an outsider.

Tertia laments the cruelty of her persecutors, who beat her as ceaselessly as monks in a temple beat their "wooden fish," the hollow sounding-block (originally fish-shaped) which accompanied their orisons. Her plaint makes for a fine irony, when a few minutes later Sister-in-law recites the name of the Buddha as she strikes her. An earlier scene (16 in the *Sixty Plays* recension) ended with Tertia's brother and his wife plotting exquisite refinements of Tertia's torture: the jars for her drawing of water to be rounded at the bottom to prevent her setting them down to rest herself, and drilled with holes to make them leak continuously; the mill ceiling to be lowered to prevent her standing upright. Touches like these seem to come straight from folklore, from some archetypal primer on how to maltreat a Cinderella. Tertia's cry, "Heaven does not answer, Earth does not hear" comes similarly from an ancient common source of lamentation. It is the cry heard in the third act of the most famous of all Yuan dynasty tragedies, Guan Hanqing's *Maid Dou Wronged (Dou E yuan)*. Maid Dou, suffering the rod and awaiting the executioner's sword for a murder she did not commit, sings:

> *Heaven and Earth, you who should sort out fair from foul. . . .*
> *you have slipped into fearing the hard and cheating the soft,*
> *pushing your boat as the current happens to flow.*
> *Earth, when you can't tell good from evil*
> *how can you call ourself Earth?*
> *Heaven, when you confuse the worthy and foolish*
> *you pose as Heaven in vain!*

—a kind of questioning of the gods drawn by overwhelming misfortune from the depths of popular piety.

The horror of Tertia's predicament—pregnant, close to parturition, too weary to move the heavy millstone, rejecting the suicide option only to be beaten one more time for "idleness"—comes to seem so intolerable that our actors break the tension with the clown's reminder that all is only stage play after all, this is no millstone but a drum from backstage. Tertia herself seems to conform to the lightened mood with her polite, semi-satirical request to Sister-in-law not to overexert herself by further beating. The humor turns bitter when our villainess adds a gross hypocrisy to the abundance of her other faults. She continues beating Tertia to the rhythm of the Buddhist rosary, the repetition of the name of Amitabha (Omitofo). The practice reflects the belief of the Pure Land sect that one who dies with this name of the Buddha on his or her lips will be translated at once into the heart of a lotus flower in the temporary paradise of the Pure Land. Here the soul will hear the sound of the preaching of the Law, which cannot fail to secure eventual release from the wheel of perpetual rebirth.

The vanity of Sister-in-law's aspirations strikes us the more forcefully as her exit reminds us of her ultimate fate in the play, which is determined with a remarkable degree of cruelty. Again this seems to belong to the folklore that arises from a brutal way of life, to a sort of archetypal wish-fulfillment for the punishment of the powerful and vicious. In the final reunion scene in the *Sixty Plays* version, the hero pardons Tertia's greedy brother for the sake of continuance of the family name. But he reminds Ugly Sister-in-law of a sarcastic vow she once made, and gives instructions now for its highly melodramatic realization:

LIU ZHIYUAN: Bring that woman before me. Now didn't you once say, back in the old days, that if ever Master Liu made a name for himself you would light a candle to illuminate earth and sky?

SISTER-IN-LAW: That's true, I did.

LIU ZHIYUAN: How can I pardon this harpy? You there, have my staff prepare fifty catties of aromatic oil and a thousand feet of hempen cloth, and make this harpy into a candle to light up the heavens, so that I can vent this spleen.

(Exeunt attendants with cries of assent)

BROTHER: Burn the bitch properly!

Ugly Sister-in-Law has been the ringleader throughout the defrauding of Liu Zhiyuan and the sixteen-year enslavement of his wife Tertia, but even so the husband's final comment comes as a shock—from the horrors of a fairy-tale world rather than from any kind of realistic representation. It is of a kind with the formulaic threat of the Giant that Jack kills: "I'll have his liver and lights for my supper tonight, and his blood for my morning dram!"

This Grand Guignol ending is surely a survivor from earliest versions of the play. It is noteworthy, and a point in favor of the folkloric authenticity of the *Sixty Plays* recension, that this ending belongs only to that version, though Ugly Sister-in-law is the chief villain in all versions of *The White Rabbit*. In the earliest surviving version of the play, the Chenghua version I will describe shortly, she is reminded of her contemptuous vow to light a candle, but then pardoned along with her husband. In the Xie Tianyou version, with which we shall conclude, she is allowed a long speech of repentance for her misdeeds before she suicides, onstage, by the time-honored method of dashing her head against stone steps.

THE HERO LIU ZHIYUAN

But who is this Liu Zhiyuan and how does he let his wife get into the predicament of giving birth to their child attended only by a wicked, jealous and hate-filled sister-in-law? Not the most concise, but surely the most colorful answer to this question is given again by the *White Fur Robe* recension. One of the reunion scenes preserved here from late in the play involves Liu Zhiyuan's return, incognito, to his native village, where he questions a herdboy as to the identity of the woman he has just seen drawing water (who is actually, as the audience well knows, the wife he has been parted from for sixteen years). The herdboy, another clown role performed in broad Suzhou dialect with its complement of atrocious puns and the coarsest of street slang, gives his own highly seasoned version of the events the play has earlier recorded. He is of course unaware that he is telling his tale to its subject, Liu Zhiyuan himself, whom he refers to as "Beggar Liu, the thief:"

HERDBOY: There was this old Squire Li of Li Village here, with his missus old Dame Li, and this particular year he goes to the Silkworm God's temple to make sacks of rice.
LIU ZHIYUAN: Sacrifice.
HERDBOY: Right you are, sacrifice, sacrifice. And he takes in this fellow called Beggar Liu, the thief.
LIU: Ha! You shouldn't slander people behind their backs.
HERDBOY: Ploughing a field or hoeing a crop, not a thing did this fellow know anything about, all he was good for was fighting with spear or staff, or handling livestock. Now on his farm old Squire Li had this horse called Piecrust.
LIU: Piebald.

HERDBOY: All right, Piebald. But how do you know?

LIU: There are horses called this.

HERDBOY: Nobody could tame him. But the little candle-burner takes one look at Beggar Liu and says to himself, "So it's you, is it?" Beggar Liu grabs one handful of his mane and leaps right up on to his back, and does that little candle-burner ever take off! Clickety-clack, there and back, just one end of the village to the other and he's completely broken in! Seeing this Liu is such a phenomenon, Squire Li gives him this Third Maid, Tertia, that you just saw drawing water, for his wife. And who knows what was so magic about Beggar Liu at the wedding ceremony, but when he made his kotows to the old couple he kotowed them stone dead, right there and then!

LIU: How can you kill somebody just by kotowing to them?

HERDBOY: I saw it with my own eyes, one kotow, one dead, two kotows, two dead, that's how he kotowed them to death. Then with Squire Li dead, the uncle didn't know what to do so he split the inheritance into three shares.

LIU: Three shares? How?

HERDBOY: The first for the eldest son, Li Hongyi, the second for the second son, Li Hongxin, and the third for Beggar Liu.

LIU: What! He was not a Li, how did he get a share?

HERDBOY: There was a reason for it. When Squire Li was alive he never laid by a dowry for Tertia when she married, so he gave them that ten-acre melon patch up there on Sleeping Ox Ridge to make up for it. But that place is haunted by a blue-faced Smelly Demon.

LIU: Melon demon.

HERDBOY: When Squire Li was alive he would often slaughter a pig or a lamb for a sacrifice, and that's why the demon didn't come out. But when the old squire died the eldest son wasn't about to make any sacrifices, and so the demon starts showing himself by day, and at night he comes out and gobbles people up. So eldest son and his wife talk it over, and they get Beggar Liu good and drunk with hot wine and cold, and they tell him, "The melons are ripe just now and there's a lot of melon thieves around." So they persuade him to go guard the melons. Beggar Liu doesn't realize it's a trick, he staggers straight off to the melon patch. First watch nothing happens, second watch all quiet, but when it gets to the third watch, aiyo! I don't want to tell you!

LIU: Why don't you want to tell me?

HERDBOY: 'Cause if I tell you I'll be spirited off in the night.

LIU: Don't be afraid, you've got me here.

HERDBOY: Big deal, you're here. Ai-ya! What do you know, soon as it gets to third watch, out pops that melon demon. Wow! Can you imagine what that melon-demon looked like?

LIU: What did it look like?

HERDBOY: Head like a watermelon, neck like a canteloupe, trunk like a wintermelon, arms like cassavas, thighs like cranshaws, ass like a honeydew, balls like acorn squash, and a good long ding-dong more like a crookneck than anything else. Plantain-leaf fan a-waving in his hand, out he strolls all lah-di-dah to take the evening breeze. Looks to the east, looks to the west, and says, "Ha! Whence this scent of a human all alive? Whence this scent of a human all alive?" That old Beggar Liu takes one look at the melon-demon, runs straight up to him and gives him a clout over the earhole. "I was just joking," says the melon-demon, "what did you want to give me such a clout for? Just for that I'm going to eat you up!" And he stretches his great maw wide open and swallows Beggar Liu straight down.

LIU: So he got eaten alive?

HERDBOY: That melon-demon didn't know his stuff. If you're going to eat somebody you have to give it some thought, at least strip him of his clothes first, get him bare as a radish and you can swallow him nicely, what's wrong with that? But that melon demon was in such a tizzy, he gobbled him up clothes and all. Well, Beggar Liu starts flailing around in the demon's guts with his "opening the four gates," his somersaults, his tiger-springs, and pretty soon the demon feels all the spittle in his throat dry up. "I'm good and thirsty, a cup of tea would go very nicely. I'd like a nice drop of Pine-lichen, or perhaps some Mustard-leaf." But where was he going to find a cup of tea in that melon patch? He lollops off to the fishpond, opens his maw and guzzle-guzzle, in no time at all he drinks the fishpond dry. Down there in the demon's guts old Beggar Liu is saying to himself, "Watch out! Flood coming!" And he starts swimming. He tries the "dragon-fly," then the "millrace," and then he treads a mite too hard and gives the melon-demon a pain deep down in his belly. "Aiyo! Aiyo!" yells the demon. "What a belly-ache! It's the trots I've got." So he jams his front paws against a couple of pine trees, points his backside up at the sky, and crack, like a thunderclap, he twangs Beggar Liu clear out to Coldland.

LIU: Iceland, you mean?

HERDBOY: Well, ice is cold, isn't it? Like they say, ice cold, icy cold. Well, never a word from Beggar Liu since he left, and brother and sister-in-law trying to force her to remarry but she won't, so she's in trouble! As

punishment she has to carry water all day without stopping. Ta-da, ta-da.
At night she has to turn the millstone till morning light. Ta-da, ta-da,
crack.

LIU: What's the matter?

HERDBOY: String broke. Money please.

LIU: How many years ago was all this?

HERDBOY: Sixteen years since.

LIU: And how old are you?

HERDBOY: Fifteen.

LIU: If you're only fifteen now how do you know what happened sixteen
years ago?

HERDBOY: I can explain: my daddy was a laborer for the Lis and when he
came home at night to sleep with my mom it was all the Lis did this and
the Lis said that. I was trapped down there in my mom's belly and
couldn't help hearing every word.

LIU: That Liu Zhiyuan is back here now. Do you think you'll recognize
him?

HERDBOY: Pooh! I'd recognize that sonofabitch if he were burned to ashes.

LIU: Well, do you recognize me?

HERDBOY: You? You look like my son.

LIU: Ha! I am Liu Zhiyuan.

HERDBOY: What? Beggar Liu, you? Aiyo! Trouble! I've got to go tell the
boss, Beggar Liu has come back for his wife. I'd give you a good
thrashing, but you could never stand it. I'm off to tell the boss, Beggar
Liu has come back for his wife.   (*Zhuibaiqiu* 3, "Madi," 165–169)

To the herdboy, Tertia is the deserted wife of Beggar Liu, a village ne'er-do-
well but for his martial skills, which make him something of a "phenomenon." Poor Squire Li has been conned into bestowing his daughter on this
penniless horse-wrangler only to drop dead together with his wife at the
wedding ceremony, the two of them "kotowed to death." The herdboy has no
explanation for this weird incident.

We, in contrast, are aware that Liu Zhiyuan is destined to become Emper-
or of China. For commoners to receive kotows from him would amount to an
intolerable lèse-majesté, an act contrary to the principles of universal
hierarchy—even though Liu is nothing more than a stableboy at this stage of
his career. The only solution to the impasse is to have Tertia's parents drop
dead on the spot. The herdboy sees this "with his own eyes," even though he
admits later that he was still in his mother's womb at the time. His account of
the fight with the demon of melon-patch far outshines any earlier version in

its Munchausen inventiveness. Evidently folkloric sparkles had continued to crystallize around the Liu Zhiyuan legends in the centuries through to the eighteenth, along with accretions derived from a more modern consciousness (Iceland, for example, was unknown in China before, at the earliest, the advent of European priests in late-Ming times). The herdboy is so pleased with his own eloquence that he makes bold at the end to pose as a balladsinger, demanding money for a broken string on his lute, "ta-da, ta-da." He has neither fear nor respect for the stranger who is questioning him: "You look like my son" is a gratuitous comic insult, as the speaker puts himself in the exalted place due to the other's father.

The audience enjoys this dramatic irony all the more because it knows very well who Liu Zhiyuan is, whether or not it has ever seen a complete performance of *The White Rabbit*. His story has survived in more genres of the popular performing arts than has that of any other hero. His appearance in actual history was quite brief, as successful general and founder, Gaozu, of the Posterior Han dynasty during the tenth century era of the Five Dynasties. He ruled for one year before passing the throne to his son, who closed out the history of the dynasty as Emperor Yindi (948–951).

Liu Zhiyuan's life is told in a wide variety of sources, in the standard histories of the period, in a popular chronicle or *pinghua* of Song-Yuan composition, in a chantefable or ballad-medley of the Jin dynasty (twelfth–thirteenth centuries), and in a Yuan *zaju* play. The last is no longer extant, but the other texts survive, the chantefable in an incomplete form which has been reconstructed by modern scholarship.[1] The *White Rabbit* romance plays present much the most detailed portrayals of Liu Zhiyuan, but they change the lighting of their subject in some remarkable ways. In the histories he is depicted fairly straightforwardly as a military adventurer. In the ballad-medley he is "romanticized and idealized," turned into "a paragon."[2] This process of embellishment is a reflection of a most profound Confucian myth, that the founder of a dynasty must needs be a worthy hero, just as the last emperor of a line must perforce be a degenerate.

The same process that romanticizes Liu Zhiyuan also turns his subordinates from brutal thugs into engaging rogues. Shi Hongzhao and Guo Wei were men-at-arms who rose to general rank in the service of Liu Zhiyuan. Shi was (rightly or wrongly) suspected of treachery and murdered on the orders of Liu's son during the latter's brief reign as Emperor Yindi. Guo Wei eventually established a short-lived dynasty of his own, the Posterior Zhou, which held a particularly wobbly sway from 951 to 960. Shi appears only in a minor role in the Liu Zhiyuan plays, Guo Wei not at all. In real life both of these men were thieves, extortionists, and killers. Shi married a common prostitute,

Guo secured a wife of some means on whom he sponged to good effect. Both became the foci of legends, and a late Ming collection, *Stories Old and New (Gujin xiaoshuo),* contains a version of some of these as they circulated among storytellers of the Yuan and early Ming times. But first we should see what the standard history says about Shi Hongzhao:

> As a young man Hongzhao roamed about in search of adventure. He was a bad character and a bully. A robust walker, he could cover seventy miles in a day and could walk as fast as a horse gallops. . . . Hong-zhao's behavior as a general was strict and stern, and he used few words. Any man under his command who showed the slightest sign of insubordination would be beaten to death on the instant, and on account of this his troops obeyed him in fear and trembling. . . . Hong-zhao sent troops to perform police duties in the capital. They killed and massacred, and guilty and innocent alike perished. If a man at this time, in broad daylight, chanced to raise his head on the street, he was cut in two without compunction. If a drunken man showed disobedience to a soldier in the marketplace, the soldier would trump up some accusation against him and he would be publicly executed. When any man was accused of an offense, the runners would state the case to Shi Hon-gzhao. All Shi needed to do was raise three fingers as a signal, and the runners would at once cut the offender in two. Among punishments inflicted were the cutting out of tongue or lips, hamstringing, and feet-crushing. (*Wudai shi,* 107; *Xin wudai shi, 30.*)

And here is an incident involving Guo Wei:

> Guo Wei was once walking in the marketplace where there was a butcher who used to impress the bystanders with his daring. Guo Wei, who was drunk, called out to the butcher to cut up some meat for him, and scolded him for cutting it the wrong way. The butcher bared his belly, and showing it to Guo cried, "You are a brave man—do you think you are brave enough to kill me?" Guo Wei at once stepped forward, picked up the knife, and stabbed him to death. All present were horrified but Guo remained unmoved. Runners arrested him, but his patron secretly secured his release out of regard for his daring. After sending him into hiding for a time the patron received Guo back into his service.

> (*Xin Wudai shi,* 11.)

In contrast, the *Gujin xiaoshuo* story "Shi Hongzhao in the Fights of Dragon and Tiger and the Meetings of Prince and Minister" presents Shi Hongzhao as a jolly rascal and Guo Wei as a chivalrous gallant. On one occasion when Shi is short of money he steals a cooking-pot, but he is scrupulous to forewarn the owner, advising him to keep a careful watch on his door that night. As the editor of the collection comments, "Even when a hero steals, it is open and above-board." Guo Wei's callous killing of the butcher is transformed in the story into the gallantry of a knight-errant. Idling in the marketplace, Guo comes across the son of a certain Shang, a rich man well known in the vicinity. The youth is engaged in setting some roughs to break up a vendor's stall. Asking his reason, Guo learns that the youth is angered by the vendor's refusal to sell him his pretty daughter:

> Guo stood forward and said to the wealthy youth, Shang: "All must cultivate goodness and right. Though a false heart be hidden in a dark room, the eyes of the spirits are as lightning. Your honor should not be lured from the correct path by the lust for a woman." In a quiet voice, Guo Wei suggested that the young man remount his horse. But the youth's temper flared, and he blustered, "Who are you? . . . This is none of your business. You men, give this fellow a beating for me." Enraged, Guo Wei replied, "I give you advice in good faith, and you order your men to beat me. You do not know what I am like." He seized young Shang with his left hand, while with his right he drew from his hip the dagger he carried in his clothing. His hand rose and the dagger fell, and what became of young Shang's life?—
>
> > The desire to rid the world of injustice
> > Reveals the mighty leader of men.
>
> (*Gujin xiaoshuo* 15.)

Just as stories like this one of Shi Hongzhao create martial or chivalrous heroes out of historical roughnecks, so do the plays revolving around Liu Zhiyuan spray whitewash in all directions. One of these directions is the domestic. The future emperor's marital life is at least as important as his prowess at arms—much more so, indeed, to the playwright. The brilliant career to come makes him a desirable match, if only someone has the necessary discernment. But will he honor the commitment made during his years of poverty and obscurity?

Here, once Liu Zhiyuan is put on the stage as male protagonist of a romance play, he finds himself playing opposite another very powerful character-type, the virtuous but neglected wife. This woman stands at center stage in practically every one of the earliest southern plays we know about. She is the "partner of one's porridge days," as the pioneer sinologist Herbert Giles tellingly translated the phrase. She is the first wife, whom a man marries in penurious youth, then leaves behind in his pursuit of ambition, whether with sword in hand on the frontier or wielding a brush in the examination halls of the capital. Her archetype is Zhao Wuniang, Fifth Sister of the play *The Lute*. Her husband Cai Bojie is rising rapidly at court while she lingers in the home village far away. She lives on what little rice a famine has spared—she has given the kernels to her husband's aging parents, whose service is her sole concern. As she forces the husks down her throat, almost gagging on them, she apostrophizes them in a powerful aria:

> *If I don't eat you, you husks,*
> *how can I escape starvation?*
> *If I try to eat you*
> *how can I swallow you down? . . .*
> *Chaff and grain, once close united*
> *blown by the winnower to fly apart*
> *one so worthless, one so prized,*
> *just like this slave and her worthy husband,*
> *no time set for our reunion.*

Husband, you are the grain

> *the grain is gone I know not where*

and I, slave, am just like the chaff

> *how can chaff save those who are starving?*
> *As now, my husband gone*
> *how can I provide the dainties his parents need? . . .*
> *I compare myself with these husks—*
> *the husks at least have found someone to eat them,*
> *but my poor bones*
> *who knows where they will be buried?*

> (*Pipaji* 25.)

Tertia is a fully accredited member of this school of deserted wives, placed before our eyes in the most pathetic predicament of all as she slaves at her millstone up to the very moment of giving birth.

These early *chuanqi* plays may not have been very vociferous—or very successful—in their championing of women's rights, for the Ming and Qing dynasties sustained and if anything intensified the general subjection of women to the masculine interest. But the suffering of their heroines must have come across with great power, as it still does. Their popularity with the feminine sector of their audience ensured their survival, and the menfolk at least were sensitized to the plight that could so easily overtake a woman when she was regarded as a chattel or as a mere source of potential revenue for the family. They were reminded, too, that loyalty and integrity were due not only between friends, but also from husband to wife in the hierarchy of Confucian relationships. Some of the plays roundly condemn their protagonists for deserting faultless wives. In one prototype of *The Lute,* Cai Bojie is struck by a thunderbolt in retribution for his heartlessness. Later versions argue his case, psychological complexities accrue, and by the time of the fully fledged Gao Ming version of the fourteenth century, from which we have just quoted, Cai is portrayed as the almost distraught victim of a dilemma of conflicting loyalties to family and state.

But subtleties of characterization have little place in the early, popular versions of *The White Rabbit.* It is almost as though, having launched themselves on a stage presentation of Liu Zhiyuan's rise to fame and fortune, the companies performing *The White Rabbit* in Yuan or early Ming times gradually succumbed to the power of the deserted wife figure who dominated virtually every other play their audiences loved. So Tertia's role grew and it was her scenes, not Liu Zhiyuan's, that people remembered when the play was spoken of—most of all, the famous and pathetic scene of giving birth by the millstone.

The contribution of the deserted wife motif to the life history of Liu Zhiyuan is somehow less important. It is enough that he is marked out by fate to establish a dynasty. Magical portents distinguish him. Squire Li is induced to accept this penniless gambler as son-in-law when he witnesses celestial portents of future greatness, a fiery aura surrounding Liu's sleeping form while snakes glide in and out of his nostrils, submitting to this imperial dragon as their lord. As a warrior hero he is not called upon to show much tenderness for Tertia. When she fearfully enters (in scene 1 2 of the Mao Jin version) half expecting to find her husband's corpse in the melon patch where he has just battled the demon, Liu hides in order to eavesdrop on her, to test her reaction to his presumed death (such testing of a wife's loyalty is a sadly prevalent motif in Chinese theater to this day). Liu's songs of parting from Tertia as he goes off to the army are perfunctory. He predicts that Tertia's brother and sister-in-law, in pursuit of family gain, will insist that she remarry. "If it's a man no better than me, don't marry him. If he's a better man than I am, marry him and that's that." Halfway up the ladder of promotion, Liu takes his general's daughter to wife without ever revealing that he is already married. Sixteen years after his parting from Tertia, when their son has brought about their reunion and accuses Liu of neglect of her, his response is to deflect all blame on to the wicked brother and sister-in-law, and we have already seen the cruel form his vengeance takes in the burning of the human candle. Although the *White Rabbit* plays made a definite contribution toward developing a consciousness of the oppression of women in traditional China, they certainly seem to have made no attempt to create a sympathetic husband out of Liu Zhiyuan.

THE EARLIEST SURVIVING VERSION

Among the old things swept away during the planned insanity of the Cultural Revolution were the tombs of a family surnamed Xuan, who in the fifteenth century owned land in Jiading county, outside modern Shanghai. The Australian scholar Anne McLaren reconstructs the course of events as follows:

> Some time after the stormy period of the "Smashing of the Four Olds" in 1966, a squad from the People's Liberation Army was sent down to the area, presumably to suppress factional violence. The military lacked land and building material for barracks and looked covetously at the expansive clan burial grounds, which were situated on prime farming land and contained an abundance of stone memorial slabs and bricks suitable for use in construction. . . . In anticipation of moves by the PLA to appropriate the burial grounds, [some of the villagers] . . . proposed to build a pigpen on the site. This idea fitted in with the aims of "Smashing the Four Olds," which called for the destruction of all vestiges of China's "feudalistic" past, and with the local policy of encouraging supplementary farming. Thus it came about that the only way for the villagers to "save" their ancestral graveyard and its resources was to raze it to the ground. The scores of tombs, most of them unmarked, were desecrated; memorial arches and statues were destroyed; memorial slabs were carted away to prop up sheds or serve as doorsteps and foundation stones. The pigpen was built, but the soil proved too marshy for pigs and the project was aborted.

By the time MacLaren visited the area in 1986:

> all that remained of the original burial grounds was a small lake (part of the original moat surrounding the central tombs), and a few battered statues of sheep, lions, and horses which had once stood proudly in a dual colonnade before the ancestral tombs. Empty pits, the remains of the unfortunate pigpens, dotted the barren field which was scarred with stones and debris.[3]

Already by 1972, when archaeologists arrived from Shanghai to investigate what was left of the once imposing array of graves, their contents were in total disarray. But there was one compensation at least for the savage rupture of five centuries of ancestral sacrifices and the smashing of the Xuan tombs: their contents proved to include one item immeasurably precious to us. It was a set of texts of old chantefables—and one play, none other than our own *White Rabbit*.

It appeared to the team from Shanghai that the texts had been retrieved from the tomb of a Madam Xuan, the wife of a sub-prefect named Xuan Chang. Dr. McLaren's subsequent investigations have cast doubt on this, and in fact it may never be possible to determine the sex of the member of the clan with whose corpse the texts were buried. But on the strength of the supposition that they had indeed come from Madam Xuan's tomb, I had speculated as follows:

• No doubt the intention was to ensure that her spirit would not lack the entertainment she had always enjoyed in life; perhaps also it was to commemorate the great merit she had acquired as a patroness of ballad-singers and actors, for a person of means could aid in bringing the masses of the people closer to enlightenment by subsidizing the presentation of plays or other popular entertainments at the temple. Whatever the purposes, the placing of the texts in her tomb gives us a strong reminder of the importance of the female sector to the old-time audiences for these shows.

I would like to let these speculations stand, to emphasize the part played by women of the gentry class in supporting and sponsoring the productions of traditional popular literature. The reader will understand that, like my reference below to Madam Xuan's post mortem puzzling over the orthography of the texts, I am engaging in supposition here rather than statement of cold fact.

The value of the texts recovered from the Xuan tombs lies less in their literary quality than in the exceptionally early date of their manufacture. Most of the ballad-tales that dominate the collection were printed between the years 1471 and 1478 of the Chenghua reign-period, shortly before the tomb was sealed, and just about the time when a number of Europeans believed they were inventing the art of printing. The publisher was the Hall of Eternal Obedience in the capital, Beijing. The ballads, in long strings of heptameters, present popularized versions of events from the chronicles of earlier dynasties, or edifying tales of filial sons, or the brilliant feats of detection of the incorruptible eleventh-century Judge Bao—about half are devoted to the exploits of this beloved hero of stage and story. They are rare survivals of a medieval crowd-pleaser, the kind of versified romance that was chanted, sometimes by blind minstrels, usually with drum accompaniment, at temple fairs or in the marketplace, and they are particularly prized because they are almost two hundred years older than any such ballads previously known to scholars. The single play in this treasure trove is no less precious. It is the version of our *White Rabbit* play that is now accepted as the earliest surviving printed text of a play of the southern style. We do indeed possess versions of thirty northern-style plays, *zaju,* actually printed a century or more earlier, during the Yuan dynasty when the plays were composed, but these texts are sadly incomplete, consisting for the most part of arias only, without the surrounding dialogue. (It is amusing to reflect that whereas Yuan printers considered only the arias worth printing, early Western translators considered the interest of the plays to be confined to the dialogue and omitted the arias as superfluous, so that between the Yuan edition and the eighteenth-century translated version of the same play it was possible that very little text would be shared!)

The *White Rabbit* play had been delighting audiences for many years, perhaps three centuries. With the growth of a semi-literate public of townsmen, shopkeepers, and the wives of gentry like our Madam Xuan, an enterprising Peking publisher saw a market for reading copies, and dressed up his product accordingly with crude but lively prints that are among the earliest full-page illustrations still surviving. One of the six woodblock prints shows Tertia turning her mill while Ugly Sister-in-law stands by with rod in hand. Another shows the grown youth Bittencord riding to the hunt, which will lead him to his mother. The text is obviously for readers, more than for actors who would learn their parts from teachers rather than from scripts, and so stage directions are minimal and even indications of who is speaking are not always clear. And this was no precious sacred transmission of the words of Confucius or the Buddha, nothing to be inscribed letter-perfect for all eternity. So poor is the quality of the spelling, in fact, that it seems in places as though its was dictated to the school dunce, who understood nothing of the meaning but simply wrote down the first character that came into his head for whatever sound he heard. Scholars in consequence owe a great debt of gratitude to the Classics Press of Yangzhou for the editorial work that made possible their fine edition of 1980. Thanks to them we can now repair the text of the poem by Qin Shaoyou that is recited in the prologue to the play, in such a line as *Zhan ting zheng zhao,* "momentarily halt traveler's oars." Since the paper of the original found in the Xuan family tomb had rotted where the fourth character should be, we have no idea whether the scribe had got the right *zhao* for "oars" or whether it might have been "morning," "reflect," or something else. We do know that he got each of the first three characters wrong: "stand" for "momentarily," "listen" for "halt," and "true" for "traveler" (the last error suggesting the southern origin of the scribe in his failure to distinguish the nasalized final). "Stand and listen to true . . ." for "momentarily halt traveler's oars"—if we didn't already know how the poem should read we would have little chance of guessing, and Madam Xuan must have scratched her head in the next world over many passages similarly mangled.

The Yangzhou editors issued our text very handsomely, in traditional thread binding and silk covers, punctuated, and with suggested corrections for almost all the erroneous characters. They give us great help also by providing indications of where the play should divide into scenes. In late Ming editions of plays, as is well known, scenes are not only clearly separated but numbered and given individual titles. Even without such specific marking we should be able easily to distinguish the beginning of a new scene. It will often open with a predictable formula: enter so-and-so, alone or with companions. After singing a short aria he or she recites a special entrance verse, and follows this in turn with a brief self-introduction in spoken dialogue. A specially structured exit verse may also mark the ending of a scene.

But our tomb text of *The White Rabbit,* as printed in Beijing in the 1470s, resembles the earliest manuscripts of southern-style plays in lacking any kind of division into scenes, and has not yet developed the full set of entrance or exit conventions that would make it obvious where scenes begin or end. At times the text resembles a novel rather than a play, and reinforces our understanding that this a reading version, complete with illustrations, for Madam Xuan to entertain herself with in the next world. Although stage directions are few and even distribution of speeches is not always clear, the text is surely based on performance on the popular stage of the time. The play is evidently structured by scenes, and the scenes are evidently measured by clearance of the stage rather than by plot incident.

This point is made very clearly in an article on the structural and musical features of the Chenghua *Baituji* by Sun Chongtao, who has written extensively on the play and must be accounted the leading authority on its history.[4] In his view, the Chenghua text illustrates the early practice of scene division in accordance with the convenience of the acting troupe in bringing its members on and off the stage, rather than with the conventions developed by late Ming editors of regarding a scene as coterminous with a plot incident and so marking it by means of a scene title, entrance and exit verses, and other signs. The most obvious signal our text gives of scene division is when a short quatrain is used on entrance or exit and is spaced across two whole columns of the text. In other places, the last personage occupying the stage is marked as exiting prior to the entrance of a new character. This clearing of the stage is equivalent to beginning a new scene, and almost always will be marked and numbered as such in later editions of the play.

But sometimes such cleared stage occurrences are harder to spot. One has to pay close attention to define the point at which a new personage enters and those previously on stage take no further part, having evidently exited or having been perhaps in a different location altogether. (Since there is no scenery, audiences simply have to deduce from the dialogue that the characters are in jail, at home, or outside the city gate, or wherever.) We may take the normal definition of a scene in plays of this kind to be a grouping of personages in a particular location. When the stage clears and a new grouping begins, usually we are to understand that the location has now changed also. In this way the total number of scenes can be very large, over fifty in some cases. The Chenghua *White Rabbit* has twenty-six scenes, compared with thirty-three or thirty-nine for the more elaborate later versions. (It is also possible to count, as does Sun Chongtao, twenty-four scenes for the Chenghua version and thirty-two for the late Ming *Sixty Plays* version, including the prologue in each case.)

It is a notable contribution by the Yangzhou Classics Press to have facilitated our reading of the Chenghua text, so that on the one hand we can overlook the innumerable orthographic errors, and on the other hand we can more easily recognize the structure of this version and compare it scene by scene with later ones.

PRELIMINARIES

One unvarying convention of the southern-style drama is to open with a formal prologue, recited by the player of the *mo* or older male roles. This earliest known text of *The White Rabbit* has a more elaborate prologue than most: the Dutch scholar Wilt Idema gives it pride of place in his discussion of the whole question of *chuanqi* opening scenes.[5] What the *mo* actor recites is of particular interest in that it gives us some vivid clues as to the sort of occasion on which a fifteenth-century performance might have been staged. Evidently we are in no large commercial theater, such as did in fact exist in the pleasure quarters of the capital and other cities, but at a banquet, in the reception hall or garden pavilion of some mandarin's residence. It is toward evening on a day of festival. The prevailing atmosphere of well-wishing and benediction is established by the opening quatrain, which calls for an ordered nation, upright officials, virtuous wives, and filial sons. We smell the incense as its smoke ascends from bronze burners, summoning the guardian spirit of the troupe to attend the feast. Since both banquet and play may be expected to last almost indefinitely, we may assume that the more privileged guests are comfortably seated with a good view of the small stage, whether this is a carpeted space at the end of the hall or a separate pavilion in the garden, perhaps viewed across the water of an artificial lake.

With "white tongue in red mouth," emblematic of the strongest language, the prologue-speaker exorcises all evil spirits by sending warnings through earth and sky. Then to the clamor of drums and wooden blocks, struck to shake the heavens, he sings a song of invocation to the immortals of the realm of music. His song is evidently intended for the ears of fairy beings, who alone will understand its import, since the words consist entirely of the nonsense syllables *li, luo,* and *lian* repeated in various permutations to fill a metrical pattern of forty-five spaces. The *mo* follows up his invocation by reciting a lyric verse by the romantic eleventh-century poet Qin Shaoyu. It is a lament of parted lovers, whose images of desolation—withered grass, rustic gate, wintry crows, and the lighting of lanterns—are appropriate enough to the drama of a deserted wife that is about to be performed. The poem finished, the speaker remarks that only a man of talent (as, obviously, he regards Qin Guan) should compose poems, just as only a hero should be entrusted with a sword. With this latter comment he presumably is making a neat switch to the hero of the play, Liu Zhiyuan, though it is just possible that the host of the banquet is a military official.

Still he has not yet introduced the offering of the evening. First comes the dictum that without action and clowning there can be no drama, then the request that the audience kindly overlook, or as he puts it "smother beneath a brocade coverlet," any errors they may find in libretto or musical interpretation.

"It is no longer early in the day, which is to say it is evening," the *mo* continues, "therefore let me indulge in no more of this banter but ask the brethren backstage whether they have prepared a play for us today."

"We have had it ready for hours," comes the reply from offstage.

"Since you have it ready, what is the play and whose story does it present?"

"It is the play of the *White Rabbit,* in which Li Sanniang at the milling-ground accepts the seal, and Liu Zhiyuan dressed in brocade returns to his native place."

What the offstage voice is announcing here is the full title of the play, which in two prosimetric lines captures the climactic moment of Liu Zhiyuan's return in glory, "dressed in brocade" as generalissimo, when he offers his seal of office in token of his rank and as pledge of his fidelity to his wife, the long-neglected Tertia (Sanniang). The identical lines are recited again by the hero, just before the finale of the play (Chenghua version only).

The seal is fashioned, according to Liu Zhiyuan's own description of it, from forty-eight ounces of gold. It might otherwise have been an intricately carved objet d'art of jade or marble, but the stage prop representing it is merely a brick-sized chunk of wood wrapped in a yellow bandana. The actor playing Liu Zhiyuan accedes to Tertia's request for a token by delivering this into her custody. He then steps out of character to announce with a flourish that this climactic action has now been performed. It is just one more instance of distancing, when the actor in his proper persona (like the prologue-speaker at the beginning) informs the audience of the completion of the essential action. All that remains, after this announcement, is the finale, in which all celebrate the happy outcome of events.

To return to our prologue: "Whom do we have to thank for this play?" the *mo* continues, and answers himself: "We have to thank the writers of the Yongjia Guild, who sat there by lamp and window's light, loaded the brush good and full, and compiled this top-class tale of filial love and integrity." Yongjia means Wenzhou, the cradle of southern-style drama, and all that *mo* is really doing here is to authenticate the white rabbit's pedigree.

The speaker boosts his "top-class tale": "See it a thousand times, always an excellent play, each time it's performed always a new experience." And he goes on to narrate the bald outline of the plot, this being the one irreducible duty of the prologue-speaker and in many later plays virtually his sole function: by the late Ming a prologue often consisted of nothing more than such an outline, preceded by a simple aria picking up one or two features of the theme.

The *mo* of the Chenghua text rounds off his prologue with the following quatrain, which once again will serve to remind the solitary silent reader (not least Madam Xuan beyond the grave) of the merry festivities at which the play originated:

> Trim the candles to brighten the scene,
> Start the feast, summer silks arrayed.
> Here comes Liu Zhiyuan himself,
> Silence, all! and see what's played.

THE TEXT

The copy of *The White Rabbit* recovered from the Xuan family tomb, as we have said, seems to have been a text meant for reading (hence the prologue speaker's apology for any misspellings), rather than an acting version for the use of the troupe. At the same time, much of its interest comes from the fact that the text was evidently based on contemporary stage performance. One indication of this is regarded by Sun Chongtao as indisputable: In scene 7 the wicked sister-in-law urges her husband, Li Hongyi, to poison Liu Zhiyuan so as to make way for them to marry off Tertia to a richer husband. Li Hongyi demurs:

LI HONGYI: No way, wife, no way, you're trying to do me in! That city magistrate will arrest me and they'll take me to some deserted spot and put me through it with a "fairy points the way and off flies the swallow." Then when I own up they'll drag me to the west corner, sitting west facing east, tie me up, and stick a placard down my neck, "the criminal Li Hongyi, for poisoning," and the executioner will lift his sword, one chop, off with my head, and then I'll be sent for a conscript soldier.
WIFE: How can they send you for a conscript after they've cut your head off?
LI HONGYI: They say the remission rate's a very poor one in this Chenghua reign.

> (The "flying swallow" was a contemporary form of judicial torture; the remission rate involved the payment of money, goods, or labor in exchange for remission of sentence.)

One of the beauties of this Chenghua text is that "what's played" includes not only such a topical reference as this, but in addition many of the crudities and irrelevancies that were edited out of later versions as the play matured, so that we can still get some idea of the fun the early groundlings enjoyed. Take the simple matter, for example, of signing the divorce papers which the villainous relatives try to force on Liu Zhiyuan. In this Chenghua version alone, Liu signs with his hand-print, Tertia's brother with his footprint, and the Ugly Sister-in-law with her backside, sitting on the paper to leave, so to say, her assprint. It is a merry piece of clowning, but has nothing whatever to contribute to the action and sadly disappears from the later recensions.

THE MANDARIN VERSION

And now at last we turn to what we shall classify as our "mandarin" version of the play, the polished production that bears the name of Xie Tianyou. It bears also the imprint of the publisher, the Fuchuntang or Hall of the Prosperous Springtime, in Nanjing in the late decades of the Ming dynasty. It can hardly be described as having been a popular version, since it seems to have survived, prior to its reprinting during the first decade of the Peoples Republic, in two copies only. The two seem to have been printed from the same blocks. One is to be found in the Beijing Library, the other, printed slightly later, with captioned illustrations, is in the Library of Congress in Washington.

Xie was evidently far from the front rank of late Ming dramatists. One other play of his, *The Fox-Fur Robe (Huqiuji),* survives in fragmentary form, and another eight plays are known to us by title alone. The contemporary connoisseur Qi Baojia assigned all of Xie's plays to the sixth category, next to the lowest of the seven he distinguished.[6]

Xie Tianyou was a native of Hangzhou, or perhaps as some say somewhere in Henan province. He was active around the year 1596. Nothing more is known of him beyond the alternative personal names he used.[7] Xie's *White Rabbit* belongs to a totally separate line of descent from the family of texts we have been considering thus far. The overall pattern of action changes little from one tradition to the other, but the actual text, whether dialogue or arias, coincides only in a few lyrics here and there, specifically in Xie's scenes 10 and 14, corresponding to *Sixty Plays* scenes 8 and 11 respectively. Evidently the two systems represent different musical traditions. The system represented by the Chenghua, *Sixty Plays,* and *White Fur Robe* texts was an older system based on the Gaoqiang musical tradition (arias from this system are preserved in early Ming songbooks), but its arias were set ultimately to the dominant new Kunqu music. Texts of the Xie Tianyou system were written for Yiyang and its related musical styles, and in fact, although Xie's play itself was not widely disseminated, the musical tradition it belonged to was clearly a popular one in late Ming performances of *The White Rabbit,* since several contemporary collections of selected arias contain *White Rabbit* scenes that resemble the corresponding songs of Xie's text rather than those of the other, earlier system. Moreover it is the arias of the Xie system that survive into many later local drama versions of *The White Rabbit.*[8] It is an index of the complexity of the total picture that the Xie version should present a more "literary" textual surface and yet that it should have evolved from the less-refined traditions of local drama, whilst it was the cruder text of the Chenghua system that was adopted by the elite, super-refined musical drama of the Kunqu school and is consequently represented in the *Sixty Plays* collection.

In essence Xie's version writes the whole thing over, converting the old melodrama into a domestic problem-play considerably different in feeling. It adds new scenes for a total of thirty-nine (the Mao Jin recension had thirty-three), and includes no less than six scenes covering Liu Zhiyuan's military career. The most elaborate of these is scene 23, where Liu Zhiyuan, challenged in his claim to be appointed general of the vanguard, sets up an array that impresses his generalissimo and is given the command. The kind of magical thinking represented by this construction of an array owes a great deal to Daoism, but it is part of Xie Tianyou's personal philosophical baggage rather than an element of the old folklore that was rife in the early versions of the play.

Even the title itself, to which we have not yet paid attention, came originally from a folkloric motif, that of the magical creature who aids the hero in his quest. The eminent drama specialist Wang Jisi has suggested that the original warren of the white rabbit is to be found in the play *Wu Hou yan* by the Yuan dramatist Guan Hanqing.[9] In this play Li Siyuan's hunt leads him to reunion with his father, the Posterior Tang Emperor.

The topos of the white rabbit who leads the way is in fact not restricted to drama. In the celebrated episode of the "true and false Li Kui" in ch. 43 of *Outlaws of the Marsh (Shuihu zhuan)*, it is a white rabbit that leads the true hero to the impostor. Ch. 37 of *Journey to the West (Xiyouji)* has Sun Wukong metamorphose into a white rabbit that leads its hunter, the prince, to his father's ghost.[10]

In the early versions of our *White Rabbit* plays Bittencord, Liu Zhiyuan's son, has grown to the age of sixteen in his father's camp and is unaware of the existence of his mother. A white rabbit, wounded in the hunt by the boy's arrow, leads him to a well, which is the site of Tertia's servitude. Xie Tianyou's version of the play uses the white rabbit for title. As usual the first scene is prologue, where the answer to the question, "What play today?" is "The history of the white rabbit, in which Squire Li takes in Liu Zhiyuan as son-in-law, and mother and son are reunited by the tiled well." In the brief outline of events spoken by the *mo* player there is mention of the jealousy of Tertia's brother and his wife, the birth of Bittencord (Yaojilang), the fifteen-year separation (not sixteen as in the earlier versions) of Liu Zhiyuan and Tertia, and their ultimate reunion.

The odd thing is that there is no mention in this outline of the white rabbit, or only in a very oblique way. Then, later, scene 34, which is exclusively dedicated to Bittencord's hunting expedition, seems to go out of its way to avoid reference to any encounter with or pursuit of any rabbit. Bittencord's first aria instructs his generals to hold their arrows poised to shoot at sight of rabbit, but soon he is complaining:

> My white horse passes one hamlet after another,
> no sign of roebuck or fawn, deer or rabbit.

In his second aria he sings at length of the success of his goshawks in their hunting of the wild swan. It is no rabbit but a mute herdboy (compare the

voluble clown of the *White Fur Robe* scene!) who leads them in search of re-
freshment and shelter to the village where Tertia resides. Not until scene 37
does the play acknowledge its debt to the legend that lies behind its title,
when Bittencord sings to his parents of his adventures, how he

> Hit a rabbit but lost its track
> seeing only an old greybeard, hoary-headed,
> who rode on mists and straddled the clouds
> and led us to a village
> where a woman wept as she drew from a well.

Professor Ye Kaiyuan of Lanzhou University has made a detailed comparison
of the Xie Tianyou *White Rabbit* with versions surviving to the present day in
several traditions of local drama.[11] In his view this sudden appearance in the
text of an "old greybeard" is intelligible only by reference to an episode re-
tained in local drama but eliminated by Xie, in which the god Taibai jinxing
"Gold Star of the Great White Spirit" dispatches the rabbit to guide Bittencord. This is, indeed, not the only point of the play at which Xie Tianyou in
his rewriting leaves inconsistencies (another is the confusion, earlier in the
action, between melon-demon and sword-spirit).

Interestingly enough, the writers of a recent Taiwan television version of
The White Rabbit, for performance by a Huangmeixi troupe, seem to have
identified the "old greybeard" as the metamorphosis of the rabbit itself: by
the modern magic of the TV camera a cuddly rabbit turns, late in the play,
into a stately white-haired sage to provide supernatural assistance as required. But as Professor Ye points out, the need for assistance from the white
rabbit disappears from Xie Tianyou's version since the meeting between Bittencord and his natural mother is no longer coincidental (or rather heaven-
ordained) in this version, but is mandated by the father Liu Zhiyuan in an
access of remorse.

Xie downplays or rejects outright several other folkloristic features aside
from the figure of the white rabbit itself. Whereas Liu Zhiyuan's battle with
the melon-patch demon is straightforward fairytale in the early versions, and
expanded later as we have seen into first-rate farce, Xie invests his scene 17
with strictly human dimensions of ironic character interplay. Liu Zhiyuan has
been soused with liquor in advance through the trickery of his brother-in-law,
and he opens this long scene with arias (to northern tunes) celebrating the
glories of drunkenness. The demon has been established in the previous scene
via a short monologue, in the kind of scene lacking arias which is not unknown but not common in southern drama. In scene 17 he is given no words
and is quickly vanquished, but Liu himself is too overcome by wine fumes to

explore the magic cave without a good snooze first. When Tertia arrives with food, Liu comments wryly that "It would have been more helpful last night" (to sober him up before his fight). There is mild but effective comic irony, too, when Tertia stumbles on Liu's sleeping form and fears that the demon has stolen his soul away.

In the Chenghua and *Sixty Plays* versions Liu Zhiyuan assures Tertia that he will not return until he wins success, official rank, and the means to avenge himself on his brother-in-law. These, he says, are his "three refusals to return" (*san buhui*). It is a formula reminiscent of Cai Bojie's "three failures to resist" (*san bucong*) and "three failures of filial love" (*san buxiao*) in *The Lute*. Such formulas seem to bespeak a popular tradition in which they are code-names for recognition of a theme, and in fact the *Pipaji* prologue uses the full title *San bucong Pipaji*. Folk formulas of this kind are completely missing from Xie Tianyou's play.

Xie considerably reduces the elements of slapstick or farce. Scene 6 of the Mao Jin version, for example, gives Squire Li scope for a comic turn when he observes the portents of Liu's future greatness. Liu is asleep in the stables, and snoring. Squire Li is convinced that it is a violent thunderstorm and has an aria of panicky reaction. Then he sees Liu lying there, but rather than resolve his fears the sight brings on fresh panic, for he mistakes the magic aura surrounding Liu for evidence that his farm is on fire. Xie retains none of this, but invents a new scene 6 of his own which, picking up the hint from the early versions, shows Liu Zhiyuan taming a horse that no one has previously been able to manage. One would think the scene is hardly stageable—the stage direction reads quite simply "Enter horse, which Liu Zhiyuan tames." But the text seizes the opportunity for a display of erudition, with an aria about famous steeds of the past, themselves emblematic of the qualities of the outstanding hero.

It is fair to ask, then, just what Xie Tianyou is doing when he takes the trouble to provide the *White Rabbit* with an all but completely rewritten text. First and foremost he is rehabilitating the hero, Liu Zhiyuan. The old legends took the historical figure of a roughneck who founded a short-lived dynasty and furnished him with various forms of supernatural aid, proving to all that the will of Heaven prevails even when its raw material is no more than a disreputable gambler. It is a theme found in other works of popular literature: witness the portraits of Shi Hongzhao and Guo Wei in *Gujin xiaoshuo* 15, where the domestic life of the heroes is again an important element. Xie Tianyou is not satisfied with all this. For a man to rise to the dragon throne, in his view, calls for a full complement of Confucian virtues, and he therefore presents us with a Liu Zhiyuan cast in a noble mold. There is a certain wildness about his boyhood to be sure, but Shakespeare's Prince Hal is not the first of the world's great literary heroes to have risen sun-like above the clouds of a stormy youth.

Liu's poverty-stricken state is explained by the early death of his parents (an extraordinary proportion of *chuanqi* protagonists are orphans, perhaps to avoid intolerable complications in the obligatory final reunion scene). Liu's outstanding talents have gone unrecognized by an ignorant world, and it is frustration on this score that drives him to the life of a gambler.

Liu Zhiyuan, in this version of his story by the late Ming dramatist Xie Tianyou, is considerate of his wife and has ready explanations for his fifteen-year absence from her, the consequence of stern duty at the frontier. He is magnanimous to Tertia's weak (not wicked) brother, who has allowed his ill-favored and sadistic wife to inveigle him into robbing Tertia of her inheritance. He is, after all, of gentry background (his social status has in fact been steadily improving ever since the earliest chantefable version of his story). Unlike the Liu Zhiyuan of the early popular versions of the play, the Liu of Xie's text is recognized as a distant cousin of the Li family. He has immersed himself deeply in military lore and can (and does) cite historical precedents for any situation that arises.

In the popular versions of the *White Rabbit* play, things just happen. With Xie Tianyou there is a new attempt to explain motivations, to interpret psychologies. Tertia's Ugly Sister-in-law is the chief villain in all the recensions. But only Xie Tianyou takes the trouble to trace the source of her hatred of Tertia. Her monologue in Xie's scene 11 reveals her motivation to be jealousy. As daughter-in-law, she has always had to take a back seat to the daughter of the house. The incident of the bill of divorcement, in the same scene, is given much more plausibility than in the earlier versions. There, Tertia's brother most unconvincingly browbeats Liu Zhiyuan (a peculiarly spineless "hero" at this point of the action) into writing the bill at dictation. When it is written Tertia simply enters abruptly and tears it up. Xie invents a more elaborate stratagem, and then has Liu Zhiyuan foil it, as a hero should, by his own ingenuity.

In scene 11, Ugly Sister-in-law cooks up a scheme whereby her husband, away from home at the time of Tertia's wedding, pretends on his return to be infuriated with his wife for consenting to it (to the extent of participating as mistress of ceremonies), and stages a fake beating. Thereupon his wife pleads with Liu Zhiyuan to save her life by writing a bill of divorcement of Tertia. This will assuage her husband's wrath, and she will return the document to Liu, she swears, when she herself is out of danger. Liu Zhiyuan in his turn pretends to be taken in and writes the bill, but using a mode of expression which cleverly shows that he is writing under duress. Tertia's uncle, the mediator, explains to her brother in scene 12 that the bill has no chance of standing up in a court of law and that Ugly Sister-in-law's stratagem has failed.

The brother's motivation for his maltreatment of Tertia is similarly a matter to which only Xie Tianyou among the *White Rabbit* dramatists pays much attention. In scene 29 Dou the majordomo and his wife, en route to commit Tertia's baby son to Liu Zhiyuan's care in Binzhou, discuss the brother's conduct. Dou's wife is inclined to excuse him, taking the view that Tertia's plight is entirely the product of the sister-in-law's malice. Then in scene 31 the brother has the stage to himself for a monologue in which he laments his wife's cruel nature and domineering ways, and plans to lighten Tertia's burden by secretly engaging a substitute to relieve her at her chores.

A curious and oddly impressive instance of Xie Tianyou's greater concern with his characters' psychology occurs in scene 38. This is the major scene of the reunion of Liu Zhiyuan and Tertia. When she learns that her husband has taken a second wife she weeps in fear that she cannot compete now, after all her sufferings, for her husband's favor—and he agrees that indeed her looks have gone! The sad truth to life of the situation comes out the more clearly when we compare it with, for example, scene 27 of the roughly contemporary play *The Gold Sparrows (Jinqueji)*, in which first wife, on learning of her husband's taking of a second, coos sweetly: "So my husband has taken a new little sister to join the household! He is to be congratulated!" Tertia, in contrast, goes so far as to contemplate suicide (again), but Liu Zhiyuan consoles her, denies that he has been faithless, and ends the scene realistically weighing the dilemma of which wife should take precedence (the dilemma is finally resolved, of course, in Tertia's favor).

This late Ming dramatist Xie Tianyou failed, obviously, to provide a *White Rabbit* that would drive all its predecessors from the stage. Still we gain some likely clues to what the late Ming public wanted from the changes we see here, where the stark figures of legend from the early Liu Zhiyuan melodramas are domesticated, given new psychological dimensions, and painted in shades that would resemble more closely their counterparts in Ming society. The peasants of the early chantefable have become gentrified, and Tertia enters the cloistered state of the classic late Ming young lady. Her first meeting with Liu Zhiyuan in the different recensions tells us volumes about the advance toward respectability. In the early versions, the father Squire Li simply marches in upon his wife and daughter with Liu Zhiyuan in tow. But by the time Xie Tianyou comes to rewrite the play around the turn of the seventeenth century, the Li family has been hoisted up the social ladder and its code of moral conduct for women has reached a high level of rigidity. A special stratagem is needed to engineer an opportunity for Tertia to catch a glimpse of a prospective spouse, and an entire scene of the play is devoted to this development. This is scene 8, in which Tertia's father and uncle scheme to have Liu Zhiyuan, newly engaged in their stables, sweep out the reception hall of their residence while Tertia spies on him from behind a screen. It is a situation of high artificiality (though of universal comic character), whose value lies mainly in its scope for romantic badinage, as Tertia responds with appropriate bashfulness to her maid's teasing. At the same time, it is a pleasant indication of the old squire's willingness to take his daughter's wishes into account instead of simply forcing her, as in the early versions, into marriage with the man of his choice.

However we may judge the theatrical effectiveness of Xie's rewriting of *The White Rabbit,* his play certainly works quite well as closet drama, as a text for private reading. And his rendering of the childbirth scene should play reasonably well on stage, with its minor battle between Tertia and Sister-in-law, and with the occasion for spectacle offered by the entrance, attended by demons, of the God of Earth. The early versions of the scene, with a representative of which I opened this chapter, have no gods but merely a stage direction for Bittencord's birth. It is unlikely that Tertia would do anything so crude as to reach down and simply pull out the rag doll from beneath her skirt. More probably a stage hand, clad in black and thus by convention invisible, entered at the appropriate moment and deposited the doll in her arms.

Xie Tianyou must have had some reason for dissatisfaction with the propriety or decorum of the proceedings, and so provides Bittencord with a divine escort into the world. In fact the descent of the Earth God, or spirit of the locality, to aid Tertia in her delivery is consistent with the kind of supernatural grid which Xie superimposes on his play, giving a new sense of unity to the whole.

No sudden fires flare out, no snakes glide through nostrils, even the White Rabbit itself practically disappears from the play that bears its name. But in place of these casual glimpses, Xie patiently constructs a whole edifice of supernatural support for the historical event of Liu Zhiyuan's royalty. Thus the melon-demon, for example, changes utterly in Xie's text. He becomes a guardian spirit and is assigned a solo scene to explain the predestined role he has been waiting to fulfill since the Han dynasty (historical precedent, to a Ming man of letters, being as necessary as air to the maintenance of life). The Earth God also, who aids Tertia in her delivery, like the melon-demon is conscripted into a grand Daoist scheme of things to obey the dictates of the Jade Emperor and assist in the incarnation of a celestial body, the Crape-myrtle Star, as the baby Bittencord destined to rule as Second Emperor of the Latter Han.

So in various ways Xie Tianyou has tried to produce a White Rabbit play that would resolve some of the problems posed by the early popular versions, questions as to the character of Liu Zhiyuan's heroism, or the reasons for the cruelty to Tertia, or in fact the central question of what kind of entertainment this was to be—swashbuckler or domestic problem-play (resolved in favor of the latter). He sacrificed a great deal of robust merriment by cleaning up the text. His lyrics every now and then offer a fresh image or a happy mode of phrasing. Whether this is sufficient compensation for what he lost is no doubt a matter of taste, but some credit is surely due to this almost forgotten figure of the Ming theater who devised his scenes, we must assume, not for the temple stage or for his village neighbors, but first and foremost for the enjoyment of the mandarins of his acquaintance.

THE "BIRTH AT THE MILL" SCENE
AS REWRITTEN BY XIE TIANYOU

The first of the poetic images Xie Tianyou builds into his verse for the new version of the birthing scene is that of close-matched stones, *tuanyuanshi,* the millstone and its fixed base, representing Tertia's brother and his villainous wife. The millstones are round and close-fitting, so *tuanyuan* is an apt epithet for them. But roundness (fullness of the moon) in Chinese imagery suggests also union or reunion, as in the grand reunion, *da tuanyuan,* which normally closes each *chuanqi* play. Tertia's brother and his wife are a complete household in the union of the two of them, a sister is an unnecessary addition. But only one of the two has a heart of iron, just as the two millstones possess only one fixed pivot. When Ugly Sister-in-law later in the scene claims "it was your brother told me to beat you," she is lying. She herself is the author of Tertia's sufferings. The brother is much less vicious, playing a role more like that of Cinderella's father vis-à-vis the Ugly Stepsisters.

The more poetic lines, in general, naturally go to Tertia. Some of them offer images of an original or at least unhackneyed sort, like the

> layered cloud-laden hills beyond the gate
> not high enough to block the approach of sorrow.

The hills are still high enough, we must infer, to obstruct her view of the road her husband must return by—a poignant reminder of her deserted state.

When later, very shortly before the moment of birth itself, she refuses to "make plaint to the east wind," she calls up multiple associations. The east wind, like the spring in Western imagery, turns the fancy of the young to thoughts of love, in this case Tertia's longing for Liu Zhiyuan. But the east wind would also bear her plaint to the border where Liu Zhiyuan is fighting, which is more to the point here.

Bearing these references is mind, I conclude now with the birthing scene from Xie Tianyou's totally rewritten version of *The White Rabbit:*

Scene 27: Tertia Li by the Millstone Gives Birth to Bittencord

SISTER-IN-LAW (*enters*):

(*TUNE: SHUANG TIAN XIAO JIAO*)

Traps and tricks
how cunningly contrived!
Fetch the water, mill the grain as well—
how much of this drudgery can she stand?

I've made her cut off all her hair, this worthless little Tertia, and I've thrashed her into working as a slave, fetching water by day and turning the millstone at night. It's getting dark now, I must see that the millstone's in order and make her come turn it. It's like they say,

A pair of close-matched stones
the pivot an iron heart;
only a few steps round,
it'll grind you, once you start!

Hurry up, Tertia!

TERTIA (*enters*):

(*SAME TUNE*)

Long-drawn-out vexation
suffering, and who to hear my cry?
Bitterly I resent their cruelty, my brother and his wife
And wonder will they ever cease this grinding punishment.

Burn the beanstalks to cook the beans
that bubble in the pot:
"Stalks, your roots and ours were the same—
why must you burn so hot?"

Because I would not consent to remarrying, my brother and sister-in-law
made me cut off my hair and set me to turning the mill. They beat me,
too, so that all I can do is go on. (*She greets Sister-in-law*): I heard you call me,
sister-in-law. What do you want me to do?

SISTER-IN-LAW: Third Sister, your brother has ordered me to supervise your
milling of the grain. Three things you are forbidden: first, to complain
against your brother or sister-in-law; second, to be idle; third, to speak
of Liu Zhiyuan. Any time you break any one of these rules you get
punished. In fact I'll just give you a beating right now as a lesson.

TERTIA: You've no need to be like this. I'm ready to do the milling.

> (*TUNE: XIANG LUO DAI*)
> *Myriad sorrows knot my entrails——*

sister-in-law, can't you see

> *the stone's too heavy for me to turn,*
> *how can I move a single step?*

What I resent

> *is the hard hearts of my brother and his wife*
> *that make them so cruel to me!*

SISTER-IN-LAW: So you're complaining against your brother and sister-in-
law again! (*She beats Tertia*)

TERTIA:

> *You have struck us apart, husband and wife*
> *matched in bliss as phoenix pair,*
> *and tried to force a second mate on me.*

SISTER-IN-LAW: If you were only willing to remarry, never mind turning the
millstone or getting beaten, I would never say a single word to scold
you.

TERTIA: Sister,

> *how could I go against all decency?*

SISTER-IN-LAW: Why do you slack about and refuse to turn the stone? (*Beats
Tertia*)

TERTIA: Oh! When we are sisters, how can you beat me so viciously? I've
given in to you this last time or two, out of consideration for my
brother's face.

SISTER-IN-LAW: Talk like that and I really will beat you, and what can you do
about it?

TERTIA: Sister,

> *your heart is the heart of a snake or scorpion*

and oh my brother,

> *you forget we are fruit of one mother's womb.*

SISTER-IN-LAW: You think I'm afraid to beat you some more, when all you do is complain about your brother and me?

TERTIA: You've no cause to beat me! (*She seizes the rod and beats Sister-in-law, who dodges*)

> *I am the proper daughter of the house,*
> *you are the daughter-in-law whose place is in the kitchen.*

It's always been said,

> *the great should receive what's due to the great,*
> *the mean what's due to the mean.*
> *Own daughter to the worthy Squire Li,*
> *how can I be subject to such heartless abuse?*

SISTER-IN-LAW: Sister, you may beat me now, but tomorrow when your baby arrives you'll need me to look after you.

TERTIA: I've been at fault. If in a day or two I bear a son, and these two plot to take his life, I shall have suffered all this abuse for nothing. All I can do is watch my step and play them along for the time being. (*She kneels*) Sister, I was at fault just now, please bear with me for my brother's sake.

SISTER-IN-LAW: Third Sister, please get up. It's nothing to do with me, it's your brother told me to beat you. I won't beat you any more. Just get on with your grinding now, I'm off to bed. (*Exit*)

TERTIA:

> *Thatched eaves and crumbling walls, a lonely watch,*
> *the layered, cloud-laden hills beyond the gate*
> *not high enough to block the approach of sorrow.*

Thank goodness my sister-in-law has gone. Let me try for a while to force this millstone round.

> (*TUNE: WU GENG ZHUAN*)
> *All I can manage, a few staggering steps,*
> *weary as I am, how can I swing it round?*
> *I think back to my parents' careful nurturing—*
> *when did I ever need step outside the door?—*
> *yet now I slave to turn the mill and fetch water.*

Ah, pity me,

> *the beauty I once had all perished,*
> *soft cheeks drawn in, slender waist now haggard.*

Ah Heaven, rather than go on suffering such abuse, better to hang myself and end it all.

Yet before I choose the road of the ill-fated—

(*She weeps*) I do wrong to think like this. I remember when we first parted, there in the melon patch, I told him I was carrying a child, and he said, "Tertia, take care of yourself here at home. If it is a son you bear, this will be the continuation of the line of the Lius."

Before I choose the road of the ill-fated,
what of the ten months I have been with child?
If I should die

ah, then I fear

the end of the Lius' posterity.
Let it rest, let it rest,
however worn my looks
as spring flowers follow autumn moon
somehow the empty days go by.

And yet I am too weary to turn the mill, and faint too with hunger. Let me rest here against the millstone for a while.

(TUNE: XIA SHAN HU)
Since you left me, Master Liu,
somehow the year's reached autumn,
and by now surely you've unfurled your whip
and on your swift steed Flying Yellow
outdistanced all your rivals.
For your sake I have toiled,
borne insult and ignominy,
but how to withstand the anxious fears
that rise in the heart, that rest on the brow
that you should prove a false hero
unmindful of your old love?
Do not cast me off
for lust of wealth that lies behind red gates:
how would I shed the sorrow,
condemned to face dim lamp, lone shadow for partner?

(SAME TUNE)
Parted a few months
it seems three autumns lie between us.

I raise my eyes, where clouds wrap distant hills,
watching till sight fails for your returning boat.
Do not cast me off,
to sigh for favor short-lived as dew at dawn.

No! He is a

man of mark,
a noble champion,
how could he sink to petty betrayal?

Ah, sorrow!

Crickets at door and window
cree-creak, cro-croak,
and in thoughts of the fate of Tertia Li,
captive to grief
grievously wronged
my eyes fill with a rain of tears.
Eaves-pendants clatter in the wind,
a hubbub in the doorway,

but who spares a thought for me,

consigned to anxious doubts in empty room.

But oh what misery, I can sit here no longer, there's still a whole basket
of wheat left, and if I don't finish milling it my brother and his wife will
scold and beat me. But it's so hard to turn!

(TUNE: ZHU YUN FEI)
Millstone so heavy, so hard to turn,
and in still of night, no one to hear my plaint,
in travail I endure time's passage
still to preserve this body alive.

Ah me,

my man far off at edge of sky,
I wait and wonder.
Far distant is the border's dust
like a sea in the sadness of recollection
yet never have I made my plaint to the east wind.

(She mimes the pangs of labor)

(SAME TUNE)
Suddenly comes the pain,
my ten months' term fulfilled now quick as counting.
Longing so for this confinement

I steel myself to endure.
Ah, but the haggardness of my flesh
makes it harder still,
the pain strikes deep to my heart.
Life and death in the balance
soul quits body, weary eyes flicker open.
(*She collapses to the floor. Enter the God of Earth bearing Tertia's son as a baby in his arms, and followed by attendant demons.*)
EARTH GOD:

From the Ninefold Heavens I bear the Golden Boy,
driving six dragons that ride the tinted clouds.
As the Crape-myrtle Star leaves the sky, new heir to imperial
  throne,
the Palace of the Jade Empyrean is bathed in a glow of blessing.

Behold me, Birth-delivering Spirit of the Ninefold Heavens. Whereas Liu Zhiyuan of Shatuo is destined in days to come to achieve highest rank, with Tertia Li by his side as Imperial Consort, and whereas the ten months of her term are now fulfilled, therefore His Majesty the Jade Emperor has decreed the incarnation on earth of the Crape-myrtle Star, and has commissioned me to deliver the babe out of Tertia's womb. Hear my command, Tertia: in time to come this child will achieve great eminence. Make no demur, but have the child carried at once to Binzhou. Let there be no mistake or delay (*He deposits the baby*)

Light is shed through earth and sky
that men need grope through dark no more. (*Exit*)

TERTIA (*waking*):   Strange! Strange! Surely someone was giving me instructions!

Limbs grown lax, hard to stir.
Good fortune has brought my babe to birth
good fortune too has preserved my life from harm.
But the umbilical cord is not yet severed.

Where am I to find shears here in the mill? What am I to do? I shall have to bite through the cord myself! Ah!

All is bloody, how can I open my mouth
suffering strikes my heart!
(*She mimes biting through the cord*)
The cord is bitten through,
teeth are flecked with blood,
cries choke my son, I grieve for bitter pain.

(*She cradles her baby and gazes down at him*)
(SAME TUNE)
So strange a dream!
When I was lying on the floor then in a faint
it seemed a spirit brought this child to me,
a son, however strange his birth
still so much to be loved!

Ah Heaven, when I have suffered such hardships, how I rejoice now in the happy gift of this child's birth! (*She sighs*)

Smiles come unbidden to my cheek
as I reflect
how closely face and form
are modeled on Master Liu!

Now I believe the ancient saying, dragon begets dragon and phoenix phoenix,

and indeed, a tiger father will beget a tiger son!

The spirit said this child will be a great man some day, and that I must send him to Binzhou. But I am still to weak to act, how am I to find anyone to take him? I must seek out my uncle tomorrow and discuss with him what can be done.

ENVOI:

Thankful am I to receive the spirit's message
that here is the Crape-myrtle Star descended from the sky.
The word that he is destined for future greatness
furnishes a dream to delight a mother's heart.

(*Liu Zhiyuan Baituji*, scene 27)

Two Icons of Xi Shi, Legendary Beauty

The blowfish or puffer, as is well known, is highly prized as a delicacy but must be prepared with great care if it is not to prove fatally poisonous. A particularly succulent part of its soft white underbelly is known to the Chinese cuisine by the name of "Xi Shi's breasts," and the deadly lusciousness of this flesh may surely provide an appropriate symbol for the ambivalence men have demonstrated whenever they tried to picture the glamorous Xi Shi: in one light, the epitome of desirable, fragile beauty, and in another a peril to be avoided at whatever cost. Fox ladies, succubi—all later representations of Woman as irresistible destroyer owe much to this early paragon of beauty.

Her name is not the easiest thing for the poor foreigner to pronounce, whether romanized in old fashion (Hsi Shih or Shi Shy) or new, as here. If you started to say "she sure is pretty," and stopped just short of the "r" in "sure," you might come close to it in English, but perhaps it might help also to think of a certain dish of steamed baby squid, which is known by the name of "Xi Shi's tongue," slithering down the throat of a gourmet—that is about the way her name sounds. The meaning of the name is "Favor of the West," and we could call her West Maid, or invent some such name as Occidia or Occidana, but because the syllables Xi Shi are known to every Chinese schoolboy we shall obediently preserve, in what follows, the name by which she has been so timorously cherished for twenty-five hundred years.

Poets through the centuries have written about Xi Shi in every known genre. In two Ming plays, *The Girl Washing Silk (Huanshaji)* and *The Plantain Kerchief (Jiaopaji),* her roles are almost diametrically opposed, reflecting the double vision described above: in *The Girl Washing Silk* she is victimized as tragic heroine, in the second play she is quite farcically libeled as a would-be immortal nymph or nymphomaniac.

烏鵲填橋
催渡何

LIANG CHENYU'S

The Girl Washing Silk

The Girl Washing Silk is celebrated as the play that established Kunqu as the dominant dramatic style, the elite, elegant style which endured for three centuries and is still favored today among the most dedicated aficionados of the classical theater. The original Kunqu, "songs of Kun(shan)," were set to local tunes from the region close by Suzhou, but the composer Wei Liangfu, who is credited with developing the style to maturity, evidently drew eclectically from other local schools. The music he created, according to the contemporary critic Xu Wei, "in its flowing beauty, slow tempi and far-reaching quality, excels all the other three principal styles."[1] This music of Suzhou is renowned for its excellence just as are the Suzhou landscapes, the Suzhou girls, and the mellifluous tones of the Suzhou dialect and, to set the coping stone on the structure of his play, our dramatist Liang Chenyu used ancient Suzhou itself as its primary setting. Liang, whose dates have been estimated as ca. 1521–1595, based his story on historical events of the fifth century B.C., when Suzhou was the capital of King Fuchai of the feudal state of Wu, and as his title suggests he gave pride of place in his scenario to the fate of the beautiful Xi Shi, the maiden discovered washing

The Girl Washing Silk: Xi Shi dances.

lengths of silk by the side of a stream but so soon to fall victim to the inter-state intrigues of the day.

We have several purposes in selecting four of the play's forty-five scenes to describe here. Xi Shi's situation is both central to the play and profoundly ironic, when she is sacrificed by her own lover to King Fuchai in the attempt to seduce him into political impotence. This irony is most effectively brought out in scene 23, "The Recruitment of Xi Shi," and it is with this scene that we begin our commentary on the play. We follow with scene 25, "The Dancing Lesson," which we translate in full, since Liang Chenyu takes the opportunity of this scene to present in dramatic form his own esthetic of the theater. The succeeding scene, "Committing the Son," has nothing to do with the Xi Shi motif of the play but deserves at least our passing attention by reason of its enduring popularity on the Kunqu stage. The fourth scene we examine, which again we translate in full, is scene 30, "Gathering Lotus," which epito-mizes at once the glamour and the poignancy of Xi Shi's position as favored consort of a detested tyrant.

SCENE 23: THE RECRUITMENT OF XI SHI

The man who enters is evidently a person of consequence. He is preceded by twin files of retainers who bear reverently before them the pearl-hung head-dress and brocade gown appropriate to the use of a palace beauty. The man himself wears the girdle of a high officer of the court. He is Fan Li, minister of state to King Goujian of Yue in the fifth century B.C., a time of strife between this southern state of Yue and the principality of Wu, in the lower Yangzi Valley. In company with his royal master Fan Li has only recently been re-leased from three years of imprisonment in Wu. Now he is approaching Net-tle Village, home of Xi Shi, the country girl whom prior to his captivity he chanced upon at stream-side, fell in love with, and vowed to take as bride.

He fears the pomp of the procession will startle the quiet rural scene, and orders his retainers to wait at the edge of the village while he enters alone. He leads them off, leaving the stage clear for the solo entrance of Xi Shi. Faithful through three years of pining, she has had news of Fan Li's return from captiv-ity in the land of Wu and now yearns anxiously for his visit. The first line of her entrance aria reminds us that her great beauty is of the delicate, pensive kind, which makes even a frown seductive:

> *Fall comes, spring passes, brows remain locked*
> *what year will end this melancholy?*
> *My lamp's bright gleam last night seemed to understand*

but I place no trust in magpie's chatter
before the eaves at dawn.

Both the flaring up of a lamp wick and the chatter of magpies are good omens, but Xi Shi in her timid self-mistrust is wary of accepting them.

While she waits for Fan Li, she tells us, she passes the time plying her needle, and one version of the scene has her seated at this point, miming the actions of sewing.[2] Embroidering birds and flowers on silk jackets or slippers to keep oneself out of mischief seems more appropriate to the genteel young lady of Ming times, when the play was written, than to the simple country girl of the Xi Shi legend. But in any case the village girl had plenty of sewing of her own to do. When all other chores had been completed there was always the making or mending of shoes, and this was done by stitching together layer upon layer of cloth to form the soles. As her Western counterpart found with the knitting or darning of woolen socks, it was a never-ending task. But put it on stage, and it provided excellent scope for mime. Slender fingers pluck the needle from its lodging-place in swept-up chignon of hair above the temple, then select a length of thread from the basket by the feet. Depending on the mood and pace the scene demands, the seamstress may make many passes before the imaginary needle is threaded, and the nonexistent thread drawn to satisfactory length and daintily bitten off. She may mime pricking her finger, or dropping her needle, or losing count of her stitches and having to start over. Whatever variations she introduces, she will be sure to demonstrate the most fluid ease of gesture as hand draws out thread then swoops again to its task.

Fan Li reenters, his ministerial robes now concealed beneath a plain traveling gown. Xi Shi is inside her cottage, and so by convention the two are still invisible to each other as he paces the stage, setting the rustic scene in a brief monologue:

> Asking my way here I have been told that Xi Shi's cottage
> faces a flowing stream and a green hill rises behind. A
> stand of tall bamboos beyond a low bridge, a thatched
> dwelling where the flowers bloom thickest.

Her gate is shut because her father is away, only her sick mother keeps Xi Shi company. Fan Li refrains from knocking for some time, hoping that she will come out if he waits. Then he coughs, then calls out. When she asks from within "Who's there?" he will not say, but waits for her to open the gate and finally recognize him.

This slow hesitancy in bringing the two together hardly matches the mood appropriate to a lover returning from three years of absence. But there is excellent reason for Fan Li's tentativeness. We are at the central moment of the play, the midpoint of the midmost scene, and Fan Li has come to summon the girl he has scarcely seen, not to the marriage ceremony she eagerly anticipates, but to the extraordinary sacrifice that is the core and cause of their entire story. The kingdom of Yue is no match for Wu in military terms and is only slowly recovering from its defeat three years previously. Guile is called for if the rival is to be weakened and Yue's disgrace avenged. As luck will have it, King Fuchai of Wu is a notorious old lecher. If Yue's King Goujian can only persuade him to accept as a tributary gift a consort of sufficiently seductive charms, Fuchai might, at one and the same time, be misled into belief in Yue's submissiveness, and distracted by pleasures of the flesh, neglect such matters of state as the proper maintenance of his own armies. Fan Li's fellow minister, Wen Zhong, has proposed this "seduction stratagem," but it is Fan Li himself who, when all other candidates have been rejected, has volunteered his own beloved, the exquisite Xi Shi, Favor of the West, for the fateful mission to Wu.

The Xi Shi legend had already begun to enliven Chinese literature by the beginning of our era, when Zhao Ye compiled his *Annals of Wu and Yue (Wu Yue chunqiu)*. The name of Xi Shi is mentioned more than once in texts earlier than that, but whereas Fan Li and Wen Zhong and the kings Goujian and Fuchai are historical figures, Xi Shi may never really have existed at all, simply a necessary invention as the embodiment of outstanding feminine allure.

A laconic comment in an ancient text characterizes Fuchai as a ruler who preferred court entertainments to the regulation of his subjects' affairs, and Zhao Ye, writing his annals, seems to have seized on this weakness as the explanation for Fuchai's defeat at the hands of the kingdom of Yue. There must be a moral lesson to be learned from the event, so the argument goes, this self-indulgent ruler must surely have been distracted, and obviously by a woman—a real Xi Shi of a woman. Dancing girls, singers, and musicians were quite customary gifts between one court and another; and so Zhao Ye, out of all these elements, concocts his legend.[3]

The tale is made all the more acceptable by its southern setting. As E. H. Schafer writes:

> For the Chinese, the south had always been the land of seductive women and attractive landscapes. An imperishable tradition has the locus of these delights in ancient Viet (Yue)—that is to say, chiefly in modern Chekiang, south of the mouth of the Yangtze. The chief denizen of this archaic wonderland in the late Chou period was an unlettered country

girl—a supreme beauty. Her name was Hsi Shih. . . . Hsi Shih has always been the Cleopatra, the Thaïs, and the Queen of Sheba of China. She is every southern beauty—and yet she is unique. Her radiant loveliness was still celebrated in T'ang times. Here is Li Po:

> Hsi Shih, a woman of the streams of Viet—
> Luminous, ravishing, a light on the sea of clouds.[4]

In another poem, "The Song of the Roosting Crows," Li Bai (Li Po) brilliantly evokes the drama of Xi Shi's sojourn at Fuchai's royal court:

> The time when the crows are roosting
>   on the terrace of Ku-su
> Is when, in the Wu king's palace
>   Hsi Shih is growing drunk.
> The songs of Wu and the dances of Chu—
>   their pleasure had not reached its height,
> As the green hills were about to swallow
>   a half side of the sun.
> From waterclock more and more drips away
>   from the basin of gold with its silver arrow,
> And they rise and they watch the autumn moon
>   sink down in the river's waves,
> As in the east the sun grows higher,
>   what shall their joy be then?[5]

—as we shall see, this poem is itself evoked detail by detail in the scene "Gathering Lotus," which we translate below.

Su Shi (1037–1111) was only one of many later poets who made various embellishments of the Xi Shi image. He began a vogue for comparison of West Maid with West Lake at Hangzhou, already a famous tourist attraction. This is his quatrain entitled "Drinking Above the Lake in Clear Weather Followed by Rain":

> The water's brightness, vast and rippling, looks best in clear
>   weather;
> The mountain's color, vague and misty, stands out even in the
>   rain.
> West Lake is like West Maid:
> Whether the makeup's light or heavy, it always looks just
>   right.

Further elaboration of the legend develops a romance between Xi Shi and Fan Li. Lu Guangwei's *Wu di ji,* a work of the Tang period, contains a tale of Xi

Shi's taking three years to reach the land of Wu and bearing a child to Fan Li en route. Her ultimate fate depends on which text one is reading. She may, variously, be drowned by the people of Wu or drown herself to redeem her virtue, be strangled by royal command (as in the Song dynasty ballad by Dong Ying), or be rescued by her lover Fan Li and sail off with him into the mists of romance. This last solution, which not surprisingly is the one our romantic playwright favors, is the contribution of Yuan Kang of Eastern Han in his *Yue jue shu*, slightly later than Zhao Ye's *Annals.* It is referred to again by the ninth-century poet Du Mu, who writes of

> Xi Shi sailing down from Suzhou
> With Fan Li in a single boat.

The lost Yuan play *Fan Li Returns to the Lakes,* by Zhou Mingdao, however, has the hero despair of receiving fair treatment either from the king or from Xi Shi, who has denounced him: Fan Li apparently ends this play by sailing off alone.[7]

Evidently Xi Shi presented a most appealing romantic image to the poets. Liang Chenyu, the author of *The Girl Washing Silk,* goes all the way toward a romantic glossing of her story by having Fan Li fall in love with her *before* the inception of the "beautiful spy" stratagem. By so doing he solves certain critical problems and creates others. He acquires a complex romantic motif well-suited to the conventions and length of the *chuanqi* form. He is able to move at once from introducing the male lead to bringing the heroine on stage. Normally this is done in successive scenes, the second and third respectively (scene 1 constituting a prologue), but Liang chooses to introduce both characters in his scene 2, "Spring Stroll." Here, at the very beginning of the action, he locates a charming love scene. This first coming together of the lovers, prior to the complications, separation, denouement, and ultimate reunion that the *chuanqi* plot demands, can thus be presented in *The Girl Washing Silk* as a totally lyrical, uncomplicated celebration of love before the high concerns of state take over.

To introduce Xi Shi in an early scene, on the other hand, as required by *chuanqi* convention, but without having her meet Fan Li, would raise the vexing question of finding something for her to do. Interchanges with her family would be out of place in this play, which centers on the high policies of royal courts, and the appearance of a rival lover, though a common enough device in these plays, would be an unwelcome extra complication in a plot already headed for great complexity. Xi Shi and Fan Li must be portrayed as free agents, figures of high romance, they must meet early in the action, and having met they must necessarily fall in love. The dramatist can then go on to work out the diplomatic entanglements of Wu and Yue in the ensuing scenes, reminding the audience briefly (scenes 9, 17) of Xi Shi's pining, until as we have observed we reach the center point of the play with scene 23, "The Recruitment."

But with this structural problem solved, the dramatist is faced with a severe problem of motivation. How can Fan Li not only assent to the sacrifice of his betrothed to the lusts of an enemy king, but actually propose it on his own initiative? If this can be made plausible, then the love-plot gains greatly in poignancy, in paradox, in exactly that quality of the "remarkable" (*qi*), which is at the heart of *chuanqi* romance. The playwright's task is not mimetic, we are not dealing with psychological realist fiction. The *chuanqi* stage itself, with its elegant music and elaborate conventions, is not the place for probing investigation of psychological states, of motives or responses. The audience already "believes" in Xi Shi and her story as received legend, if not historical fact. The task is to develop to the fullest extent possible the glamorous potential of the story, its poignancy and pathos. Cheaply done, the Xi Shi story could be mere titillation. Liang Chenyu's worthier contribution is the loyalty and devotion of his lovers, to each other and to the king they serve, which raise the sordid intrigue to the high sunlit peaks of romance.

The key to Liang's solution is the characterization of Fan Li as supremely loyal servant of his king. His dedication has brought him little reward beyond high office itself: his early counsel of caution is ignored (scene 5) and the Yue armies suffer defeat in consequence. Accompanying King Goujian and his queen into captivity, he has served them with devotion and invented stratagems to secure their release (scenes 15, 16). While in the land of Wu, Fan Li has observed two woefully negative models of subject-prince relations in Wu Zixu and Bo Pi. Wu Zixu is himself the hero of legend and cult, the archetype of the avenging son: his heroic adventures are recalled in scene 12, "A Discussion of Honor." As minister to King Fuchai of Wu he suffers the Cassandra fate, his prophecies of doom are ignored and he cuts his own throat in obedience to royal command in scene 33, "Loyal Unto Death."

Wu Zixu's fellow minister at Fuchai's court, Bo Pi, is played by the buffoon actor (*chou*). Bo Pi is a self-serving and treacherous sycophant, whose simultaneous flattery and deception of King Fuchai are prime factors in the ultimate collapse of the state of Wu. In the first part of the "Gathering Lotus" scene, translated in full below, we see his clownish attempt to pass off tribute from the state of Yue as his own private gift to Fuchai, a gift moreover that draws attention to the grossly overpopulated royal harem, smelly as a stable in the summer heat——a typically coarse lead-in from Bo Pi to the main body of the scene in which dainty palace maidens attend the lovely Xi Shi, culling delicate lotus blossoms from the autumn lake.

How is Fan Li to distinguish himself from a sycophant like Bo Pi and yet avoid the fate that befell brave Wu Zixu? All he can do is sacrifice every last shred of his private interest, even his love for the secluded virgin Xi Shi, to the overriding claims of his country's need. As he rides to Nettle Village in the "Recruitment" scene, stern Confucian duty conflicts with private desire in his monologue:

> The King my master has searched the country over for a beautiful woman to present to the King of Wu, and has found none fit to serve. In face of so urgent a national need, how can it be proper to begrudge one solitary woman? I therefore made bold to propose Xi Shi to my master, who has ordered me into these hills to bring her forth. Yet this is the abandonment of a virgin maid and the betrayal of our sworn bond. I am distressed at heart——what to do for the best?

The Confucian scale of values, which would weigh "one solitary woman" as a matter too trifling to cause concern, is not likely to have a sympathetic appeal to even the least feminist-minded modern audience. But Fan Li as well as Xi Shi must sacrifice for the king, as his agonizing in this speech makes clear. What is more, his love for Xi Shi in no way blinds him to her destructive potential. He must sacrifice in a double sense, as a subscriber to the Confucian view of the femme fatale, the beautiful woman as temptation to disaster. At the very end of the play, Fan Li sails off with Xi Shi not just as her lover but also as her knowing and committed victim. He is no simple hero disappearing into the sunset with his bride, but a more complex figure. In his entrance verse in the concluding scene 45, "Sailing the Lakes," he recites:

> Say not my abduction of Xi Shi lacks forethought!
> I fear her power to overthrow my country and delude my prince!

——he is taking her away, he confesses, to prevent her from ruining his own king as she has ruined King Fuchai of Wu!

Critics have considered this a defect in the play, a weakening of the portrayal of Fan Li as admirable lover and a defamation of Xi Shi as heroine.[8] Such a view seems anachronistic, too much a product of liberal modern values. I believe on the contrary that Fan Li's words here complete the pattern of patriotic self-sacrifice that provides the central meaning of the play. Fan Li has accomplished his life's mission by leading his king to the defeat of Wu. He is in debt to Xi Shi who has sacrificed her virtue to this end, but he owes it also to his own king to render harmless the lethal weapon of Xi Shi's seductive power. He pays both debts at once by sacrificing *himself to Xi Shi* in withdrawal from public life; yet at the same time, to round out the pattern of the *chuanqi* romance, he does indeed achieve a triumphant finale with his beautiful though battered bride by his side. As for the defamation of Xi Shi: in her arias in the "Gathering Lotus" scene, as again and again throughout the play, we hear the humane voice of the dramatist Liang Chenyu, his recognition of her pitiful position *despite* the menace represented, in the inescapable traditional view, by her irresistible loveliness.

But all this is far in the play's future action. To return to scene 23: the dialogue that ensues when Fan Li has gained admittance to Xi Shi's cottage fully reflects the central conflict of love and duty. A poignancy of feeling still comes through despite the archaic elegance of the language. Fan Li opens with an apology for his long absence that nevertheless stresses the primacy of his obligation to his royal master:

> My salutation to you, lady. Because of the hardships that befell my prince, who is as a father to me, I was detained in a land apart and compelled to neglect our solemn pact, and this I deeply regret.

By the generosity of her response, Xi Shi provides Fan Li with the opening he needs to broach his theme. She says:

> I learned, sir, the details of your captivity. But matters of state are of the highest importance, whilst matters of marriage are of the slightest. How could you betray the expectations of the multitudes for the sake of one insignificant woman?

She has left Fan Li's way clear. Still hesitant, he begins:

FAN LI:　Lady, there is something I must say to you, and I am afraid I must be blunt.

XI SHI:　Don't be afraid to speak.

FAN LI:　It had been my intent to bring about the joyful union of your name, lady, with mine, in anticipation of a lifetime of happiness together. How could I have foreseen the loss of my home, the destruction of our nation, my prince fettered, and myself his minister taken into captivity. It was my good fortune to devise a modest stratagem, which secured our master's release and return to his kingdom. Now, observing how King Fuchai of Wu indulges in every excess of licentiousness, giving himself over to drinking and debauch, my royal master seeks the services of some seductive beauty who will even further inflame Fuchai's lusts. We have searched throughout the land without finding the right person. As I pondered the matter I concluded that you alone possess truly supreme beauty of face and form, and I chanced to speak your praises before the

throne. His Majesty conceived the desire to seek your help in this
stratagem, but I had no inkling of your readiness to assent. This is why I
now presume to visit your dwelling, solely to inquire whether you will
be willing or no. Lady, what is your view?

One wonders if when a sixteenth-century performance of the scene had
reached this point, there might have occurred to some member of the audience
a wry reflection on how the "modest stratagem" would have been presented to
a peasant girl in the rough old days of feudal rivalries—some poor virgin
who would, presumably, have been scrubbed clean and thrown into Fuchai's
bed without any conceivable necessity of a word of explanation to her. Fan
Li's diplomatic delicacy in the play may, in fact, be seen as a sign of the recognition that was beginning to stir in the society of late Ming times that women
after all might be creatures of human mold. In Liang Chenyu's play Fan Li has
not, as we see, gone so far as to commit his betrothed to the wicked will of
King Fuchai. Ostensibly at least, acceptance or rejection of the mission is up
to her, even though Fan Li's "chance" praise of her before the King of Yue
makes the pressure on her irresistible. She seeks an escape route, first in conventional modesty and then in an appeal to the sanctity of their betrothal:

> I am no more than a simple village girl, in calico skirt and with a thorn
> for hairpin, unfitted to utter pearl-smooth notes and dance with
> peacock-feather fan in the "courts of Chu and Qin." Furthermore, I have
> suffered with grieving heart through the three years that have passed
> since I promised my hand to you. I beseech you, sir, to seek elsewhere in
> your efforts on behalf of our country, for I cannot switch allegiance from
> one to another as you suggest.

Fan Li repeats the overriding claims of national interest: "The survival of our
altars hinges entirely on this plan." If the two of them can only survive, then
their future union may still be effected, but the collapse of the state of Yue can
mean only death for both.

Now Xi Shi's distress has reached the level that can only be expressed in
song, and for the first time in the scene the two exchange stanzas of an aria
face to face. Everything so far has been buildup to this dramatic high point of
the scene. Xi Shi reminds Fan Li how they tore and shared, as pledge, the
length of silk she was washing in the stream when first they met. The silk is
the play's eponymous symbol, and its use as image here emphasizes the climactic nature of the situation on stage. She recalls the lonely nights she has
endured through the three years of his captivity, and predicts the pain of a
new separation, in an aria which plays with time, past and future, recalled or
imagined, in a manner reminiscent of the great Yuan plays:

(*TUNE: JIN LUO SUO*)
Three years already for our pact
a hundred years' felicity in view
when you and I by streamside tore silk for pledge.
Learning of you held captive
at court of Wu
nightlong brought pain to my heart.
Strip of silk, given and received—
what cause now for such callousness?
So cruel a fate
I who have never gazed on new horizon
to wander there in foreign land
cut off from word of you,
to fall as into deep deep well.

Xi Shi cuts a figure of pathos here, but Fan Li reveals himself in response as no less pathetic, no less a victim of national circumstance. He seems to throw himself on Xi Shi's mercy: only she can save him from the failure of his lifetime's career. In the terms of the play, Xi Shi begins to appear neither as passive instrument of state policy nor as self-sacrificing patriot, but as a heroine of romance on whose initiative depends her lover's success and her own marital future. Fan Li's aria presents the romantic imperative, the challenge of the quest:

(*SAME TUNE*)
Changing months and years since our parting
each left partnerless, alone.
Night and day you filled my thoughts
but you were further than rim of sky.
To have proved unworthy of our pact
is the great regret of my life.
Who could foresee our country's might year by year brought low
and needlessly my dear one wasting, sick.
Shame overwhelms me, for temples grizzled with nothing yet achieved.

Now I come to your door
bearing my king's commission:
the populace East of the River has none but my darling
to look to.

Lady, if you will undertake to go, then the life and death of two kingdoms will hang in the balance, and none can know whether you and I may not even yet achieve reunion.

> *I look for you to set forth at the earliest moment, do not delay:*
> *whatever marriage will come has already been predestined.*

This is the climax. Fan Li, romantic lead given the preposterous task of recruiting his betrothed for the bed of a lecherous enemy, brings it off in the end with a single aria of deep feeling. He wins both Xi Shi's assent and the audience's sympathy with his confession that, despite the lifetime of devoted service to his king that has grayed his temples, he has "nothing yet achieved." But he brings out to the full the paradox at the heart of the play: by the sacrifice of her own virtue Xi Shi can secure national honor for her lover, and in this way alone win eventual union with him.

In a few words Xi Shi gives her assent and exits to take leave of her mother, confined within the house by sickness: again, like *The Lute* and so many other plays, *The Girl Washing Silk* has little to do with relationships within the woman's family and prefers to handle them offstage. The tension is broken, and the remainder of the scene is given over to panoply with a touch of comic relief. The stage fills with the procession of Fan Li's retinue bearing the jeweled headdress and gown in which they now dress Xi Shi. The stage directions for her reentrance include an instruction for unspecified clowning: this is done by Dong Shi (Favor of the East) and Bei Wei (Splendor of the North) respectively, and probably consists largely of having these two galumphing clodhoppers shimmy around the stage in gross burlesque of the graceful Xi Shi. Dong Shi is not only as ugly as her cousin Xi Shi is beautiful, she is also heavily pregnant with an illegitimate child. Bei Wei is the village medicine woman. The conception of these two as foils for Xi Shi's beauty goes back to the earliest versions of the legend. These speak of the village girl who, told that Xi Shi was lovely even when she frowned, herself began to practice frowning in the attempt to improve her own looks and, of course, scared off everyone in sight. Dong Shi and Bei Wei are played, with exaggerated clumsiness, by male actors, the role-types of "secondary heavy" (*xiaojing*) and buffoon (*chou*) respectively. In the previous scene of low comedy they have offered themselves for the advertised position of beautiful spy, to be rejected out of hand after a whole series of scatological jokes.

Now they undertake to stand in for Xi Shi's parents in seeing her off, but their principal concern is still their own dismal chances in the marriage market:

> Sister Xi Shi, you're no "bottom shelf" piece of goods like us, this deal of
> yours is certain to succeed. But when you get to Hangzhou, think of us
> two and send us back three or four cart-loads of face powder each!

This injunction, which as usual for these role-types is phrased in full colloquial rather than the elevated archaic style used by the principals, is followed
by exaggerated gestures of boo-hooing.

Xi Shi, newly resplendent in palace robes, sings one last sad aria, trembling at the prospect before her and despairing of ever reuniting with Fan Li.
She is led in procession round the stage, the entire retinue singing in unison
about the carriage and pipes which are escorting her to King Goujian's court,
but reassuring her that the union she desires will come at last. By stage convention the "carriage" into which Xi Shi has stepped consists of two flags,
each bearing the device of a wheel. These are held horizontally, flanking her,
by an extra who walks a pace behind her. Mention of pipes in the processional
aria indicates that at this point of the scene the orchestra is augmented by
some kind of raucous trumpet (*suona* or double reed aerophone).

The procession ends with the announcement that it has now reached King
Goujian's palace. The king enters to assume his throne at center stage rear.
Fan Li is led before the throne, bows deeply and begs permission to present
Xi Shi. To the shouts of the retinue, lined up in two diagonal files, Xi Shi
shimmers slowly upstage and prostrates herself in graceful kotow before the
throne. His Majesty sings in rapture:

(*TUNE: DONG OU LING*)

Truly bewitching!
Fascination as reputed!
Allure beyond the painter's skill!

Lovely lady,

a thousand years of our royal line hang by a thread
for you alone to secure.
Only renew this withered tree
and the nation will bow before you, gracious maid.

There is a nice double-entendre in these lines. The king is addressing a
ravishing girl just recruited for court service: one might imagine that by "securing our royal line" he was referring to her potential provision of an heir for
himself, when in paradoxical fact the plan is to present her to his country's
enemy. This man, King Fuchai of Wu, is a old lecher portrayed on stage by the
"heavy" role-type, in contrast with King Goujian who is junior lead
(*xiaosheng*). The "withered tree renewed" is a common metaphor for revived
sexual activity in an old man. So Goujian's words are heard as a plea that she
excite this old fool Fuchai to waste his declining powers, as well as the hope
that she will revive the fortunes of the state of Yue.

Xi Shi modestly deprecates her own talents, but Fan Li's final aria caps the king's prediction and challenges her again to heroic achievement. Fan Li will prove himself by steadfast devotion to his country, but it is this slip of a girl who will undertake a knightly quest:

(TUNE: LIU BO MAO)
Maiden no less subtle than fair
greater boon to our realm East of the River
than myriad mounted men:
prove yourself in foreign court to earn our true respect!
Then land and sea will be secured
all beacon fires extinguished.

The king gives instructions for fifty eunuchs and a hundred palace maidens to wait on Xi Shi, and announces that the queen herself will instruct her in singing and dancing, thus ensuring audience anticipation of the glamorous scene 25, "Dancing Lesson." The king exits with Fan Li in attendance, and the courtiers, singing in chorus, escort Xi Shi on a final celebratory tour before clearing the stage.

SCENE 25: THE DANCING LESSON

Ostensibly this scene shows the Queen of Yue instructing Xi Shi in the arts of song and dance. In fact Xi Shi, simple country girl so recently brought to court from village obscurity, obviously has innate talent, she is not only breathtakingly beautiful but the epitome of grace of movement and a natural musician to boot. A single rendering, first of the song, then of the dance she was taught the previous day, is enough to convince the queen that her pupil has perfected each. So the scene is not at all a realistic presentation of a music lesson.

Such a scene does occur on the *chuanqi* stage, for example the second scene of Kong Shangren's *Peach Blossom Fan (Taohuashan)* in which Su Kunsheng rehearses the heroine, Fragrant Princess, in an aria from *The Peony Pavilion (Mudanting)*. "Your rhythm is weak," Su comments. And then: "Let the accent fall on 'spend' and 'glorious,' don't run them together. Once again! . . . The word 'showers' should be stressed, and sung from deep in the throat."[9]

The "Dancing Lesson" scene from *The Girl Washing Silk* is more simply a spectacle, a celebration on a miniature scale of the glamour of court entertainment. But it does give Liang Chenyu the opportunity to present, through the person of the queen and in the manner of Hamlet's instructions to the players, his own esthetic as dramatist, and since his play was musically the most successful and influential of the entire southern school, this is inevitably of interest to us.

Xi Shi enters alone, dressed and coiffured for the first time in the play in the elaborate style of a woman of the palace. Her new finery shines in ironic contrast with the pathos of her position as she defines it in her opening aria. She is a fallen blossom, adrift at the caprice of the fickle fate to which great beauty has always been subject. The last three lines of her aria revolve respectively around her own past, present, and future as she wonders what ultimate marital prospect she may entertain. The recited verse which by convention follows her aria announces her betrayal by her own beauty, and the succeeding monologue elaborates upon the irony of this. Both verse and prose monologue contain considerable verbal parallelism (we shall consider later the larger symmetries of the scene). She sketches the sensuous spring noon setting with lines which read, in word-for-word rendering,

| breeze | warm | bird | song | broken |
| sun | high | flower | shadows | intense; |

and her monologue opens with light touches of parallel prose, from balanced clichés ("form and face to top the world, taste and talent to surpass all others") to symmetries of syntax ("not only seduced by Lord Fan Li, but degraded by order of His Majesty the King.") She will study song and dance, as required; but she is fully aware of the "reward" such accomplishment will bring her, the privilege of being sent to an alien land to distract a lecherous old king. Xi Shi's own awareness of her situation undercuts, with its heavy irony, the glamour that follows, and turns the scene from mere show into drama.

The Queen of Yue is presented throughout the play as a figure of great dignity and courage in adversity. Recalling the three years of her imprisonment, with her royal husband, after defeat at the hands of Wu, she sings of herself on entrance in terms of widowhood, as the "not yet dead" in the chilling Chinese phrase for widow. Where Xi Shi is the spring oriole, she herself is the crane, symbol of aging, returning to the palace by moonlight.

As the foundation of her esthetic the queen declares the three essential components of perfect beauty to be beauty of feature, skill in song and dance, and deportment: "There is a style proper to singing and a posture proper to dance. Ease of manner and grace of movement—these are what one needs to

affect the feelings of an audience." As to the function of all this, she is perfectly explicit: The use of singing is to "foster the natural desires," and of dancing
to "draw people out of stagnation"—it is evidently the ill-starred King of
Wu, her mortal enemy, that she has particularly in mind.

The queen reminds us of the classical setting for our story by giving a sort
of brief lecture in which she traces the early history of music. She lists the
titles of ancient dances and of those ancient songs that according to tradition
originated among the people and were collected by the "Music Bureau" established by the emperors of the Han dynasty. Each pair of titles she lists is se-
mantically balanced, for example the songs "White Water" and "Clear Water"
or the dances "Bowed Waist" and "Soaring Sleeves." Many of the pieces she
names are mentioned in literary sources: Ge Hong of the fourth century in
Records of the Western Capital (Xijing zaji), his book of gossip about Chang'an in
Han times, speaks of the Lady Qi, consort of the founder of the dynasty, as
skilled in singing "Leaving the Frontier" and "Return from the Frontier," and
in dancing the "Bowed Waist" and "Soaring Sleeves."

The songs the queen lists were certainly sexy enough, if we may judge
from a specimen of the "Clear Water" song by the poet Jiang Huan:

> Rushes soon will cover the pond
> Pearblossom on islet soon must fade.
> When spring blood races so fast
> Spring flood can't be hard to cross.
> Cassia-wood oars scent evening breeze
> Rising moon reflects among water-chestnuts.
> Accept this gift of my sweet springtime
> And I'll step out to you on silk-stockinged feet.

The songs have local associations, for example "White Nettles," which is an
old folksong of Wu, is also called "White Hemp" after the name of a locally
produced cloth; and some have fabulous origins, like the ballad "White
Clouds," which the divine Royal Mother of the West was said to have composed for King Mu of Zhou. The queen names famous dances, like the
"Whirling Chu," which is named in the "Summons of the Soul" in the anthology *Songs of the South (Chuci),* from south-central China in the fourth century
B.C. The *Dongmingji,* a book of marvels from the Later Han period, describes
how effective the dances could be: When Lijuan, favorite court dancer of the
Emperor Wudi (reigned 140–86 B.C.), performed the "Whirlwind" dance
before the Magic Mushroom Hall, she brought blossoms from the courtyard
trees swirling to the ground. The accompanist for Lijuan was always Li Yannian, first director of the Music Bureau and thus a sort of legendary godfather

of "Music Bureau" folksong as a genre. Li Yannian in turn has his own kind of association with our heroine Xi Shi, to whom is often applied Li's famous line about a beauty capable of "overturning city and state."

Not surprisingly in view of her rank and dignity—but still in accord with the ultimately erotic purpose of her instruction—the queen prefers slow, sinuous melodies with a "liquid richness." She insists on the clear enunciation of syllables and careful modulation of the voice, and totally proscribes "wagging head, eyes tight shut, mouth awry and puckered lip"—an effective caricature of the facial contortions of a novice. The lyrics of Xi Shi's practice-piece describe the singer herself in her characteristically melancholy set of brow, but far from being tight shut her eyes emit clear beams of light. The convoluted aria—she is singing of an auditory impression of herself singing—uses conventional images: "Pearls rolling on a tray" suggest the roundness of deeper notes, "an oriole trilling from beyond the wind" suggests modulation to a whisper.

But there is another text hinted at also, a suppressed text, the song Xi Shi describes herself as singing but does not actually voice. It is clearly one of the queen's preferred slow melodies, and a sad one, for the last line of the aria Xi Shi does sing tells of "syllable by syllable the sorrows of parting, the soul about to faint away." Part of the playwright's design in his ironic structuring of the scene becomes visible, or rather audible, when we contrast the presumed slow tempo of this hidden melody with the actual aria-pattern Xi Shi uses for her practice song and repeats for her dance. This is the "Er fan Jiang'er shui" pattern, a tune to a quick beat marked by gongs and drums. Our playwright Liang Chenyu seems to have had a special fondness for this tune as evidently giving great scope to the performer. By repeating the first and a later line he worked out a variant form of it that became known (wrongly, since he was a southerner) as the "Northern" Jiang'er shui. Liang's use of the pattern for these arias by Xi Shi, the West Maid, may even have set up an association which the later dramatist Tang Xianzu catches, playing also on the poem by Su Shi we quoted earlier. In scene 15 of Tang's *Peony Pavilion,* when the Barbarian Prince is contemplating the conquest of Hangzhou, he sings to the Jiang'er shui tune:

> . . . . . think of the smile on West Maid's lips
> as on West Lake with charming grace
> she leans on oars bedecked with orchids.

When the queen turns to the subject of dance, her requirements of the dancer are that body and arms should bend and sway, rise and fall in strict accord with the rhythm of the music, and with a swift lightness that avoids disturbing the merest particle of dust. Xi Shi sings of her own dancing as she dances—a demanding feat, which calls into play techniques for control of the breathing that can still be observed, and marveled at, on the Peking Opera stage. Her aria abounds in references to her slightness of build, broad sleeves contrasting with slender body, mere pinch of waist, a tiny whirling creature who could "dance on the palm of your hand," like Flying Swallow Zhao, the celebrated but tragic consort of the Han Emperor Chengdi. Despite this ethereal lightness the dancer is firmly poised on "golden lotus buds" of tiny bound feet. The reference to bound feet is one of the many anachronisms we will find in these plays, since foot-binding was unknown in Xi Shi's day and for a thousand years thereafter. It is there for its erotic force: three-inch "lotus buds" were understood to be at least as stimulating to the Chinese male as swelling breasts to the Western. The eroticism of the "dancing" lyric, more pronounced than that of the "singing-lesson" aria, is carried further by the breeze, which playfully opens the dancer's skirt, and by the final image of her, light as a cloud above Yang Terrace, the terrace of the sun, of the male principle, where in a celebrated early rhymeprose a legendary king bestowed his favor on a goddess who identified herself as "at dawn the cloud, at dusk the rain." "Clouds and rain" or "clouds of Yang Terrace" have been synonymous with amorous dalliance throughout the centuries since this classic rendezvous.

I have mentioned more than once the occurrence of certain repetitions and parallels in the "Music Lesson" scene. Some of the symmetries of structure may be seen from a simple chart:

XI SHI	QUEEN
sings aria: "Wind in the Pines:" (*lente*); speaks entrance verse; monologue, own uncertain marital prospects	
	enters sings aria: "Wind in the Pines" (*lente*), lamenting that own career as favorite yields to role as teacher
dialogue	
requests instruction in singing	lists five balanced pairs of song titles sings aria, "Good Sister," on art of singing

(*duet, last three lines*)

sings aria, "River Water"
(modulated), about her singing   congratulates Xi Shi on her singing

dialogue

requests instruction in dancing   lists five balanced pairs of dance
                                          titles
                                          sings aria, "Good Sister," on art of
                                          dancing

(*duet, last three lines*)

sings aria, "River Water" (modulated)
   about her own dancing   congratulates Xi Shi on her dancing
thanks queen for her instruction   prescribes new lessons for following
                                          day

The scene advances like a minuet, the tune of Xi Shi's entrance aria repeated by the queen on *her* entrance, then precisely the same structure used for both singing and dancing lesson segments. The musical repetitions are reinforced by precise duplication of the prose syntax in the queen's brief histories of song and dance, respectively. The dramatist seems to be pairing everything in sight to produce his elaborately symmetrical *pas de deux:* teacher and student, song and dance, spring garden and midnight chamber (the prescribed locales for love-songs), crane and oriole (symbols of the two women), "Phoenix Starting" and "Luan-bird Gliding" (names of dances), and so on throughout the scene. The effect, both auditory and visual, must be of great charm as the queen leads her pupil through courtly rituals of the art of seduction. But the scene itself is only a microcosm of *The Girl Washing Silk* as a whole. Parallelism is carried to greater lengths in this play than in any other. K. C. Leung takes the play as evidence of the influence on dramaturgy of the examination essay,[10] called the "eight-legs" either because of its prescribed eight-section structure or because of the balanced bifurcation of its four middle sections (opinions differ). Leung traces numerous parallels within the play, which reflect "the larger symmetry of attack and counterattack, bloodshed and revenge" of its chronicle of the two rival kingdoms. The overall historical pattern of the play's events moves from initial success for Wu to final victory for Yue. The lives of the principals show a diamond pattern as they meet in Yue, separate for the mid-section of the play with Xi Shi's mission to Wu, and end in the reunion in the conquered Wu capital. Scenes are matched against each other, as for example, scenes 3 and 4, each of which displays a king (first of Yue, then of Wu) consulting with two ministers, with a resulting musical structure based on the trio. Events are arranged for deliberate recall of earlier events, as when Bo Pi's surrender to Wen Zhong in scene 40 recalls his receipt of Wen Zhong's surrender—same action, reverse direction—in scene 7.

Balance within the individual scene may on occasion give extra rhetorical force. A prime example in *The Girl Washing Silk* is scene 20, "Heroes Debate," in which the King of Wu's upright heir-apparent discusses with the noble Wu Zixu the treachery of Zixu's fellow minister Bo Pi. Each cites historical precedents, and every precedent cited points toward death as the only honorable way out for either speaker. As Leung says, "both vertical (historical) and horizontal (structural) parallelism are present here, reinforced by parallelism in music. The resulting symmetry operating at different levels adds a hint of inevitability to the sense of doom which is gradually overtaking the house of Fuchai."

Such parallels are rare in the comic scenes, but they are a feature of the more lyrical sections of the play. The lovers Fan Li and Xi Shi, from start to finish, perform as if mounted on twin pedestals. At both their first meeting (scene 2) and their final departure, when in scene 45 they sail off across the lake together, they share an exact alternation of speeches and arias. Scene 45, in fact, is a celebrated example of the alternation of northern tunes (robust, sung by Fan Li) with southern (more languid, and assigned to Xi Shi).

The scene I now translate, "The Dancing Lesson," is merely the most pronounced of many examples of balanced patterning in this elaborately mannered prototype of the Kunqu opera.

Scene 25: The Dancing Lesson

XI SHI (*enters*):

(*TUNE: FENG RU SONG MAN*)
Fallen blossoms, masterless, scattered at random—
don't blame the passing of the spring
its "fair face oft ill-fated!"
A joke, my once betrothal, best forgotten.
Midway in my mission, today I lodge in the Guest Palace:
behind whose red-lacquered gate shall I end my days?

Betrayed already by my own beauty
now loath to draw near my boudoir mirror.

It's not the prettiest face wins kindest treatment
and my fair looks have brought me only sorrow.
Birdsong dies in the warm breeze
flower shadows deepen as sun climbs high.
Maidens by streams of Yue, recall each year
how once Xi Shi gathered the lotus with you.

And why, you ask, should Xi Shi speak such lines?—Because it was my
lot to be of outstanding beauty, surpassing grace, no sooner born into
this world than granted a handsome mate; yet then seduced by Lord Fan
Li and traduced in the royal court of Yue. Ah, but surely failure and
success must be predestined—how could they depend on a fair
complexion? These past few days Her Majesty the Queen has made
special visits to this western quarter to instruct me in the arts of singing
and dancing. But when I think about it, "fair face to topple city walls" is
not something to boast about—what good is it to me if I learn to sing
and dance to perfection? I hear the tinkling of ornaments—Her Majesty
is here.

QUEEN (*enters*):

> *Relict of three years in foreign land*
> *I come now to the Guest Palace for diversion,*
> *no more to sing or dance in this my lifetime*
> *but here to catechize the "toppler of nations."*

As I begin my instruction in song and dance, see how
by the night moon a crane returns to the palace
while spring breeze carries the oriole's trill past a thousand gates.

XI SHI (*kneels and kotows*):　Your Majesty!

QUEEN:　Rise, pretty child. Understand that the term "consummate beauty"
was reserved in ancient times for one who possessed first, beauty of feature; second, skill in song and dance; and third, elegant deportment. A
pretty face is nothing remarkable if there is no proficiency in song and
dance, and skill in song and dance are no great marvel if the deportment
is not superior. Now your charming face, my dear, needs no comment.
But there is a style proper to singing and a posture proper to dance. Ease
of manner and grace of movement—these are what one needs to affect
the feelings of an audience. We had intended to appoint one of the former palace maidens to instruct you, but we feared she might corrupt or
spoil you. His Majesty was concerned, and ordered me to come myself.

XI SHI:　Favored by Your Majesty's teaching, your slave will make every
effort to do her best.

QUEEN: Then pay attention to my words, my dear: the purpose of song is to foster the natural desires, and this is why songs are sung in spring sunlight beneath the blossoms, or in the chamber in depth of night. The ancients had "White Water" and "Clear Water," "Black Clouds" and "White Clouds," "South of the River" and "South of the Huai," "Leaving the Frontier" and "Return from the Frontier." The voice should be resonant, the melody sinuous. Today in our lovely southern lands the songs "White Nettles" and "Gathering Lotus" are popular. When you practice singing today, my dear:

>*(TUNE: HAO JIEJIE)*
>
>*At the banquet, "send the dust flying, stop the clouds in their tracks"*
>*with undulating tune of liquid richness*

but avoid the

>*wagging head, eyes tight shut*
>*mouth awry and puckered lip.*

QUEEN, XI SHI:

>*With stylish grace*
>*as night advances, deep in gilded hall*
>*bring tipsy flush of spring to every cheek.*

QUEEN: Do you remember the song I taught you yesterday, my dear?

XI SHI: I do.

QUEEN: Try it for me now.

XI SHI:

>*(TUNE: ERFAN JIANG'ER SHUI)*
>*Clear and pure from scented throat*
>*but faintly heard, so pure from scented throat*
>*pearls rolling on a tray*
>*or to the damask-pillowed halls of Qin and Chu*
>*an oriole trilling from beyond the wind*
>*to stir the fragrant dust*
>*to stir the fragrant dust*
>*and halt the colored clouds.*
>*Mascara'd brows in sorrow frown*
>*while eyes emit clear waves of light;*
>*singer acclaimed for voice supreme*
>*but granted no light dalliance mid the flowers*
>*no light dalliance mid the flowers:*
>*how to escape as nightly lamps are lit*
>*syllable by syllable the sorrows of parting*
>*the soul about to faint!*

QUEEN: I didn't think you fully understood the art of singing yet, my dear,
but as soon as you opened your lips just now the notes came soaring and
swooping, the resonances lingered in the air, not the legendary Qin Qing
nor Han E themselves sang more superbly than this. Admirable, truly
admirable!

XI SHI: I believe I now appreciate the main requirements of singing. Please
instruct me in the art of the dance.

QUEEN: Then pay attention to my words, my dear: the purpose of dance is
to rescue people from stagnation, and that is why dances are performed
in the spring breeze at the banquet, or in gatherings by moonlight on
high balconies. The ancients had the "Flying Phoenix" and "Ascending
Luan," "Tangling Dust" and "Clustering Feathers," "Bowed Waist" and
"Soaring Sleeves," "Whirling Chu" and "Sunlit Ah." The body must
swoop forward or sway back depending on the music, rise and fall
according to the rhythm. Today in the palaces of Wu and Yue the
"Whirlwind" and "Whirlpool" dances are popular. When you practice
dancing today, my dear:

> (*TUNE: HAO JIEJIE*)
>
> *In performance, let grace of movement mark you out*
> *for elegant deportment, circling swift and light*
> *dipping and rising, swooping and swaying*
> *spinning no speck of dust into the air.*

QUEEN, XI SHI:

> *With stylish grace*
> *as night advances, deep in gilded hall,*
> *bring tipsy flush of spring to every cheek.*

QUEEN: Do you remember the dance I taught you yesterday, my dear?

XI SHI: I do.

QUEEN: Try it for me now.

XI SHI:

> (*TUNE ERFAN JIANG'ER SHUI*)
>
> *Gauze robe with flowing sleeves*
> *soft rippling of gauze and flowing sleeves*
> *so light, a weightless presence*
> *breeze-borne, a flicker beneath the moon*
> *swirling, spinning to her song*
> *mere pinch of waist*
> *mere pinch of waist*
> *a dancer to whirl on the palm of your hand.*
> *Now eagerly advancing*

烏鵲填橋
催渡何

The Girl Washing Silk: Xi Shi dances before the Queen of Yue.

now bashful in retreat;
gold lotus-buds so sure of step
while a fragrant breeze opens the broidered skirt
fragrant breeze opens the broidered skirt:
lustrous black locks, flower-woven, "cicada curls" by cheek
seductive-soft, cloud-maiden of Yang Terrace.

QUEEN: I didn't think you fully understood the art of dancing yet, my dear, but as soon as you began to move just now, each pose you assumed was of unparalleled grace, each movement of unmatched elegance, neither the swallow startled into flight nor the free-roaming dragon itself moves more beautifully than this. Lovely, truly lovely! And now, be sure to practise day and night, do not forget.

XI SHI: Favored by your Majesty's teaching, your slave would not dare forget one word.

QUEEN: Rest now, tomorrow we shall practise again.

XI SHI: As Your Majesty commands me.

QUEEN:

In a hundred years, thirty-six thousand feasts
daily the cups are raised to the spring breeze;

XI SHI:

the song ended, white snow drifts in spring sun
tipsy from dance, the cold moon reels to the "Rainbow Skirt."

SCENE 26: COMMITTING THE SON

Though this scene has an intrinsic interest it has nothing to do with our principal subject, Xi Shi, and so I will describe it only briefly. It is a heroic scene revolving around Wu Zixu, the legendary avenger, here concerned to protect his son from the catastrophe he correctly predicts will shortly engulf the state of Wu. Zixu has undertaken a mission to the neighboring land of Qi to arrange a suitable date for his own prince (of Wu) to invade—we are in the sixth century B.C., when even though the world has declined from the universal peace of the Golden Age, at least the courtly rules of war are still observed, surprise attack is scorned as a dastardly act, and one gives due notice of impending aggression. This, at any rate, is the view of this classical feudal age that is fostered by the Confucian historians, and evidently it is the view of our dramatist.

Wu Zixu's duty to remonstrate with his misguided prince calls him back to the Wu court, even though he knows in advance the king's rage will be his own doom. He has therefore included his small son in his embassy to Qi. Though he must sacrifice his own life by returning to Wu, he will protect his son by consigning him to the care of his friend, Bao Mu of the state of Qi. "Committing the Son" is a fine vehicle for the invocation of the whole valorous aura of the Wu Zixu legend. Here the man who has dedicated his life to avenging his murdered father now completes his service to the family line by securing the survival of his son. As the introduction to a modern-day phonograph recording of the scene puts it, the scene concerns "integrity in the service of the prince, proper feeling between father and son, and the path of trust between two friends." Three of the five relationships sacred to the Confucian ethic are here celebrated (the other two being the relationships between husband and wife, and between elder and younger siblings). Noble sentiment could hardly ask for more perfect expression in a single dramatic event. In performance the voices, near-tenor of Wu Zixu, soprano of his son, light baritone of his friend Bao Mu, contrast and blend very movingly in the arias of tearful leave-taking. The modern stage version of the scene adds some effective bits of stage business, as when at the very end of the scene the boy is induced to accept his surrogate father, Bao Mu:

SON: Where is my father?
BAO MU: Your father has gone far away.
SON: Where is my father?
BAO MU: Your father has gone far away.
SON: Where is my father?
BAO MU: (*throws open his arms*):   Here is your father!

"Committing the Son" is a rare example of a surviving Kunqu scene containing a juicy child role (*wawa-sheng*), and is still capable of making the name of an actor or actress, as witness the recent account of a performance by the Jiangsu actress Shi Xiaomei:

The Wu child as played by Shi Xiaomei very accurately expresses the son's deep love of his father. When the child regains consciousness after swooning away and realizes his father is nowhere to be seen he gives a thrice-repeated cry, "Where is my father?" Done in the traditional style, the voice grows in volume through the three cries, but Shi Xiaomei arranges things differently. Her second cry is stronger than the first, and then the third cry begins even stronger, but suddenly in mid-sentence weakens, forming a marked contrast of loud and soft. This weakening of the voice forcefully conveys the child's feelings of despair and distress in the fruitless search for his father, and so is more moving than any louder cry could be, bringing tears to the eyes.[11]

SCENE 30: GATHERING LOTUS

Our fourth and last scene from *The Girl Washing Silk* is even more popular than "Committing the Son" and even more glamorous than "The Dancing Lesson," and I give a complete translation. In "The Dancing Lesson" we saw Xi Shi in training; here we see her at work. The besotted King Fuchai has begun to feel that his soul has deserted him, and suspects that it must be wandering among the lotus blooming on the lake. He therefore orders a lotus-gathering expedition with himself and Xi Shi in the van.

A short prologue to the scene is furnished by an exchange between the king and his sycophantic minister Bo Pi, played by a performer of the buffoon role (*chou*). Bo Pi officiously presides over a delivery of tribute from the King of Yue, passing it off in the first instance as his own gift to King Fuchai, and calling attention in his clownish self-defense to his own stinginess in contrast with Fuchai's extravagance, and to the general corruption, which extends to the sewers of the pullulating royal harem. This kind of earthy reminder of physical reality is probably necessary by this point in the play, when the glamour of Xi Shi is beginning to take on a too ethereal quality; it is certainly an effective counterpoint to the gorgeousness of the remainder of the scene.

Besotted as he has become, Fuchai is not at all unaware of the peril Xi Shi represents, yet his only recourse is ever deeper indulgence in her charms. "Since Xi Shi came into the palace," he openly confesses as soon as Bo Pi has left the stage, "we have rejoiced from dawn to dusk in graceful dance and sweetest song. Though not so many days have passed, I can't count the hundreds of times we have found the 'delights of cloud and rain,' nor recall how many thousands of loving-cups we have drained together. To a bewitching grace of form and figure she joins a tender warmth of character, and it's a certain fact that these old bones of mine are destined to meet their fate at her hands."

Despite this, Fuchai announces his only hope of recovering his lost wits, the expedition in Xi Shi's company to gather lotus on the lake. Xi Shi on her entrance exchanges lines of verse with the king, recalling their love-making of the night just past. The exchange ends with the ominous lines, in which all attendants join,

> Crook the fingers: how often comes the west wind?
> Nor count the stealthy shiftings wrought by the flowing years.

(Unlike the Western gesture of counting which involves checking the fingers of one hand with a finger or thumb of the other, the Chinese practice is to bend or crook successive fingers, left hand then right. Both east wind and west wind have sexual connotations, but where the east wind is associated with spring and the turning of young fancies to thoughts of love, the west wind is the wind that brings the rain. "Clouds and rain" is the commonest euphemism for love-making; but the rain, though fructifying, is also autumnal and reminds us of King Fuchai's advanced age).

A stage direction now reads, "Boats set out with drums playing." The mid-Qing acting version of the scene specifies four eunuchs attending Fuchai on stage, and four palace maidens for Xi Shi, but the actual number of dancers performing the scene was probably limited only by troupe resources and size of stage or arena. From the launching of the boats onward, all is song. First Xi Shi sings two folk melodies, plaintive songs of lovesickness which (however much they further stimulate poor Fuchai) she is clearly dedicating to her lover Fan Li, left far behind in the land of Yue. The folksongs lead in to the high point of the scene, the exchange of arias to the tune of Niannu jiao xu, the king's aria beginning "Across lake's limpid acres, a rich brocade of clustered blooms," Xi Shi responding with "A lovely sight, waves smooth as palm of hand." Their lyrics vividly evoke the scene on stage, the lines of dancers in pink blouses and green skirts, human representations themselves of the lotus flowers they are gliding among, swaying as slow rhythms symbolize placid lake, dipping as they cull the paper flowers strategically placed in readiness. The late Ming playgoer Zhang Dai records the spectacle in these words:

> Five dancers with long sleeves and trailing sashes. As they spin, the sleeves and sashes form unbroken rings around them, and they swoop to touch the ground, rise again to circle and shimmer with the soft elegance of autumn leaves. Twenty or more maids of honor and palace attendants bearing plumes, parasols, lotus-tipped staffs, circular fans of silk, palace lanterns—a blaze of brilliance, a riot of colored brocades, the audience is stunned.[12]

While all this is going on, King Fuchai stands bemused, the huge painted face "heavy," from time to time raising his left sleeve to screen the giant wine-cup his right hand has raised to his lips. Perhaps he staggers now and then in imitation of the dancers, but his principal contribution to the glamour of the scene is the none-too-subtle erotic suggestiveness of his arias. He sings of dew sucked into heart of flower, of skirts growing moist from splash of wave, and generally makes it clear that more than lotus stems are being deflowered in his kingdom of Wu this day.

But there is more to the imagery of the scene than a simple erotic equation. The Niannu jiao arias, with their "array" of boats and their "oars by the thousand paired," hold also a suggestion of the naval might of Wu surrendered into "flower-soft hands," with the same sort of incongruity on which Shakespeare builds *Antony and Cleopatra*. The same sickly, overblown gorgeousness holds Fuchai captive as holds Antony, in the famous lines Enobarbus speaks in Act II, scene 2:

> The barge she sat in, like a burnish'd throne
> Burnt on the water; the poop was beaten gold;
> Purple the sails, and so perfumed that
> The winds were love-sick with them; the oars were silver,
> Which to the tune of flutes kept stroke, and made
> The water which they beat to follow faster,
> As amorous of their strokes. . . .

Xi Shi is a simple country girl, not Egypt's queen, but Fuchai is no less besotted by her, and his kingdom no less irrevocably lost in consequence.

"Gathering Lotus," surviving into our own age in stage performance, was included also in the anthology *Zhui bai qiu,* the collection of acting versions of such scenes from *chuanqi* plays as still formed part of the mid eighteenth-century repertoire. The text of the scene is very slightly abbreviated, but the exchange of arias discussed above is preserved intact. This is hardly surprising, for the king's aria beginning "Across lake's limpid acres" had been one of Suzhou's most popular musical treats already for over a century. That same Zhang Dai whose description of the dancers is quoted above witnessed also the great eisteddfod held annually on Tiger Hill, just outside the northwest corner of the city, to celebrate the full moon on the Mid-Autumn Festival:

> On the fifteenth of the eighth month people assemble on Tiger Hill: natives and visitors, scholar-gentry and their families, girl instrumentalists and singers, famous artistes of the ballad and dames of the stage, young wives and respectable daughters from among the common people, virile lads and pretty boys, and also drifters and profligates and young ne'er-do-wells, retainers and hangers-on, serving-men and vagabonds, all cluster like scales on a fish. They spread rugs and seat themselves wherever they can, from Shenggong's Dais, the Thousand Men Rock, Crane Brook, the Sword-washing Pool, and the Petition Shrine, all the way down to the Sword-testing Stone and the first and second gates.
>
> > [All of these are celebrated historic or legendary sites of ancient Suzhou. Shenggong, for example, was a sixth-

century monk of great sanctity. When he preached in the
great Buddhist temple on Tiger Hill, the very rocks nodded their heads in approval. As evidence of this fact, the
rocks are still there!]

Viewed from a vantage point, the scene resembles the flocking of
wildgeese to rest on the sand, or sunset clouds layering the river. When
it grows dark and the moon appears, then sounds of pipe and drum
arise from scores and hundreds of points, louder and louder, with clash
of cymbal, boom of great Yuyang tympani, moving earth and reaching
heaven, surging and boiling like thunder and lightning, so that one
could shout at one's neighbor and still not be heard. As the watches
begin, the noise of drum and cymbal gradually subsides, to be replaced
by a wealth of wind and string instruments, to which singing is joined,
all major pieces for ensemble singing like "Brocaded sails unfurl" and
"Across lake's limpid acres."[13]

"Brocaded sails unfurl," we may note, is an aria from scene 14 of *The Girl
Washing Silk*. This naming of two of its choruses (no other pieces are named)
as popular choices for festive community singing illustrates for us the contemporary success of the play, and the passage gives us a clue also to the civic
pride of Suzhou, as its citizens relive the sensual fantasies of their lecherous
king of two millennia ago.

Day is done, a short stage day: the scene began with Xi Shi rising from her
night's amours, and now after half a dozen arias the sun is setting again behind
the hills. The dancers mime the return of the boats to the shore. Fuchai,
miming drunkenness, confesses a renewed "itching at the heart," and blurts
straight out that he can't wait to have Xi Shi once more in his ivory bed. A
string of images depicts gleaming lanterns, gauze curtains, and the phoenix-
like sporting of the lovers. Xi Shi picks this up:

> Up, down, phoenix cock and hen
> in, out, bee or butterfly—
> how to fend him off?

and later, pathetically, she sings of her own sacrifice:

> Remnant wisp of fragrance, broken jade
> crushed blossom, trampled leaf
> no course but to dissemble, to endure.

However spectacular the dances, seductive the costumes, bewitching the
lyrics, Xi Shi brings home to us at the end of the scene the falseness of all this
glamour, the underlying pathos of deception, where she herself as well as the

gross Fuchai is victim. In fact the scene, as Liang Chenyu originally wrote it, contains subtle reminders throughout of the disjunction between Fuchai's lust and Fan Li's true love for Xi Shi. The later acting versions of the scene dropped these passages, intent as they were on maximizing the glamorous spectacle of the dance. The *Zhui bai qiu* version opens with the strictly conventional brief appearance of a eunuch announcing Fuchai. This is a poor substitute for the original opening dialogue between Fuchai and his clownish minister Bo Pi, who admits his expertise in cutting a dash at others' expense: "I rom- my own -antic though I gener- someone else's -osity"—a comic wordplay that has a strong satiric application to the situation at hand, for Fuchai himself is cutting a dash at the expense of Fan Li, Xi Shi's betrothed and true lover; Bo Pi is shadowing his master the king, who is quite content to "gener-" Fan Li's "-osity" by sequestering his mistress.

Similarly, two of Xi Shi's arias cut by the *Zhui bai qiu* version contain wistful questions:

> *Where is the silk-washing stream? . . . .*
> *Where is my companion of the silk-washing stream?*

These lines give the strongest indication that throughout the scene, while Fuchai is doting on Xi Shi, her thoughts are all of Fan Li. The refrain of the Niannu jiao arias,

> *Let ties between us two be close*
> *as ever-faithful mandarin ducks*

means one thing to Fuchai, quite another to Xi Shi. This irony, this dramatic conflict of character, is much reduced in the later acting version, which stresses the spectacular at the expense of psychological or mimetic values.

These omissions are to be attributed to a wish to speed up the action rather than to any kind of prudishness. In fact, although the most specifically erotic images occur in an aria of Fuchai's, which the *Zhui bai qiu* cuts, there is in the latter version a piece of stage business that is equally suggestive. Fuchai has the four palace-maidens who attend Xi Shi report the names of the varieties of lotus they have picked. Each name has a punning significance, "Western" and "Guanyin" lotus both suggesting the West Maid's beauty; and the second pair, "upside-down" lotus and "head-to-head" lotus, offering presumably a choice of sexual techniques. Xi Shi, questioned, admits to preferring the last, and the infatuated king, whose appetite no doubt surpasses his acrobatic ability, concurs one assumes with relief.

The musical structure of "Gathering Lotus" is one of Liang Chenyu's tributes to his great predecessor, Gao Ming. The latter, in *The Lute,* scene 28, "Mid-Autumn Moon-Viewing," depicted a situation in which a couple, ostensible lovers, sang together to celebrate natural splendors, but with the unhappiness of one partner running as an undercurrent throughout. Liang borrowed the same sequence of arias for his scene, and used it with at least as much effect. The tradition continued: the second scene, "Love Declared," of the famous early Qing romance *The Palace of Eternal Youth (Changshengdian)* uses again the same basic musical structure.

Scene 30: Gathering Lotus

KING FUCHAI (*enters, followed by Bo Pi*):

> (*TUNE: CHOU NUER LING*)
> Such delights the autumn brings!
> Cool breezes fan my halls of leisure
> river banks trap scent of lotus,
> a morning for intoxication.

BO PI:

> Suzhou, city of ancient splendors,
> from subjugated distant realms
> tribute bearers in endless line:
> What power can rival this land East of the River?

(*They exchange salutations*)

Your Majesty, your servant has found no way to repay your gracious favors, but today I beg leave to express a fraction of my gratitude by submitting a few trifling gifts. They are outside the palace gate—I have not presumed to have them brought in.

FUCHAI: You should not go to so much trouble, old minister of mine. What are these things?

BO PI: Plaited boxes: one hundred.

FUCHAI: What will I do with so many?

BO PI: Fox furs: fifty pair.

FUCHAI: Too many again.

BO PI: Plus: home handwoven grasscloth: one hundred thousand bolts.

FUCHAI: You're making it up. How could you have so many people at home to weave that quantity?

BO PI: Here is a card to go with it—please deign to read it.

FUCHAI (*reads out card*): "With respect: plaited boxes, one hundred; fox furs, fifty pair; grasscloth, one hundred thousand bolts, reverently presented

館娃高歌
秦篁篆

The Girl Washing Silk: Xi Shi and her maidens gather
lotus on the West Lake.

to the attention of the great King of Wu by Xie Yong, envoy of Goujian, unworthy Prince of the Eastern Sea and King of Yue, for favor of His Majesty's kind acceptance." Well, minister, I made sure you didn't have all this stuff, but you actually do. You're normally so stingy, how could you bring yourself to present it?

BO PI: The women's quarters in your majesty's palace are very extensive and in the summer they get very smelly, so I sent a messenger to the King of Yue and had him order every woman throughout his kingdom to weave day and night so that he could present you with this. So you see it's just the same as coming from me. If I hadn't asked for it, he wouldn't have had it available.

FUCHAI: You're always making gifts to people—with other people's things.

BO PI: Your Majesty knows very well what sort of person I am: it's true that I rom- my own -antic while I gener- someone else's -osity.

FUCHAI: No more joking. Since the King of Yue shows such filial submission we must write to inform him that we are enlarging his fief. What do you say to our showing our gratitude with a grant of the lands east as far as Gouyong, west to Plum Orchard, south to Gumo and north to Prairie?

> [This grant of land is authenticated by historical texts. "Plum Orchard," Zuili, from a homonym of *zui* which means "drunk," developed in legend as the place where King Fuchai became intoxicated with Xi Shi; in fact, it was the site of King Goujian's eventual destruction of the forces of Fuchai's kingdom of Wu, and the irony of Fuchai's grant of this place is evidently not lost on our dramatist.]

BO PI: An excellent plan. I'll inform Xie Yong of this and tell him to produce some more tribute. (*He exits*)

FUCHAI: Since Xi Shi came into the palace we have rejoiced from dawn to dusk in graceful dance and sweetest song. Though not so many days have passed, I can't count the hundreds of times we have found the "delights of cloud and rain," nor recall how many thousands of loving-cups we have drained together. To a bewitching grace of form and figure she joins a tender warmth of nature, and it's a certain fact that these old bones of mine are destined to meet their fate at her hands. But where my soul has fled to, this last couple of days, I have no idea. Yesterday I ordered my palace maidens to the lake to gather lotus flowers: I suspect it must be there on the lake that my soul is wandering, so today I shall go seek it

there and bring it back. Eunuchs! Go to the women's quarters and
request the company of my lady to pick lotus flowers on the lake. (*Eunuchs
assent*)

XI SHI (*enters*):

> (*TUNE: NIANNU JIAO*)
> *Maple leaves dyed red*
> *shallows' sparkling gleam*
> *and the traveler's gown grows chill.*

(*She greets King Fuchai with a bow*)

FUCHAI:

> *When the Lord of the West roamed his lands*
> *'neath a flurry of falling leaves*
> *three thousand was the number*
> *of palace maidens in his train.*

PALACE MAIDENS:

> *Crimson silks with springlike freshness*
> *powdered cheeks to dazzle the sunlight*
> *mandarin ducks on riverbank*
> *yield pride of place.*

XI SHI:

> *So misty dim——*
> *ah where is my silk-washing stream?*

FUCHAI: Have you only just now completed your toilet, lady?

XI SHI: Your Majesty kept me up so late enjoying the cool of evening that
this morning I inadvertently overslept.

FUCHAI: Can you remember exactly how it was, as we enjoyed the cool?

XI SHI: I can:

> Ice flesh, jade bones
> no drop of sweat, pure and chill
> breeze-borne fragrance from off the water
> and a bright moon peering in.
> Still not asleep
> leaning on pillow, hair tousled, pins awry.

FUCHAI:

> Rising, no sound from courtyard doorways
> watching late stars wheel by the Milky Way.
> Asking how goes the night

the middle watch already here
"Jade Rope"'s twin stars dipping down waves of moonlight.

PALACE MAIDENS:

Crook the fingers: how often comes the west wind?
Nor count the stealthy shifts wrought by the flowing years.

FUCHAI: Lady, I gave orders yesterday for painted boats with pipes and drums to be readied for us to visit the lake to gather lotus.

ATTENDANTS: The boats have long been ready. May it please Your Majesty and madam to board.

(*Boats set out with drums playing*)

XI SHI: In my homeland by the stream in Yue I learned two lotus-gathering songs. I should like to sing them for Your Majesty.

FUCHAI: Thank you, my dear.

XI SHI:

> (*TUNE: "OLD SONG"*)
> *So thick the lotus by the autumn bank,*
> *maidens come pick them, singing by their oars.*
> *Flower and fruit alike close-set in leafage,*
> *racing to pluck them, voices skim green ripples.*
> *Alas, too long a stem, root beyond reach,*
> *broken threads dangle, sharp points prick the fingers.*

> ["Threads," *si,* is a homonym of "thoughts, longings" in Chinese. The "broken threads" here are another clue to Xi Shi's longings for home and for her lover Fan Li.]

> *When comes the time of homing to the beloved?*
> *Far waters, endless hills—never look back.*

FUCHAI: Marvelous! Wine here—a big goblet for me.

XI SHI:

> (*SECOND "OLD SONG"*)
> *Lilies we pick, in skirts of lotus-pink,*
> *autumn wind ruffling the lake, the wild geese flying.*
> *Oars of cassia wood, oars of magnolia glide us by the bank,*
> *slender wrists of gauze-clad girls gently rock the sweep.*
> *Leafy islets, flower-filled pools, to the edge of sight,*
> *song of Wu, but from Yue the singer, bitterness of longing.*
> *Bitterness of longing,*

not to be plucked up—
picking lotus South of the River, already it grows late
and still he comes not home, the wanderer from the sea.

FUCHAI: Better yet! Better yet! Another big goblet here!

(TUNE: NIANNU JIAO XU)
Across lake's limpid acres
a rich brocade of clustered blooms
red bridal gown with mile-long train.
Eddying, the offshore breeze
catches one's sleeve with cooling grace.
Rising, dipping
magnolia-wood hulls a hundred in array
painted oars a thousand strong
boats of the lotus-gatherers striving for midstream pride.

BOTH:

Let ties between us two be close
as ever-faithful mandarin ducks.

XI SHI:

A lovely sight
waves smooth as palm of hand.
Melodies from hidden places
singers in secret unison.
delicate faces, skirts of gauze
all one with green of leaf and pink of petal.
In vain to think
how difficult to mend the broken root
how pearl once round lies shattered
and new thorns unbidden catch with old memories at my
  gown.

BOTH:

Let ties between us two be close
as ever-faithful mandarin ducks.

FUCHAI: Lady, if I try to compare these lotus flowers with your beautiful face, how can they match you?

Placed side by side
compare jade-smoothness, judge sweet fragrance
flower just opened

still surely longs to hide in shame.
Form and reflection
form and reflection
paired in perfection as root and heart.
Imagination starts
as delicate face turns towards sunset
dewdrops to sip from heart of flower
skirt grows damp where wavelets splash.

[In this song we see Xi Shi leaning over the lotus bed, reflected in the lake's surface, and the king's lustful imagination playing less on the religious symbolism of the lotus (in Buddhism, the pure flower growing out of the world's mud) than on its sexual reference (the opening bud representing the female sex organ, with double entendre in the dew and splashed skirt).]

BOTH:

Let ties between us two be close
as ever-faithful mandarin ducks.

(King Fuchai *reels drunkenly*)

XI SHI:

A sight for grief
hills swallowing sun's decline
wintry crows homing over the ford
while floods block passage
from this land of lake and cloud.
Chill wind, chill dew
chill wind, chill dew
how can the poor corolla bear such ravage?
Desolate, alone
amid the clustered blooms
threads of separation linger—
where is my companion of the silk-washing stream?

BOTH:

Let ties between us two be close
as ever-faithful mandarin ducks.

FUCHAI: You've made me drunk again.

XI SHI: Your majesty, the wind is blowing in again from the creek, the sun has set behind the hills, please order the boats to take us back.

FUCHAI: Eunuchs, pass my orders to the palace ladies on each boat to take up the lotus blossoms they have picked and escort my consort back to the Lovenest.

> [King Fuchai called Xi Shi by the local dialect word for a beautiful woman, *wa* "baby," and on a hillside outside Suzhou where now stands a large and famous Buddhist temple he built a special pavilion for her that was known as Guanwagong. The closest translation for this would unfortunately sound too much like a fast-food joint: "Babe's Place"; "The Lovenest" hopefully suggests the right idea.]

PALACE MAIDENS (*bearing flowers, they cross the stage in procession*):

> *Day fades*
> *magnolia oars row home barks filled with sweet scents*
> *cold tides arise, whipped up by autumn wind.*
> *Songs of the lotus-gatherers from all sides*
> *and over the three-mile curving dike*
> *the moon begins her rise.*

FUCHAI (*stares at* Xi Shi):

> *Soberly surveying you*
> *what a hateful sight*
> *red-skirted tart, fit mate for some popinjay—*

> > [The text has "green-clad youth," which is actually a kenning for "parrot," so popinjay (from an Arabic word for parrot) seems to work in nicely here.]

> *then suddenly heart itches*
> *to mount our ivory bed this instant!*

XI SHI (*sings an aside, as the* King *continues to reel drunkenly about*):

> *Up, down, phoenix cock and hen*
> *in, out, bee or butterfly—*
> *how to fend him off?*

PALACE MAIDENS:

> *Evening clouds stretch over our return*
> *sounds from above*
> *pipes playing from The Lovenest's balonies.*

We have reached The Lovenest, may it please Your Majesty and madam to enter.

FUCHAI: Eunuchs, bring red candles at once and light our way into the bridal chamber.

EUNUCHS (*do so, singing*):

A thousand files
of lantern candles gleam and sway
silks rustle down the corridors
pipe and voice sound high and clear
swirls of incense smoke ascend
musk and orchid scent the air.

FUCHAI:

A night of joy
quick, quick into the curtained bed
the two of us, twin phoenix beneath the quilt.
How should I pass it lightly by?
This glorious night is mine for wild debauch!

(*He staggers drunkenly and is held up by his* Eunuchs)

XI SHI:

Remnant wisp of fragrance, broken jade
crushed blossom, trampled leaf
no course but to dissemble, to endure.

EUNUCHS and PALACE MAIDENS:

Frost sparkles on duck-patterned tiles
the Milky Way shines clear
a fading moon glimmers down winding walks.

FUCHAI:

(*TUNE: CODA*)
Dizzy-drunk, into the bridal chamber.

XI SHI:

From the fields, cocks crow once and again.

EUNUCHS and MAIDENS:

Let joy be unceasing for lord of ten thousand years,
mistress of a thousand autumns.

FUCHAI:

Silver arrow, jar of bronze, swift drips the water-clock.

XI SHI:

See the cold moon sink into waves of red.

EUNUCHS and MAIDENS:

Songs of Wu, dances of Chu, endless delight.

ALL:

Can joy survive the brightening eastern sky?

SHAN BEN'S
The Plantain Kerchief

When Xi Shi sails off with her lover Fan Li at the end of *The Girl Washing Silk* she has not said farewell to the Chinese stage. To this day retellings of her story go on in local opera forms, in movies, and on television. Before the Ming dynasty ended she appeared in a *zaju* play, *Sailing the Five Lakes (Wu hu you)*, which is a simple lyrical piece modeled on the final scene of *The Girl Washing Silk*. The most startlingly original use of the Xi Shi character, however, was made by a man called Shan Ben, or Shan Chaxian, about whom we know little more than he himself tells us in the closing words of his only surviving play, *The Plantain Kerchief (Jiaopaji)*: that he was a man of Kuaiji in Zhejiang, who lived forty-nine years of "nothing but a dream" before waking to offer the world his comedy of the plantain leaf that magically transforms into a silk kerchief. His only other work, *The Dewy Ribbon (Lu shou ji)*, seems to have sunk without a trace. But the skillful construction of *The Plantain Kerchief*, the facile dialogue and unusually abundant stage directions, all bespeak close familiarity with the theater—perhaps that was a major part of his "forty-nine years of dreaming." Certainly the avid playgoer Qi Baojia, who died in 1645 one year after the close of the Ming dynasty, suggests this as an explanation of the play's success:

The Plantain Kerchief: Frailty and Long Xiang quarrel on their wedding night.

(Shan) Chaxian had a congenital dislike of study, which is why he could escape pedantry in his diction, and a congenital disinclination to work to enhance the family fortunes, which is why no vulgar sentiments debase his lyrics. He would often, on the other hand, don the costume of an actor or perform as an amateur musician, which is why every situation he contrives is fresh and novel, and every phrase hits the mark. (His characters) are depicted with the finest of brushes and come vividly to life. This gentleman is truly a dramatist of genius.[1]

Xi Shi, in *Plantain Kerchief,* plays the minor heroine role *(xiaodan)* and appears for the first time at the beginning of scene 4, "Magical Transformation." The heroine proper *(dan),* Hu Ruomei, whom we call Frailty, has not yet appeared, but we have been given to understand that she is the daughter of a good family of the scholar-official class, headed by one Commissioner Hu. As always in *chuanqi* plays we have already, in scene 2, met the hero, the young scholar Long Xiang. Many complications are going to ensue for these two young people, but in the beginning their romance is conveniently to hand, ready-made, for Long Xiang is an orphan, the ward of Commissioner Hu, and evidently destined as son-in-law—he will be taken into the Hu family, who will literally gain a son rather than losing a daughter. This is one of the classic situations of the "genius meets beauty" type of romance, much favored by dramatists since it relieves them of the tedium of introducing *two* sets of parents with all the attendant complications of family relationships. But the so-neatly manufactured match is about to be seriously jeopardized by none other than our silk-washing seductress Xi Shi, as she pursues the purposes of her own strange destiny.

Now at this point we have to question the veracity of our playwright friend. Xi Shi has been dead for centuries! Commissioner Hu, Long Xiang, and the rest are honest subjects of the Southern Song court. They are citizens of Hangzhou, the city by the beautiful West Lake, established as provisional capital after the Song imperial power fled south across the Yangzi in the face of invading Tartars in 1126. We are in a time and place that are strong favorites with the storytellers and dramatists for several reasons—the appeal of the natural setting, the ongoing national crisis that brings forth patriots and traitors, collaborators and noble martyrs in record numbers, and not least the massive population shifts of the period, which provide such an abundance of partings and reunions. But Xi Shi is a figure of the era before the Han and Tang dynasties, let alone the Song—what is she doing in this story?

Xi Shi has been waiting, she tells us on entrance in scene 4, for three thousand years and more. (Some hyperbole here: from Xi Shi's lifetime to the twelfth century is only half that length of years; but traditional Chinese dating systems were not conducive to the ready reckoning of centuries or millennia, and we should take this as poetic license rather than as an indication of any particular mendacity in Xi Shi's makeup.) Her successful seduction of King Fuchai, she informs us, brought down not only the state of Wu in collapse and ruin, but also the wrath of Heaven on her own head. She has been condemned to reincarnation in the form of a white vixen; she is a fox-spirit.

As she tells us this she is standing before us in white robes, and she bears the title, she announces with some pride, of Great Sage of Frosty Splendor. Evidently she already enjoys something very close to immortality. But she is none the less kin to foxes and dwells in a hole in the ground. In three thousand years of alchemical effort she has come close to perfecting the pill that will complete her proper destiny. One ingredient alone is lacking: this is semen, the male essence to counter the excess of femininity with which—very plausibly—she has hitherto been afflicted. She has determined that Long Xiang, our hero, shall supply the missing ingredient. Her task will be to inveigle him into doing this by impersonating his bride-to-be, Frailty.

Such an adventure should present no difficulty to a fox-spirit with the amatory armament and experience of Xi Shi at her disposal. The playwright, on the other hand, must decide whether he wants one actress to play both parts, Frailty and Xi Shi. The result would be a satisfactorily convincing impersonation, but it would involve the most painstaking arrangement of entrances and exits, it would overload the poor *dan* actress who had to sing both parts throughout, and it would eliminate some juicy opportunities for farce with the two female leads on stage at the same time.

To the rescue come the conventions of stage dress and makeup. Even a small troupe would not find it too difficult to locate two *dan* players sufficiently close in height and figure, for no girl of unusual height or degree of plumpness would ever have sought her living as a *dan* actress. Take the two actresses, dress them as young ladies of quality in silk jacket and embroidered skirt of identical cut and color, and trust to the thick rouge and white of the *dan* stage makeup to disguise the individual facial features and to the kingfisher feathers and pearls of elaborate but identical hair ornaments to complete the deception.

Now it becomes possible for Xi Shi to appear on stage at the same time as Frailty. At first she does so surreptitiously, as she spies on her intended victims: the audience can see both women, but by stage convention the personages on stage cannot necessarily see each other. In later scenes Xi Shi alternates with Frailty on stage, to the bamboozlement of the hero who, of course, cannot tell one from t'other; toward the end of the play the truth is out, and Xi Shi the fox-fairy and Frailty the modest young bride can confront each other openly on stage.

Even though dress and makeup render the two female leads identical in appearance, the audience can at once recognize which is which by the flirtatious liveliness of the free-spirited Xi Shi. Frailty, in contrast, moves with slow deliberation, has her glance perpetually lowered, and behaves with the utmost decorum. As she sings on her first entrance, in scene 4:

> *Toilet completed, hands still rouge-scented*
> *tiny curved feet inch forward bashfully;*

shortly afterward, in her first full aria, she asserts her decorous concerns against the temptations of any idle garden amour:

> *I put aside my busy needlework*
> *to help my parents pass this day of leisure*
> *and yet my maiden heart*
> *not held by garden scene,*
> *accustomed more to pricking out phoenix patterns*
> *than plucking idle flowers amid willow groves.*

Very obviously, these are not the sort of sentiments Xi Shi would be likely to voice—the audience, unlike the bewildered romantic lead Long Xiang, can be quite sure who is who as the comedy progresses. .

The Plantain Kerchief is a complicated and uneven play that offers some superb domestic comedy in its first half but deteriorates into a farrago of fanciful inventions from about scene 24 on. We shall follow Xi Shi's progress in her quest for immortality as far as the major and very lengthy scene 17, whose second half I translate. To lead up to this it will be necessary to look at scene 6 in some detail and to make brief reference to a handful of other scenes along the way.

SCENE 6: THE KERCHIEF PRESENTED

Her plain white robe now exchanged for the identical costume worn by the demure Frailty, Xi Shi enters alone to open the scene and begin her campaign. She has already found more uses for her magic than merely to transform herself into a copy of Frailty. She has cast a mild spell on Frailty's mother, Madam Hu, causing her sufficient discomfort to bring the dutiful son-in-law-to-be, our hero Long Xiang, to inquire after her health. Anticipating his arrival, Xi Shi now prepares the object that provides the play with its title. Plucking a spreading plantain leaf, she tranforms it with a breath into a silk gauze kerchief. On this she proceeds to inscribe a poem bearing a riddling message of assignation—reading the first word only of each line yields "flower - garden - evening - meeting." She tucks the kerchief in her sleeve, and waits. (We shall see later, in scene 17, the rationale for this rigmarole with the plantain leaf, when Xi Shi liquidates the evidence of her affair with Long Xiang by turning the incriminating kerchief back again into innocent leaf.)

Long Xiang is as hot-blooded as Frailty is cool. He sings, on entrance now, of his impatience to marry: if Madam wants to be free of sickness, caused no doubt by malevolent stars, she should speed up the preparations for her daughter's marriage! So full of thoughts of Frailty, Long Xiang decides deliberately to lose his way in the garden courts, and blunders up to the forbidden door of Frailty's wing of the mansion rather than her mother's. He knocks: "Who's there?" — "It's me." In Chinese life this formula never changes, one is always supposed to know who "me" is by the voice, no name is ever given even though the exchange may be repeated half a dozen times.

Xi Shi (as Frailty) opens to him and the flirting begins at once. She deliberately refuses to believe his protestation of innocent error: "You know perfectly well which is my mother's room. . . ." She recites the hoary old prohibition against the touching of male and female hands when objects are passed between one another: this suggestion of the contact of flesh reinforces, of course, exactly what Long Xiang has in mind. She threatens to report his trangression to Madam Hu, reducing Long Xiang to low bows and pleas for forgiveness. Now she has him thoroughly scared, which gives her the opportunity to work still further on his emotions. But she has gone almost too far—in his self-abasement he threatens to take his leave. Swiftly she relents, confessing that she herself is not made of wood or stone. She reminds him of what he knows full well—that Madam is confined to her sickroom, the Commissioner away from home; and then she announces that she has something to tell him, words that can come only in the form of song:

Myriad hidden longings
myriad hidden longings
a thousand different dreams—
if only I could take all night to tell you!
But so meager is my love karma
the magpies hesitate to build their bridge!

"Love karma" is a combination of *fen,* one's "share" or "lot" in general, and *yuan,* the specific affinity one shares with a predestined mate. If one has received a generous portion of such karma, then undoubtedly the magpies will flock to form a bridge for one's lover to cross over, as they do in folk belief annually on the lovers' festival, the seventh of the seventh lunar month, so that the Herdboy star, Altair, may cross the Milky Way to tryst with his beloved Weaver Maid, Vega.

Xi Shi has declared her passion in unmistakable and most unmaidenly terms. Long Xiang thanks her, but since he seems a little too taken aback to seize the initiative, Xi Shi presses on. She urges him to engage a matchmaker to secure her father's formal consent. Long Xiang admits to having long aspired to her hand, and she resumes her aria with an allusion to the founder of the great Tang dynasty, who proved his claim as a potential son-in-law by shooting an arrow through the eye of a peacock painted on a screen:

> So great your skill to hit the peacock's eye
> the very pattern of a son-in-law
> surely the red thread linking our feet
> must be secure and strong.

A folktale of the Tang period describes how the "old man under the moon" ties an invisible red thread to link the feet of those predestined to marry— those, that is, who have a proper affinity, a *yuan*.

Long Xiang says amen to her last statement with a propitiatory bow toward Heaven, and ends the aria she has begun:

> May Heaven ensure
> that on the night of red candles
> I hold you close upon my lap
> our faces pressed together
> as lovingly we decide
> whether to push or knock!

The Tang poet Jia Dao was once discovered puzzling his brains whether to "push" or "knock" at a door in the line he was composing. Long Xiang's use of the allusion in a context rather less intellectual points up the element of parody in this whole scene. The first confession of mutual regard between young scholar and virginal maid, assuming (which is most unlikely) that they had chanced to meet prior to marriage, should obviously be highly oblique, tentative, preferably wordless. Here we have talk of holding on lap, of faces pressed together, a young hero no less riggish than the relentless Xi Shi herself. The audience delights in Long Xiang's good fortune, wishes Xi Shi success—and trembles with half-pleasurable anxiety for poor Frailty, about whose true character Long Xiang is being so thoroughly deceived.

The problem of where to go from here is resolved by an interruption. Offstage shouts of "Clear the way!" announce the return of Frailty's father. Xi

Shi passes the poem-inscribed kerchief, or handkerchief, to Long Xiang, and exits. Long Xiang conceals himself out on the veranda, that is to say at the side of the stage, to avoid being caught in Frailty's room, as a procession enters from upstage right: Commissioner Hu, his boorish son Hu Lian, and a servant guiding in the doctor who has been summoned to attend Frailty's bewitched mother. Discovered, Long Xiang explains that he has been waiting to inquire after Madam Hu's health. He is asked to entertain the doctor for a moment, and they exit together.

The considerable amount of movement on and off stage at this time is to be traced to the problems of etiquette surrounding the medical examination of a woman of the gentry class. Any kind of contact, even if it were no more than visual, with an unrelated male was an offense against the rites. Exceptions were made for certain nonpersons such as servants, or monks—ladies could visit temples on festivals, or receive monks on visits to their homes. But the practice of medicine was an occupation (not a particularly honored one, admittedly) of the educated class, and a doctor could be allowed into one's wife's presence with only a little less difficulty than a colleague or drinking companion. Usually a screen would be erected to separate patient from physician, whose examination would be confined to feeling the pulse "with the back turned" (Doctor Chen, in scene 18 of *Peony Pavilion,* farcically chooses to misunderstand this ritual prescription and searches for Bridal Du's pulse on the back of her hand). If a concealed part of the body had to be indicated, a small nude ivory doll was used for the purpose. So now, when Madam Hu appears onstage (the doctor has temporarily withdrawn), she is flanked and supported by Frailty and the maidservant Blossom, who help her to a chair and begin to direct the setting of screens about her. But Hu Lian, the son, objects:

HU LIAN:　Who is this lady?
FATHER:　Idiot, it's your mother, what are you talking about?
HU LIAN:　Then, since she's my mother, it's clear she is your wife, so what kind of etiquette allows that doctor to come feeling her hand and pinching her feet, fondling her up and down?

Hu Lian, right from his first appearance in scene 3, has been characterized as an ignoramus. A standard meter for Chinese verse uses seven syllables to the line, whilst the prescribed form for the examination essay requires eight sections or "legs," and so the fatuous Hu Lian must of course claim to write "seven-legged essays" and "eight-syllable verse." He is a wastrel whose only merit is the generosity with which he distributes his patrimony among the local whores. His role-typing as a "heavy" puts him squarely in the clown category. For him to show such delicate scruples over the ritual propriety of the doctor's actions is either totally out of character—or it is parody. The context of the burlesque wooing we have just witnessed puts the matter beyond doubt: Shan Ben is here satirizing the absurd prudishness which would prevent a physician from conducting a necessary examination of his patient. As a parody of genteel manners, the episode fits snugly into the scene's overall ironies.

His father, however, follows Hu Lian's suggestion, which is simply to report Madam Hu's condition to the physician and request a prescription. As she is describing the fever that has so mysteriously assailed her, Long Xiang reenters to pay his respects. Hu Lian, in further demonstration of his extraordinary concern for the proprieties, insists that his sister Frailty leave the room to avoid the company of her intended. As she makes her exit, the comedy of errors resumes. Long Xiang, under the illusion that she is the person whose declaration of love he heard only a few minutes ago, gives her a prodigious knowing wink as she hurries past. The wholly innocent Frailty indignantly ignores him and hastens offstage. Long Xiang turns to the audience with an aside: "She's just pretending to ignore me, to conceal our affair from her brother"—the dramatic irony is piling up good and strong.

More clowning from Hu Lian ends the scene. He makes an elaborate description of a rare character he is trying to read in the doctor's prescription, which turns out to be nothing more esoteric than the graph for "ginger." Madam Hu is assisted offstage again, her illness having served its purpose in Xi Shi's plans. Hu Lian makes his last suggestion: to sponsor a dramatic performance in honor of the gods, who may thereby be induced to assist in the Madam Hu's recovery. This link between theatrical performance and religious ritual is strong in China and goes back to the very origins of the drama, and the suggestion is well received. But again we wonder if such tender solicitude is not out of character for Hu Lian, until we realize that his motives are perfectly selfish. Like any other young wastrel he is profoundly stage-struck and eager for any opportunity that will place an actress—or a young boy of the troupe—at his lecherous disposal. And so Shan Ben zeroes in on his last target for the satire that has pervaded this entire scene, by striking at the long traditions of the theater itself through Hu Lian's hypocrisy.

SCENE 16: A SPY AT THE WEDDING

Scene 16 is very short and I translate it in full. First, however, we will note the swift progress of Long Xiang's courtship both of Frailty and, unwittingly, of her impersonator Xi Shi. In scene 6 we saw with how few inhibitions Xi Shi declared her affection and with how much enthusiasm Long Xiang responded. The two keep up the pace in scene 8, the assignation in the garden (the intervening scene gives Long the opportunity to work out the message of the poem Xi Shi has inscribed on the plantain leaf kerchief). The title of scene 8 is a complex double entendre: "Picking the Real," or "Gathering the Essence," *cai zhen*. It works in both directions: Long Xiang picks ("chooses," also "plucks") the real goddess even though she is not the "real" beloved, Frailty, that he takes her for. At one point, Frailty and her maid have left the stage and Xi Shi, in the guise of Frailty, is about to return alone as she has promised. Long Xiang says in an aside, "Over there in the distance I can see my lady, on her way back here unaccompanied. Truly she must be a nymph descended from Heaven!" "Truly," of course, this is exactly what she is, the audience enjoys the dramatic irony. Earlier, Long has found the good fortune of the assignation too much to believe, and asked Xi Shi, "Is it true or false?"

XI SHI: Foolish boy. With anything in this world, if there is a true then there will be a false also.

LONG XIANG: Then . . . tell me, are you false?

XI SHI: Ah, but the false in this case is better than the true!

So Long Xiang, deceived as he is in the identity of the beautiful woman he is talking to, has "picked the real" goddess.

Xi Shi, for her part, has picked or plucked the true essence, Long Xiang's semen, which is the final ingredient she needs for her elixir (*zhen,* true or real, used now in the alchemist's technical sense of the fully refined, the perfected and magically effective). She has done this, needless to say, offstage, after a brief scene of verbal lovemaking, with teasing on her part and impatient assurances of endless devotion on his. The passage has culminated in an extraordinary stage direction:

XI SHI: If you really love me . . . (*She "tuts" into Long Xiang's ear. These "tuts" must not be sung, but tutted, with tongue against teeth.*) I am a tut-tut fragile flower, be careful how you crush me . . .

It is a gift of an exit line for the comic actress who plays Xi Shi, this character who is close to the status of love goddess, still "uncrushed" after three thousand years!

In return for Long Xiang's services Xi Shi has expressed in a monologue her resolve to aid him both in his marital quest and in his future career. Most of the scenes between 8 and 16 revolve around Xi Shi's theft of a jeweled hairpin, which she donates for Long Xiang's use as a betrothal gift (thus spiking the guns of Frailty's avaricious brother who wants a wealthier husband for his sister). By scene 15 all preparations for the wedding have been completed.

Xi Shi's impersonation of Frailty is almost over, she appears onstage only very briefly during the wedding-night scene, and once or twice in subsequent scenes. Immediately preceding scene 17, however, Shan Ben allows Xi Shi a solo appearance that effectively enlists audience sympathy for her. Close to immortal she may be, but she is still subject to all-too-mortal yearnings:

Scene 16: A Spy at the Wedding

XI SHI (*enters and sings*):

(*TUNE: YUE SHANG WU GENG*)
Poetic lines form as petals fall
birdsong sounds from mate to mate
deserted is sweetbriar arbor
cold and lone the plantain palm—
what pains, to obtain a single drop from magic horn!
Tonight the two, the two of them, devoted couple
there to take their joy
while I am here cast off, rejected
and only further saddened
by sultry summer rain on lotus leaves
drop by drop and drip by drip, incessant patter
starting and shaking maiden soul
with thoughts of road to refuge.

—Such efforts as I have been making just lately to bring about Master Long's marriage! But tonight the matter of the plantain leaf kerchief must come to light—how am I to gloss it over? Ah, Master Long, Master Long, there's bliss in store for you tonight, and yet you have no notion of whom you owe for all this!

(*TUNE: XIANG GUI LUO XIU*)
A marriage is ordained—
but who was it took the lead?
Short of bright pearl stolen from Qin palace
what could withstand jade pestle of house of Pei?
Rejoice this night as son-in-law
rejoice this night as son-in-law.

Young mistress, 'if you want to know the road through the hills, you'll need to ask me as I pass by.' What tricks he'll be playing tonight! Such

sweet talk, such honeyed words
who could fail to credit them?

And, when that point is reached

some skilful exercise.

Ha, but it does no good to go on thinking of him. Myself here,

struggling to withstand birdsong and falling blossoms

while they

after play of cloud and rain comfort each other,

myself

lacking a thread to guide me through this desolation

while they

tangle themselves together beyond recourse.

But once that young lady discovers I was there before her, she'll be angry with me beyond all bearing. She'll say

the wren has taken the branch for itself
(*she spits in the direction of the stage exit*)

but tonight

not a twig for a perch is mine.

Ha, but I've been bothering my head about all these trivialities, and almost forgetting who I really am. I'll just pay a visit to the nuptial chamber, and there by the gleam of the red candles I'll perform one of my little marvels. After that I can get on with my own true karma, why not?

ENVOI:

Springs come, springs go, bothered by all the blossoms
but the blossoms have let the wind spread their perfume
  elsewhere.
You in your joy, grumbling the night's too short
are only stretching out my loneliness that much longer.

The falling petals of the opening aria symbolize things of beauty, briefly appreciated and then sentenced to long neglect; the mating birds, in contrast, reciprocate each other's care. Xi Shi has served to advance Long Xiang's courtship and now suffers rejection in favor of Frailty. Her skills (the plantain palm is a reminder of her tricks) brought her an experience of sexual love, but not that union which runs "between hearts, one minute thread from root to tip of the magic horn."[2] To escape the sadness of that world of the neglected courtesan that is conjured up by the imagery here, the dripping of the sultry summer rain, Xi Shi must turn her thoughts toward the ultimate goal of her magic. She must think, that is to say, of refuge, *gui,* the "return" to Dao, or Buddha, or whatever syncretic transcendence of worldly values Shan Ben may have wished for her (he does not say).

The use of paired allusions, the "Qin palace pearl" and the "Pei family pestle," is a little more problematic. The "bright pearl" may be simply the drop of semen she stole from Long Xiang's "jade pestle," in which case she is simply commemorating her own experience of Long and congratulating Frailty in advance. Alternatively, with the pearl she may be symbolizing herself, "stolen" by Long Xiang and serving as his initiator into the arts of love: she, pearl, could withstand the shock which, uncushioned in advance, would prove too much for the innocent Frailty. Her subsequent quotation of a popular proverb, "ask one who's been there already," would support either interpretation.

The arias here, consistently with those of the play as a whole, are something less than great poetry. But Shan Ben does show a certain wit, and a sensitivity to metaphors hackneyed though they may be. Hence Xi Shi's contrast of herself "lacking a thread, cut off from mortal ties" with the lovers all too thoroughly "tangled" in the toils of mutual affection.

The "little marvel," finally, that she promises to perform in the nuptial chamber, is to turn the silk gauze handkerchief back into plantain leaf, thus destroying the evidence of assignation and keeping Frailty a little longer in the dark about the liberties Xi Shi has taken as her double.

SCENE 17: NUPTIAL UPROAR

Uproar, *nao,* was an obligatory feature of the traditional Chinese wedding. When the ceremonial bows to Heaven, earth, and the ancestors had been performed and the loving cup drunk, when the guests had feasted their fill and the bride had withdrawn to the nuptial chamber—her face still concealed behind the heavy red veil—an extraordinary bit of hell-raising would commence—what nineteenth-century rural America would have called a shivaree. The bridegroom's siblings, the neighbors' children, and all the young roughnecks of the vicinity would gather inside or outside the room and "rouse the wedding chamber," *nao xinfang.* They would laugh and shout, jump about, and subject the poor bride to the most obscene and humiliating mockery they could invent for as long as the humor took them. Only when all tired of the fun would they yield at last to the entreaties of the shamefaced bridegroom. After the years of delicate nurture, the protective swaddling of the secluded young maiden, this was the reverse side of the medal, the dropping of the mask of decorum and ceremoniousness. Western observers, missionaries and others, condemned the practice as barbaric, but it must presumably have had some extraordinary kind of cathartic effect, perhaps like the boisterous drunkenness at an Irish wake.

Scene 17 of *The Plantain Kerchief* presents a kind of stylized dramatic sublimation of this folk practice. It is a major and very complex scene, three times the average length. In fact the part of it translated here, the entire second half, is labeled *diao chang*, "scene pendant." This is the technical term in *chuanqi* for a kind of epilogue. The *diao chang* presupposes the prior completion of a full song-set, and consists often of a few simple lines delivered by a single character, or a couple, remaining behind after the essential action of the scene is over and all others have left the stage. In this case, the musical structure of the scene is composite. The first song-set has just ended with a coda; the "pendant" involves nothing less than a change of musical mode (from *shuangdiao* to *zhenggong*, then to *zhonglü*) and an entire new song-set of ten different tunes, followed by a double coda to finish off the whole scene.

Probably the chief reason Shan Ben labels the whole second half a "pendant" is that the grouping of characters onstage is radically diminished after the halfway point is reached. Scene 17 opens with the entrance of Frailty's parents, who in introductory arias rejoice together over the approaching festivities. The actual performance of the simple rites (the triple prostrations to Heaven, earth, and parents) is saved from mere routine and considerably livened up by the majordomo, Long Xing, whose role-type is buffoon *(chou)*. The usual form of wedding delivered the bride into the groom's household. Since Long Xiang is an orphan, his marriage will be uxorilocal, and the ceremonial in this case requires the presence of a *binxiang*, a kind of best man or master of ceremonies. Long Xing, the majordomo, having had some difficulty in securing the services of a suitable person, has decided to save trouble and expense by disguising himself behind a white beard and taking the role of *binxiang* upon himself. He does this with much joking and joshing of the principals. After he has finally wheedled a tip out of the bride's father, then one from her mother, he goes one step too far by approaching the bride herself. The maidservant, ordered to get rid of this nuisance, seizes his false whiskers and unmasks him. In his own defense—which seems to be successful—Long Xing delivers a reprise of the "true/false" motif of scene 8:

COMMISSIONER HU: What is Long Xing doing, posing as fake master of ceremonies?

LONG XING: Sir, it is the fake, not the true, that suits people in this world. As long as you can fake your way out of something, you can get away with whatever you like.

After a round of celebratory arias from bride, groom, and parents, a messenger arrives bearing an urgent summons from the imperial court for Commissioner Hu. To announce this the messenger has come down from the entrance at backstage right, all the way forward, ignoring the wedding party center-stage, which of course, occupying as it does the main hall of the Commissioner's residence, is by convention invisible to him. In response to the messenger's loud hail the Commissioner steps out of the imaginary hall (attendants opening the doors from either side) and stalks with slow, swaying dignity downstage to join the court envoy. From this officer he receives, reverently in both hands, a yellow silk scroll bearing the Emperor's orders, which he reads aloud. He is to leave at once at the head of fifty thousand troops to undertake the defense of the region to the north against Tartar attacks. The Commissioner orders that the envoy be rewarded, then returns to the wedding party to inform them of his imminent departure. Madam Hu must see to it that the wedding observances are properly concluded, the bride is admonished to show due fealty, and the two young men of the household, the new son-in-law and Hu's own son, are urged to apply themselves industriously to study for the state examinations.

This first half of the wedding scene ends on a rousing martial note as four generals, the Commissioner's staff, enter to escort him to his new assignment. Each wears a gorgeous brocade robe over his armor: in actuality, high-ranking officers really would wear rich brocades into battle, small steel plates sewn into the material to compose a suit of mail that would thus be practically as well as psychologically effective.

Extras carrying multicolored banners precede the generals on their entrance and line up at either side of the stage as the four swagger across it. The actors portraying the generals belong to four different role-types and are perfectly matched in terms of physique and stance, gait and voice quality: they are respectively older male, juvenile, minor heavy, and buffoon, or *mo, xiaosheng, zhongjing,* and *chou,* though for this appearance the last two are given no clowning to engage in. On the head of each general is an elaborate winged helmet, from his back protrudes an array of flags. The height of the actors and the majesty of their bearing are further enhanced by deep, wide skirts beneath whose hems we can see black boots with white soles fully two inches thick. The four terrifying warriors flank Commissioner Hu, the civilian scholar-official who is their commander, and sing, in unison, arias proclaiming their martial ardor and resolve. The fatuous Hu Lian, the Commissioner's son, cues his father to a stirring exit line by suggesting a stirrup cup. "As I march against the foe, what need of wine cup to sustain me?" roars out the baritone voice of the Commissioner in the last line of his aria, and with gongs and drums, flags and banners, the procession sweeps offstage.

Left behind are bride and groom, who will occupy the stage together for most of the scene's second half, and Madam Hu and the maid Blossom, who reopen the proceedings:

Scene 17: Nuptial Uproar

MADAM HU: Take up your candle, Blossom, and guide the young master and mistress to the nuptial chamber.

BLOSSOM: Very good, ma'am.

(*Candle in hand,* Blossom *leads* Long Xiang *and* Frailty *on a circuit of the stage,* Madam Hu *bringing up the rear*)

[The procession indicates that the party is retiring from main hall to bridal chamber.]

MADAM HU:

(*TUNE: QI NIANGZI*)

Welcome them into the chamber, lacquer-bright and orchid-strewn

(*She weeps*)

yet parting comes as joy begins.

[Madam Hu's weeping is occasioned by the departure of her husband to the wars. *He* exited with a fine flourish; now *she* is given the opportunity to deliver one of those philosophic sentiments—sorrow born in the midst of joy—so beloved of Chinese audiences.]

BLOSSOM (*tugs at Madam Hu's sleeve and speaks in a stage whisper in her ear*): This is a fine act of merit of yours tonight, Madam.

MADAM HU (*surveys* Long Xiang *with a pleased expression*):

Such a handsome young son-in-law

(*She surveys* Frailty *in turn*)

and my child a pretty little thing—
now is their time to fulfill
the bliss of the night of red candles.

Blossom, stay close at hand to attend their needs. (Blossom *assents*)

I feign my pleasure for public view
concealing secret sorrow!

(*Exit* Madam Hu)

BLOSSOM: Young master, young mistress, Madam has left us, and now I'll
hand over the stage as well and get out of your way.

FRAILTY: Stay here to look after us, Blossom, don't go.

BLOSSOM (*laughs*):   Ai-ya, young mistress, you'll just have to put up with it as
best you can tonight, *I* can't take your place. And you, Master Long,
you'll need all your technique. My young mistress knows her way
around here, and if she once slips out of your net, there you'll be in the
middle of the night with no idea where to hunt for her, and *I'm* keeping
out of your way. Like they say,

tender sapling unused to wind and rain—
let the Lord of the East be gentle with her now!

(*Exit* Blossom)

[The pert maidservant is one of the richest roles in the
Chinese comic repertoire. The all-time audience favorite
in this role is Hongniang, "Red Maid," of the *Romance of
the West Chamber*. Even though this is the most famous of
all Chinese plays, in fact, going back to a Yuan dynasty
original, nowadays in Peking Opera presentations it is
most commonly known simply by the name of *Hongniang*
rather than by its original title. Here in our present play,
Blossom's impudent speech teases both bride and groom,
and reminds us of the special nature of this wedding, that
the groom is entering the bride's family. Normal procedure is of course the other way around, and the bride on
her wedding night, in effect, no more than a terrified
teenager locked in a strange place with a youth she has
never seen before. Blossom sagely advises Long Xiang
to be gentle or he will literally lose his bride. She makes
it clear, also, that she herself is not the kind of com-
plaisant slavey who will be willing to take the place of
a reluctant mistress in the master's bed—"*I'm* keeping
out of your way!" The "Lord of the East" is a mock-
heroic reference to an ancient deity to whom female sha-
mans sang hymns, posing as the beloved to solicit his descent.]

LONG XIANG (*laughs*):   You know your way around, lady, no mistake about
that! So who needs a lecture from this maid of yours? Ah, lady, lady!
(Frailty *ignores him*) Out there in the ancestral hall you played the role of

new bride, but here in your chamber we're old acquaintances all the same! (*She continues to ignore him, and turns away when he offers her the loving-cup*)

(*TUNE: SI YUAN CHUN*)

Laughing in lantern's light we drain the communal cup,
then hand in hand, the pair of us, we enter the conjugal bed.

(*He takes her hand but she jerks it away*)

Now to retie the double lovers' knots!

(Frailty *hurries to the far side of the stage*)

Uh? I'm afraid something must have upset my lady:

No more for now of this talk of former joys.

> [These lines, like the next utterance by Frailty, are obviously delivered aside to the audience.]

FRAILTY: Hah!

These things he's saying—for whom are they intended?
Deep within, what can I feel but alarm?

LONG XIANG:

My shame, as broken reed to stand beside jade tree!

FRAILTY:

Each word he utters false as it could be!

LONG XIANG:

yet fallen petals follow flowing stream—

FRAILTY: Hah!

When did stream treat petals tenderly?

> [Frailty must in the end respond to Long Xiang's outrageous insinuations of previous familiarity (outrageous from her point of view, since she is ignorant of Xi Shi's existence). It is well suited to her status and character that before addressing Long directly, she first makes an aside to the audience. When she does overcome her bashfulness sufficiently to respond at least on verse, she proves quite tart. His phrase, "broken reed," suggests himself as unworthy partner—she is the precious "jade tree." Unfortunately, she is also the "fallen petal," which in the original as in English has something of the suggestion of the fallen, and deserted, woman. It is this insinuation of her loss of innocence that she counters with an attack on the callousness of men, unfeeling as the stream that bears the petals away.]

LONG XIANG: Lady, what possesses you to keep up this pretence?
(*She spreads her fan and turns away, ignoring him*)
Lady, after all we've been through to reach this day!

(*TUNE: FEN HAI'ER*)

Hotly I've eyed this moment's "sharing of one branch"——it seems a thousand days since our garden tryst!

FRAILTY: Oh!

Lifelong secluded in chamber, never one step outside——how could you invent so groundless a tale?

[*The Plantain Kerchief* is a sort of Chinese variant, with the sexes reversed, of the Amphitryon motif, used by Western playwrights from the days of classical Greece until as recently as Jean Giraudoux. In Plautus' comedy *Amphitruo,* the gods Jupiter and Mercury disguise themselves as Amphitruo and his slave respectively in order to accomplish the seduction of Amphitruo's wife. In the Chinese case, it is of course the goddess (so to call her) Xi Shi who substitutes for the rightful spouse. Shakespeare concocted his *Comedy of Errors* by grafting the theme on to the basic plot of another play by Plautus, the *Menaechmi.* With Frailty's denial here we might compare the bewilderment of Antipholus of Syracuse, accused by Adriana of denying her, his own wife:

ADRIANA: Ay, ay, Antipholus, look strange and frown;
Some other mistress hath thy sweet aspects;
I am not Adriana nor thy wife.
The time was once when thou unurged wouldst vow
That never words were music to thine ear,
That never object pleasing in thine eye,
That never touch well-welcome to thy hand,
That never meat sweet-savour'd in thy taste,
Unless I spake, or look'd, or touch'd, or carved to thee. . . .
ANTIPHOLUS: Plead you to me, fair dame? I know you not:
In Ephesus I am but two hours old. . . .]

LONG XIANG: I've been at fault, no point in raking over these things of the past. Come to bed now.
(*Frailty ignores him. Offstage the watchman strikes the third quarter of the third watch.*)

Clepsydra's urgent drip——

> [The watchman is not exactly "dripping," but beating a wooden block. Long alludes to the archaic water clock or clepsydra which, by dripping water at a measured rate, floated an indicator to the time of day. The dripping of this instrument is the auditory image most frequently used in old lyrics for time's slow wasting.]

(He starts to remove her hair ornaments, but she fends him off)

Lady, it's true enough, "the new one is most excellent," but what about the old one?

Please now unbind your hair——
(He tries to blow out the lamp, but she shields it with her fan)
blow out the lamp, we'll rest where none can see.

(Xi Shi slips onstage unobserved and spies on them)

> [It is an effective stoke of dramaturgy to bring Xi Shi onstage to witness the lovers' dispute yet take no part in the exchanges. The sour grapes of Xi Shi's monologue, scene 16, suggest her huge enjoyment of Frailty's present predicament—enjoyment she presumably communicates to the audience with knowing winks as she peers from her "hiding place" through the crack of the imaginary door.]

FRAILTY:

(TUNE: FU MA LANG)
Scholarly youth, yet so careless of the rites
so rude to me, here where nuptial cup is raised——
what can it mean?

(She makes to leave the room)

LONG XIANG *(barring her way)*: Where do you wish to go, lady?

FRAILTY:

Before my mother, to argue who's right, who's wrong!

LONG XIANG: You have your say, I'll have mine.

FRAILTY: Why, what will your story be?

LONG XIANG: Of how you gave me a bright pearl and a silk gauze kerchief, and made an evening assignation with me in the garden.

FRAILTY: Oh! Devil-talk! What bright pearl did I ever give you?

LONG XIANG:

The night-gleaming pearl, no other.

> [This legendary pearl is also known as the "whale's eye." Several gems with properties of innate light are mentioned in early books of marvels.]

The Plantain Kerchief: Frailty and Long Xiang, quarreling on their wedding night, are spied on by Frailty's mother and maid.

FRAILTY: Oh! And what silk kerchief?

LONG XIANG:

That green gauze kerchief, there for me to find.

(Blossom *steals onstage to listen, then brings on* Madam Hu *also. Both come downstage, listening.*)

[Like Xi Shi, they are outside the imaginary walls of the nuptial chamber within which the newlyweds are squabbling. This is obvious to the audience, since no one has opened any doors or crossed a threshold.]

FRAILTY:

(*TUNE: HONG SHAOYAO*)

Wild words spilled out at random—
who ever gave you pearl or kerchief!

LONG XIANG:

Yourself, with your own hand, both pearl and kerchief
for evening assignation in the garden.

FRAILTY: How can you rave this way?

LONG XIANG: If I am raving (*he searches in his sleeve*) then who was it gave me this kerchief? (*He draws the kerchief from his sleeve, but* Xi Shi *puffs a breath of air from her hiding-place*) Oh! A kerchief, for all to see—how did it turn into this plantain leaf?

[No sleight of hand is required here: the square of cloth Long Xiang draws from his sleeve is plain kerchief on the obverse, embroidered plantain leaf on the reverse, and needs only be turned around before the eyes of the audience. The ability to perform sleight-of-hand tricks was not required of the *chuanqi* actor in general. But when a role called for a particular skill, it would be developed to meet the demand. Only an accomplished acrobat would attempt the Monkey King, for example—in fact, he would have trained for it since childhood. I once heard the Czech scholar Dana Kalvodova describe how in modern *Chuanju* (Sichuan Opera), a god is at one point required to change facial color several times very rapidly. For this stunt the stage is prepared in advance with small piles of differently colored powders. The actor somersaults so that his face passes within an inch or two above one of these piles. At the appropriate split-second he puffs so that the powder flies up, adhering to his oiled and sweating face and changing its color. He displays the effect to the audience, then moves on to somersault above the next] pile, and so on. In comparison with a "special effect" like this, the trick of palming a silk kerchief and substituting a plantain leaf would be simplicity itself—particularly since the deep sleeves of the man's gown were in normal everyday use as "pockets."]

FRAILTY: Hah!

Possessed by demons, for all to see! (*She weeps*)

Oh father, mother, how could you bestow

daughter of honored house
on so disreputable a son-in-law!

LONG XIANG: Lady,

accept this plantain leaf as "red leaf envoy"
and with its aid we'll make a perfect match.

[*The Poem on the Red Leaf (Ti hong ji)* was a contemporary play by Wang Jide, based on the Tang story of a lady who wrote a poem on a red leaf, which she floated down along the palace drain. The finder of the billet doux eventually won her hand.]

FRAILTY (*stamping her foot*): Worse than ever! Where is Blossom? Blossom! (*As she stands there desperately calling,* Xi Shi *slips out.* Frailty *makes to open the door but* Long Xiang *bars her way.*) Blossom! Blossom! Call my mother here, at once!

BLOSSOM: Here, young mistress, I'm here, and madam your mother as well.

(Madam Hu *clamps her hand over* Blossom's *mouth.* Frailty *shouts again, and flings the door open.* Madam Hu *and* Blossom *enter.* Long Xiang *stamps his foot angrily and goes to stand at the far side of the stage.* Madam Hu *and* Blossom *raise their candles to peer in turn at* Long Xiang *and* Frailty *in opposite corners of the stage.*)

[This may well be the longest stage direction in all of Ming drama. It marks the climactic moment of the play, the point of extreme alienation among the principals, and comes exactly halfway through the text. Xi Shi's surreptitious visit (she has exited immediately before this moment) has reminded us of her behind-the-scenes manipulation of the fates of the newlyweds; now we get a veritable tableau of disaster, bride and groom as far apart as the stage will allow them to stand, their position a net result of the action of the entire first half of the play. The second half will be devoted to their reconciliation, in the

classic mold of comedy. A total structure of this kind
would lend itself admirably to performance over a two-
day period (five or six hours—a long afternoon—each
day). By placing this dramatic moment or tableau so close
to the end of this longest scene in his play, and exactly at
the halfway mark, the dramatist displays his concern for
retention of his audience through day number two.]

MADAM HU: Oh dear!

(*TUNE: NAN SHUA HAI'ER*)

When tonight should see a couple in harmony
how is it the lantern shows one east, one west?

Good son-in-law! (Long Xiang *sighs*)

Too annoyed for words, Master Long can only sigh!

My child!

(Frailty *weeps, hiding her face behind her extended sleeve*)

[She has previously hidden her face behind her extended
fan, but the fan plays no part in the gesture of weeping. It
is folded and tucked into the bodice. With the fingers of
her right hand (the thumb always as inconspicuous as possible for the player of women's roles) she draws out the
yard-long white silk "water-sleeve" from her left wrist to
it fullest extent horizontally before her face. She has lowered her head, which is turned slightly to the right, and
now stands motionless, half screened by the extended
sleeve. She then touches the edge of the sleeve to each eye
in turn in a gesture of drying tears.]

And why do Frailty's eyes glisten with tears?

Good son-in-law!

BLOSSOM: Young master!

(Long Xiang *takes no notice*)

MADAM HU: My child!

BLOSSOM: Young mistress!

MADAM HU: My child, what was it you wanted to tell me when you called
me here?

BLOSSOM: Why won't you say, miss?

FRAILTY (*points at* Long Xiang): He . . . . (*words fail her*)

MADAM HU: Hah!

Opens her lips
only to shut them again!

(TUNE: HUI HEYANG)
Husband and wife till you reach a hundred
your marriage begins tonight:
turn anger now to joy, end this division!

BLOSSOM:

Let the bride show a little more patience—
for the sake of your maidservant's face!

[For the wedding night to pass off smoothly a well-regulated household was required, and for the household to be well regulated the personal maid of the "young mistress" bore a heavy responsibility—even though this nuclear household, within the larger family residence, was only a few hours old. Blossom is concerned not only for the loss of face that discord involves, but for her own skin as well, for she could be beaten for failing to secure harmony between her mistress and new master. The jingles she now addresses to each in turn are designed to persuade Long Xiang to take the initiative ("cock pigeon chases hen") in making up the quarrel, to let the annoyance pass and accomplish his wooing of Frailty before sleep overtakes her; and to persuade Frailty in turn to yield to her husband's marital demands.]

Young sir,

Dawn coming soon
cock going to crow
folk get sleepy—
let it go!

(Long Xiang *takes no notice, and she turns to* Frailty)

Young miss,

Cock just crowed
sun came out
sleepy or not
can't do without!

(Frailty *takes no notice either, and she turns back again to* Long Xiang)

Young sir, no need to look any farther, just watch that cock-pigeon *wark-wark-wark-wark* chasing after the hen! When were we hens ever supposed to chase after you cocks? Why don't you listen to little Blossom and make it up? (*She tugs at* Long Xiang's *sleeve, but he shakes loose*) Oh!

So you're playing hard-to-get too!

LONG XIANG (*points at* Frailty):   She——

    stands there reviling me——what can I say?

FRAILTY (*points at herself*):   I . . .

> [In the Chinese manner, she points not at her own chest but at her nose.]

    stand here unwilling to put up with his insults!

(*She bustles agitatedly offstage*)

MADAM HU: Hurry, Blossom, ask her to come back.

BLOSSOM (*hastens off after* Frailty, *but reappears almost at once*):   Oh dear, my young mistress has gone straight to Madam's room to sleep in your bed, and she refuses to come back. She'll come only if Madam herself goes to fetch her.

MADAM HU: Then you stay here, Blossom, and try to bring the young master round, while I go myself. (*She exits*)

BLOSSOM: Young master, the apricot blooms prettily, but it's sour when you first taste it. How can you be so ignorant that you need *me* to show you the way? She's

> (*TUNE: LÜLÜ JIN*)
>
> *so young and innocent*
> *it's tenderness she needs*
> *to turn her head a little.* (*She kneels*)

Watch me:

> *suppose you just kneel to her——*
> *she'll be sure to come round.*
> *But when the cage-bird flies away*
> *what are you going to do?*
> *Longing looks won't fill a hungry belly,*
> *you're left with a flute and no hole to play it by!*

> [Blossom displays not only the pertness of the witty and resourceful servant, but folk wisdom also. Her speech and aria here string together one proverbial expression after another. The flute with no hole is a clear sexual reference, but it is worth noting also that this was the instrument used to accompany performers as they left the stage in the old Song dynasty variety show, so that there is also the inference that Frailty has left Long Xiang's stage sadly bare.]

LONG XIANG: Well, what you say makes sense. Please go to her at once and ask her to come back.

BLOSSOM: Good enough. Tonight's the night for you to prove yourself behind the gauze bed-curtains. I'll run your errand for you! (*She exits*)

LONG XIANG: And yet . . . a silk gauze kerchief, clear and plain, and all at once it turns into a plantain leaf! The young lady took exception to my reminder of our past adventures, and went off in a huff, putting me out of temper too. Well, I'll sit here for a while till Madam Hu and Blossom have brought her back, and then we'll see what can be done.

(*He stretches back in a chair and mimes falling asleep*)

> [He has full sleeves, though not so voluminous as the heroine's "water-sleeves." He folds his right sleeve behind his head as he leans back in the (upright) chair, and holds his left sleeve before his face to indicate sleep.]

XI SHI (*reenters*):

(*TUNE: YUE NEN HAO*)
Hide the tail but show the head,
hide the tail but show the head—
how I blush to think of it!
Scurrying back and forth,
now to inscribe a poem on his lapel.

(*She folds back the neck of* Long Xiang's *gown to expose the lining, then takes a brush from her sleeve and writes out the poem, reciting it as she does so*)

Plantain leaf and kerchief, one and the same,
metamorphosed by fairy maid.
In the Eyes of Heaven Mountains, at Dragonboat time
she will direct your future path.

> [The Eyes of Heaven Mountains, Tianmushan, rise from the shores of Hangzhou Bay, near Haining, and so are not too far away from Hangzhou, where Commissioner Hu's residence stands. "Dragonboat" is the festival held on the fifth day of the fifth lunar month, when boat races are held, supposedly to seek the watery resting place of the ancient poet Qu Yuan.]

Ah, Long Xiang,

a goddess who's "heard the Way" is beyond your reach,
her heart borne by lake waters far, far from here. (*She exits*)

[Xi Shi here refers to the popular legends that portray her, after the completion of her ruin of the state of Wu, as sailing off with her lover Fan Li across the Five Lakes. Since this action supplies the last scene of *The Girl Washing Silk,* it would be well known to Shan Ben's playgoing contemporaries.]

LONG XIANG (*wakes up*): Uh? I just sat down—must have nodded off. (*He looks down at his collar*) Strange—two columns of characters on the lining of my gown, the ink not yet dry. With my lady off in the inner apartments, who could the writer be? (*He reads the poem aloud*) This is some kind of marvel! (*Takes off the gown*) I'll put this one on the inside and examine it later at my leisure. (*He switches his outer and inner gowns*) I shall need to be careful when my lady returns.

[The onstage changing of dress is a commonplace. Black-clad assistants lend a hand, just as they appear from time to time, theoretically invisible, to move the table and chairs. Long Xiang is dressed for his wedding, and so particularly colorfully. His outer and inner gowns, equally elaborate in the quality and extent of embroidery, would be carefully matched in shade.]

A goddess took brush in hand, but kept her secret close;
now modesty inhibits speech,
words crowd the tongue, but how to excuse what's past?
And how conceal the thudding in my heart?

MADAM HU (*reenters, clutching at Blossom's sleeve with one hand while with the other she pushes* Frailty *before her*)

(*TUNE: HONG XIU XIE*)

[The aria pattern *Hong xiu xie,* "Embroidered Red Slippers," is a joyful tune as its name suggests, red being the color of joy and therefore of weddings. Like several such allegro patterns it involves reiteration of ends of lines or whole lines; all the lines are in any case short, mostly trisyllabic.]

Gentle daughter, make up your mind, make up your mind!

BLOSSOM: .
Here's Blossom right behind you, right behind!

MADAM HU, BLOSSOM:
Time of joy
day of bliss

what a happy
union this!

(*They thrust* Frailty *through the doorway.* Frailty *stumbles over the high threshold; as she does so,* Madam Hu *and* Blossom *seize the occasion to bar the door from the outside.*)

> [The (imaginary) door, which is double, has bolt-hooks on both sides. The actors may therefore mime the action of sliding the bolt to open or close the door either from inside or outside—the one essential is that they remember (as the audience surely will) which side the door was bolted by the *last* actor to pass in or out!]

Cross the painted threshold
bar the lacquered doors,
cross the painted threshold
bar the lacquered doors. (*They exit*)

LONG XIAN (*takes* Frailty *in his arms—she ignores him*):   My lady! My lady! (*She makes no response other than to lower her head*) It's all my fault, I said the wrong things. Come, raise your head, and come sleep. (*She takes no notice*)

> (*TUNE: WEI SHUANG SHENG*)
>
> *Still you refuse to raise your head—*
> *shall husband and wife fail of their joy this night?*

(*Offstage a cock crows; he turns in the direction of the sound*)
> For shame!
>
> *It maddens me, this overzealous dawn-announcing cock!*

(*The cock is joined by several others*)
> Shame, shame!
>
> *If I have to strangle them*
> *I'll stop the noise these flea-bitten creatures make!*

(*Still* Frailty *refuses either to raise her head or to make a sound.* Long Xiang, *his arm about her shoulders, leads her offstage.*)

Frailty's silence is more effective than either dialogue or aria could be at this point. It brings the scene, and the first half of the action, to a moving close. The highlights of the play, considered as romantic comedy, are now past, though good comic situations continue to stem from the "Amphitryon theme," the substitution of sex-goddess for innocent bride. By scene 21 Frailty has learned of the existence of Xi Shi, whom she insists on referring to as "that monster" (Long Xiang, horrified, substitutes "sylph"). The comedy of errors continues through scene 23, with Xi Shi still impersonating Frailty and Long Xiang hard pressed to tell which of the two is aboard the dragonboat with him on the excursion to the Eyes of Heaven Mountains. But Frailty's reconciliation with her husband, after the disaster of the wedding night, is fairly quickly accomplished, and the clever domestic comedy of the first half of the play fades out almost completely after scene 23.

It is replaced by a meander of more or less fantastic plot developments as Xi Shi completes her own ascent to godhead and along the way repays Long Xiang for the favor of his vital gift. She secures his success in the examinations by a trick that elevates scene 26, "Uproar in the Examination Hall," from the category of stock scene by injecting an element of novelty in keeping with the high level of invention of the play as a whole. (Examination scenes are so inevitable a feature of these plays about young scholars that they can sometimes become "stock" to the extent that when the libretto arrives at this particular plot development it will read merely "Scene number so-and-so: examination scene as usual.")

In scene 26 of *The Plantain Kerchief,* the examiner sits with Long Xiang's paper before him. The paper has actually been written by Xi Shi, with a magic brush borrowed from the God of Letters, but this presumably counts as divine aid rather than simple cheating, given the worthy nature of the hero. Next to Long's paper lies one written by the grandson of Qin Hui, the treacherous Song minister and a favorite villain of the traditional Chinese theater. The examiner weighs the papers one against the other, picking up each in turn. "This one has the style," he says of Long Xiang's. Then, picking up the other paper, "but this one has the influence!" Long Xiang's prospects look bleak, until the examiner begins to notice what the audience has been aware of for some time, that thunder begins to roll when young Qin's paper is touched, turning to fairy music when Long Xiang's paper is taken up. Since he fears the wrath of Heaven even more than he fears Qin Hui, the examiner decides to nominate Long Xiang as Prize Candidate.

Qin Hui attempts revenge by sending Long Xiang on a hopeless military mission, which gives Xi Shi, now serving as his guardian angel, a chance to display even more of her skills—and of her celestial connections—in effecting his rescue. By scene 34 Long Xiang has been appointed to the Hanlin Academy, the exclusive metropolitan coterie of scholars selected to fulfill the literary obligations of the throne. Xi Shi herself has been promised a temple in her honor. Even now Shan Ben adds two more scenes, which provide an additional layer of supernatural interpretation of everything that has transpired. Among other things, one of the legendary Eight Immortals explains that Long Xiang and Frailty are in fact incarnations of two servants of the goddess Queen Mother of the West. They have been banished to earth for committing the indiscretion of falling in love. In the concluding action of the play, they are given golden pellets that will restore their immortal attributes.

As domestic comedy *The Plantain Kerchief* is first-rate; as fantasy romance (that is, unfortunately, for most of the play) it is run-of-the-mill. Compared with *The Girl Washing Silk,* Xi Shi's major stage vehicle, it has not been successful. It was certainly performed: Qi Biaojia, whose appreciative comment on Shan Ben was quoted earlier, recorded his attendance at eighty-six plays between the years 1632 and 1639 and listed *The Plantain Kerchief* as one of them.[3] It is still read today because of its inclusion in the major late Ming reprint series of *Sixty Plays* edited by Mao Jin. But neither the play itself in abridged form nor any of its separate scenes seem to have survived into the eighteenth-century or later repertoires. The *Zhui bai qiu* anthology of scenes still being performed around the year 1770 contains seven scenes from *The Girl Washing Silk* but not a single scene from *The Plantain Kerchief.* A modern scholar's list of scenes from southern-style plays still in the repertoires of Shanghai troupes at the turn of the twentieth century includes no less than eleven from *The Girl Washing Silk,* but again not one from *The Plantain Kerchief.*[4]

Probably we must seek the main reason for this failure in the inferior musical quality of Shan Ben's play. The late Qing scholar Wang Jilie asserts the preeminence of the musical aspect of southern drama in the following words:

> The composer of a *chuanqi* play may use a remarkable story and beautiful diction, but if he does not properly fit these to the musical modes his work cannot be imposed on the throats of singers; he may match the modes and harmonize the notes, but if he pays insufficient attention to arrangement [*pai chang,* the selection of song-sets and their distribution among the different role-types in a scene], his work will never make it as far as the carpet [i.e., will never reach the stage]. Unfortunately, not too many men of letters are capable even of writing song lyrics; as for understanding the joys and sorrows, the labors and rewards of stage production, or knowing how an audience may be moved by what it sees and hears, men with these capacities are fewer still. That is why the romances they compose, however beautiful their language, fail to win popularity on the musical stage, while plays put together by the actors themselves may manage to win acclaim.[5]

Evidently *The Plantain Kerchief* had no musical appeal to compare with *The Girl Washing Silk,* whose arias as we already noted were sung by the entire assembled crowd on Tiger Hill outside Suzhou at the Mid-Autumn Festival. Few critics have bothered to comment on Shan Ben as a composer, but the fellow dramatist and fiction writer Ling Mengchu objected to his habit of adding lines to the last aria in a suite:

> A good line now and again, but too often harsh and lacking polish. As for his addiction to the double coda, this is unorthodox even for the Yiyang school. The registers do include such a pattern as the double coda, but who wants to hear it again and again? Moreover, when a coda line is doubled, how can there be any "lingering resonances?"[6]

Like the language of its lyrics, then, the music of Shan Ben's play struck contemporary ears as commonplace, less than impressive "even for the Yiyang school" (which used old popular tunes in contrast with the new, refined Kunqu melodies of *The Girl Washing Silk*).

Where *Plantain Kerchief* scored was in sheer entertainment value. We can easily visualize the spectacle of the lotus-gathering scene in *The Girl Washing Silk,* the waterborne dancers in their pink and green costumes, and there are other moments in the play that offer a good swirling show of onstage action. But when it came to spectacle, a performance of *The Plantain Kerchief* brought a whole three-ring circus into town. Its author is constantly inventing excuses to drag in some form of popular entertainment.

His earliest opportunity is scene 3, since by convention the first scene is prologue and the second merely introduces the hero and his circumstances. Not until scene 3 does the playwright get the chance to send his hero and friends on an excursion to the West Lake, where they (and the delighted audience) make a wide sampling of its pleasures: a juggler and sword-swallower, a vendor of erotic paintings (by the famous Ming masters Tang Yin, Qiu Ying, and Zhou Chen!), a snake-charmer and monkey trainer, and a troupe of actors who perform for them one of the celebrated recent plays of the eccentric Xu Wei. Scene 22 offers a whip-dance and a sword-dance, Scene 27 a man-versus-tiger wrestling match (one of the hoariest of all stage spectacles, recorded from Chang'an in Han times).

Scene 33 calls for the onstage burning of a rebel camp, before the rebel leaders are trapped in a snow-covered pit (great scope here for tumblers and mimes). Stage directions for this play are exceptionally detailed and include plentiful sound effects: fairy music versus thunder in the examination scene, depending on which candidate's paper is picked up; sounds of watchmen's gongs and ravens' cawing, honking of wild geese and tigers' roars. Almost every scene has something special to look at, laugh at, or listen to.

But probably the greater interest we find in *Plantain Kerchief* lies in the force of its mimetic qualities, the strength of its reflection of the realities of Ming life outside the theater. From the individuality of the protagonists and the liveliness of their dialogue, we can see something of the thinking and values of people of the time. We are dealing after all with entertainments, and perhaps it would seem pretentious to speak of philosophic values in either of these two offshoots of the Xi Shi legend. Yet both *Girl Washing Silk* and *Plantain Kerchief* have something to say about the human condition, not in the sixth century B.C. nor in the twelfth century A.D., the times of their ostensible settings, so much as in the latter part of the sixteenth century when they were written and first performed. It is in this respect, the mimetic, that the two plays differ most significantly. We could describe the attitude toward Xi Shi, the one personage the two plays share, as sympathetic in each play, but the nature of the sympathy undergoes a profound shift from one work to the other.

The Xi Shi of *The Girl Washing Silk* is viewed from the standpoint of the Confucian heroic code, which dominates the play. She is woman as temptress, the beautiful lure that the man of good sense resists—or accepts, as Fan Li accepts her, only with the greatest caution and understanding of the peril she represents. The playwright's romantic sympathy for her, and the demands of the genre of romantic comedy to which *chuanqi* in essence belongs, turn this siren figure into a sacrificial lamb, a "root of disaster" redeemed by her sacrifice to the political purposes of the play's hero and his master, the King of Yue. This sacrifice is in its turn made possible by her redeeming love for the noble Fan Li, whose strength sustains her beyond the dishonor of King Fuchai's lustful bed.

The Xi Shi of *The Plantain Kerchief* may be lodged temporarily in the body of a fox-spirit, but she is viewed with much less of the old chauvinist suspicion. She is presented—with a certain amount of sniggering, it is true—in a remarkably modern, "liberated" light, as a frankly sensual woman with needs of her own, not to be subordinated to the will of the male world around her. The satire of the play is aimed not at her, but at the wholly conventional ingenue, Frailty, and her less-than-irreproachable fiancé, Long Xiang. Shan Ben is writing a full generation later than Liang Chenyu, the author of *The Girl Washing Silk,* and his assertion of the right of this love goddess to the satisfaction of her own physical needs is consistent with the age that admired the *Romance of the Western Chamber* and that gave birth to *The Peony Pavilion.*

TANG XIANZU'S
The Peony Pavilion

FLOWER SPIRIT (*enters*):
> (*TUNE: BAO LAO CUI*)
> *Ah, how the male force surges and leaps*
> *as in the way of wanton bee he stirs*
> *the gale of her desire*
> *while her soul trembles*
> *at the dewy brink of a sweet, shaded vale.*
> *A mating of shadows, this,*
> *consummation within the mind,*
> *no fruitful Effect*
> *but an apparition within the Cause.*
> *Ha, but now my flower palace is sullied by lust!*

For a long time I found the last line of this aria about as difficult to understand as any line in any of the fifty-five scenes of Tang Xianzu's *Peony Pavilion*. Not difficult in the sense that the words are particularly hard to translate into English, though none of Tang Xianzu's language is ever plain and straightforward. But puzzling—why does this last line have to be said, or rather sung, at all? We are here in the middle of scene 10, "The Interrupted Dream," the most celebrated and most frequently performed scene of the play, still today.

The Peony Pavilion: Bridal Du, in spirit form, is borne by
a whirlwind to the gate of Liu Mengmei's studio.

The Flower Spirit has made the first of his two entrances, announcing to the audience that he comes specifically to watch over the heroine, Bridal Du, to ensure that the lovemaking she is engaging in at this moment (off-stage, I hasten to add) will be a joyous experience for her. He will only appear once more in the play, in scene 23, "Infernal Judgment," when Bridal appears on trial before the Judge of the Dead. The Flower Spirit at that point successfully defends Bridal against the charge of wantonness and helps her secure permission to return to the world of the living.

So, despite the brevity of his appearances on stage, the Flower Spirit performs an important function in the plotting of this play, which is all about the power of love to overcome death. Why then does he get himself into such a logical tangle, setting out to act as a kind of pander, or at least a kindly patron, for the lovers, celebrating their passion in a set of unmistakably explicit sexual images, but then in his last line lamenting the "sullying" of his realm by—of all things—lust? He has just told us, after all, that for all the surging and trembling and dewy sweetness this is no more than a "mating of shadows." In the Buddhist doctrine of karma, every phenomenon, everything that happens is both the effect of a prior cause and the cause of a future effect. There is thus an endless chain linking all life, all action, nothing is without its cause and its consequences, even though the cause may originate in a previous incarnation and the consequence ensue in the next life rather than this present one. The act of love the Flower Spirit so obligingly and so vividly describes for us, going on at this moment in the wings there, is not, he tells us, actual, but only apparent, "no fruitful Effect/but an apparition within the Cause"—a foreshadowing of the inevitable future mating and lifelong partnership of these young lovers of our play.

So why this concern about "lust?"

The answer to this question, I now believe, is both simple and profound. Fundamentally, the entire *Peony Pavilion* is Tang Xianzu's protracted meditation on the nature of love. What we may call love he called *qing*, for which the most general equivalent would be "feeling." *Qing*—I will continue to call it "love"—in its highest development, as true love between man and woman, includes sexual attraction, physical passion, but also sentiment, empathy, devotion, the virtues of that broader love that exists also outside the sexual relationship.

There is no doubt about the mutual sexual attraction between the lovers of *The Peony Pavilion,* the aristocratic maiden Bridal Du and the young scholar Liu Mengmei. In pursuing their story through the scenes of his play Tang Xianzu has them make love, via the most lyrical and picturesque imagery, no less than three times. The occasion the Flower Spirit has just described for us, in scene 10, is the first. The second time is in scene 28, "Union in the Shades," which is translated below. But in scene 36, "Elopement," Bridal Du is still proclaiming her virginity. Their first lovemaking, she reminds Liu Mengmei in that scene, was in her garden dream before they had ever met. The second occasion was subsequent to Bridal's death from pining. Summoned from the shades by Liu's own yearning as well as by her mother's pious memorial prayers, her soul or shade, *hun,* has visited her lover in the night. She confesses, recalling later this second act of love.

> *Hidden longings possessed my ghostly form,*
> *too feeble to resist*
> *the surge of the male force.*

But then she claims:

> Master Liu, I am still a virgin. . . . That was my ghostly form: only now do I bring you my real self.

At the level of social convention, Tang Xianzu has avoided certain censure by having his heroine retain her virgin status until this moment in scene 36, by which time the resurrected Bridal has resumed fleshly form, eloped with her lover, and safely reached at last the married state.

But the playwright's purpose runs deeper than this. He is celebrating *qing,* and physical love is a part of *qing,* a part to be exalted. But *qing* itself is more than sexual love. True feeling demands authentication. The lovers' ecstasy, portrayed with a zest that has kept these scenes for ever in the repertoire, is in fact, as the Flower Spirit fears, no more than lust until it has been tested. Liu Mengmei must conquer more than Bridal's maidenhead. He must overcome his fear when he discovers his beloved to be a ghost. Then, further even to this, he must banish all revulsion over the disinterment of her corpse, and have faith in the power of his love to resurrect her physical body. And Bridal, in her turn, must hold fast to her love for him in the chill of the grave and through the shadows of her ghostly wanderings.

The sequence of scenes between 28, "Union in the Shades," and 32, "Spectral Vows," develops the love between Bridal and Liu Mengmei to its highest pitch. By this stage of the action of the play Bridal has been three years dead, victim of love-longing, pined away for love of the young scholar Liu whom she has never met, but who has appeared to her and wooed her in her garden dream of scene 10. She has faced trial in the underworld, and the Judge of the Dead has granted her plea to return to the world of the living where she must accomplish her predestined fate of union with Liu. Liu in the meantime has chanced upon the garden of Bridal's dream, where her body is buried, and there among the rocks about the peony pavilion he has discovered the scroll bearing her portrait, painted by herself in the days of her pining.

Enamored of the demure beauty of the portrait Liu calls out to her. His cries summon the wandering soul of Bridal, which is responding also to the ritual prayers of the Daoist priestess, Sister Stone, charged with the maintenance of Bridal's garden shrine. Here, from scene 27, "Spirit Roaming," is the lead-in to Bridal's first entrance (subsequent to her trial before the infernal Judge) as a wandering soul. A young visiting nun asks Sister Stone the purpose of the evening mass she is preparing to celebrate. Incense perfumes the text as they exchange lines of verse prior to launching into their arias of prayer to the appropriate Daoist goddesses for Bridal's return to the mortal world:

Scene 27: Spirit Roaming

SISTER STONE (*sighs*):   Ah,

> young mistress of the house of Du
>> three full years departed;
> tonight her soul is summoned
>> to ascend the ninefold Heavens.

YOUNG NUN: So this is your purpose.

> For sacrament of prayer
> this is a favored time;
> let me with incense and burning lamp
> assist the holy celebrant.

SISTER STONE: You are welcome to do so.

(*Bells and drums sound offstage*)

CELEBRANTS: We request our head to offer incense.

SISTER STONE: In honor of the First Consort of the Southern Dipper, charged with mortal matters, and of the Lady of the Eastern Peak, charged with reincarnations:

(*She offers incense and prostrates herself*)

> (*TUNE: XIAO NAN GE*)
> *Flames of newly kindled fire*
> *incense of highest excellence*
> *devotions offered on behalf of Bridal Du.*

CELEBRANTS (*prostrating themselves*):
> *Clouds of incense wreathe about our banners*
> *delicate music soars aloft on breeze.*

O holy ones

> *in your immeasurable majesty*
> *receive this fragrant soul*
> *swiftly into Heaven's height;*
> *or if her mortal longings still persist*
> *and she would live again in human form*
> *then let her be reborn as maid or man*
> *and grant that she may find*
> *a partner for eternal bliss;*
> *let her not once again*
> *perish so young.*

SISTER STONE: I reflect that the young lady died of her passionate grieving for the flowers, and so today I have picked a sprig of flowering apricot to present before her in a consecrated vase.

> [Sister Stone's "grieving for the flowers" is a metaphor: the grieving that led to Bridal's death was for the passage, unloved, of her flowerlike youth. The sprig of apricot is emblematic of Bridal's beloved, Liu, whose personal name Mengmei translates as "Dream-of-apricot"; and it is beneath a flowering apricot tree in the garden that Bridal's body, by her own wish, is buried. Liu's surname itself means "willow," which is why Bridal at one point apostrophizes him as "beloved 'Apricot,' dearest 'Willow.'"]

(*She makes obeisance before the "spirit tablet" bearing Bridal's name*)

> *In purified vase*
> *under cold spring sun*
> *set one last spray of apricot*
> *its waxen blooms still red.*

Ah young mistress,

> *spirit so determined—*
> *by whose side do you walk*
> *in fragrant dream?*

CELEBRANTS: Tell us, revered teacher, what is represented by the consecrated vase, and what by the sprig of apricot?

SISTER STONE:

> *Within the hollow of this vase*

is held the mortal world
while her poor self
just like this fading apricot
watered but rootless
still brings a fragrance to our senses.

CELEBRANTS: Young lady, may you accept this offering and find

cool balm for your flesh,
sweet fragrance for your soul;
if you would return to mortal world
cannot this sprig of apricot
serve as your canopy?

(*Sound of wind offstage*)

SISTER STONE: Most strange! A whirlwind rustles and strikes chill!

(*Booming of bell offstage*)

CELEBRANTS: The hour of the evening meal, let us eat before we return to
bring our ceremonies to a close. Truly,

before morning mirror we laid aside
all inconstancy,
now bell of evening interrupts
our song of "Pacing the Void."

(*ALL leave the stage*)

The nuns' closing verse reminds us of the world of Daoist magic they inhabit.
The mirror of the morning toilet recalls to a nun her abjuration of worldly
vanities, at the same time as it reassures her of her spiritual health. As Wolf-
ram Eberhard comments in his *Dictionary of Chinese Symbols:*

> It was popularly believed that mirrors made spirits visible, and one still
> finds today so-called "magic mirrors" on the back of which strange pat-
> terns appear when they are held in certain ways. . . . Buddhist priests
> used these mirrors to show believers the form in which they would be
> reborn. If a man looks into a magic mirror and cannot recognize his
> own face, this is a sign that his death is not far off.

The chanting of "Pacing the Void" accompanies a kind of ritual dance in which
a Daoist paces out astrological patterns to place himself and his congregation
in tune with the universe.

Now, as scene 27 continues, Bridal makes her spectacular ghostly entrance. This has already been announced in Sister Stone's line,

A whirlwind rustles and strikes chill!

—the whirlwind is nothing more or less than the customary means of trans-
portation for a ghost, which is why living beings shiver when one approaches.
Bridal is a new ghost, and in fact only temporarily in this state at all since she
has received the Judge's permission to return in due course to the world of
the living. She comes now borne from the terrace at the very edge of the
nether world, from whence the souls of the dead may catch a glimpse of the
home they have left. The actress playing Bridal at this point whirls in to
the sound of clashing cymbals and her own loud wailing. She makes a swift
round of the stage before allowing the flimsy gauze of her skirt to settle about
her, and begins her aria with face hidden by upraised flowing sleeve:

BRIDAL DU:

> *(TUNE: SHUI HONG HUA)*
> *In spirit form, as in a dream*
> *from Home-gazing Terrace I come*
> *where graveyards silent lie in shimmering night.*

(She starts at the offstage barking of a dog)

So, it is only

> *false promise of the shadows—*
> *a puppy barking at the stars.*
> *Cool and dim*
> *springtime shade of flowering pear.*

Ah, here is the pavilion of the tree peonies, and here the peony walk,
and all neglected and overgrown, for three years have passed since my
parents left this place.

(She weeps)

> *Crumbling wall and weed-grown path*
> *so deeply wound my spirit.*
> *Now as I gaze, whence comes*
> *dull gleam of ghostly lamp?*

(She listens)

> *Ah me, surely the sound of human voices!*

(She recites in verse):

In former days, daughter highborn
cherished as hoard of gold
but now the stream flows on
the blossoms have faded:
alas for this passionate flower
of the noble house of Du,

self-willed beyond recourse
tonight I count the stars alone.
In life and death
passion was all to me
and how can passion be withstood!

You see before you the spirit form of Bridal Du. My death came of a
dream, besotted with passion and longing for love. It happened that the
tenth judge of Hell was relieved of his post, and for three years I lodged
in the women's cells with none to despatch my case. Then it was my
good fortune to meet with a judge who took pity on me and granted my
temporary release. This is a night of bright moon and gentle breezes and
I roam at will. But here is the old garden to the rear of the study—how
can it have been turned into an Apricot Blossom Shrine? How deeply this
distresses me!

(*TUNE: XIAO TAO HONG*)
Despair tortures bowels
of one who seems to wake from drunken dream.
Who will make restoration
of my remaining years?
No sister from the ghostly ranks keeps me company,
alone I straighten gauze robes that trailed on the ground.
I pace my realm
of shadows amid forms
where dew settles on breeze,
cloud obscures Dipper
and moon endures eclipse.
First watch, the flowers shadowed—
(*She starts at the sound of chimes in the wind*)
my heart suddenly catches in fear
but it is nought but the sound of chimes
in breeze beneath eaves of shrine.

How sweet this scent of incense!

(*TUNE: XIA SHAN HU*)
Smoke of incense clouding
where lanterns glow and shimmer,
I shiver at the sight
of saintly portraits mounted high.

What holy images are these? So, the Lady of the Eastern Peak and the
First Consort of the Southern Dipper. (*She performs a deep kotow*) The spirit
of Bridal Du kotows before the holy ones. From my obscurity

bring me to the light
that in full clarity I may be fated
    to find rebirth in human form!
Let me read these charms: so, this shrine is in the charge of Sister Stone,
and here is a mass for my ascension to Heaven. Ah Sister Stone, I am
deeply in your debt. Ha, and here in this consecrated vase is a spring of
fading blossom from the apricot by my tomb. Sweet blossom, like Bridal
Du herself you fade before your time, how sad!

> *But all these random drumbeats*
> *striking of bells*
> *intonings of precious scriptures*
> *break in upon my yellow-millet dream.*

> [Bridal here uses a well-known allusion to an early Daoist
> story, an allegory of a youth who came across a Daoist
> adept cooking yellow millet for his supper. The youth
> borrowed the adept's pillow, which was the usual hollow
> block; but this pillow was magic, and as the youth drifted
> into slumber he entered a world within which he under-
> went the successes and failures of an entire lifetime. He
> awoke at last to find that the millet was not yet cooked, so
> brief the dream that is this mortal life. Our playwright
> Tang Xianzu vastly expanded this story to furnish the
> framework of his fourth play, *The Handan Dream*.]

> *Stepping where roots of apricot*
> *grip the fissured earth,*
> *here let me leave some sign.* (*She weeps*)

Unless I leave some trace of my presence, how can I show my
appreciation for the devotions of these pious sisters? Then let me scatter
petals of the apricot here on the altar. (*She does so*)

> *To each petal cling*
> *myriad loving thoughts.*

I long to know where my father and mother are this night, and where
my maid Spring Fragrance. Ha, but from somewhere comes a sound of
someone moaning and calling. Let me listen.

VOICE OF LIU MENGMEI (*offstage*):   My gracious mistress! Lovely lady!
BRIDAL (*startled*):   Who calls, and for whom? Listen again!
(*The* Voice *calls again, and she sighs*)

> (*TUNE: ZUI GUI CHI*)
> *You the living, I in death*

each fated to wander alone.
One full of longings elicits
from the one he longs for no reply.
But why do you name no name of her you love?
On my solitary spirit
who would ever call?
Voice of mystery
calling continually
yet pausing ever and again.

(*The* Voice *calls again*)

So, in some guest-room of the shrine

some wandering scholar
rambles in his sleep.

(*TUNE: HEI MA LING*)
From heart I thought devoid of love
longings arise
as he calls and calls again.
I shudder chill, and bitter tears start up.
Ah me, could this be him I saw in dream,
beloved "Apricot" or dearest "Willow"?
For I recall
such a pavilion by flowered pool
was witness to our innocent play
of breeze and moonlight.
And yet what starry union
could be the destiny of a lonely ghost?

I would go at once to find out what I could, but the Dipper turns, Orion
wheels, and I may not linger!

(*TUNE: CODA*)
What is this waving now of temple lamps?

NUNS' VOICES (*offstage*):   There are sounds of someone at the shrine!

(*A* Novice *stealthily enters and looks about. A second whirlwind rises.*)

BRIDAL:
I set embroidered banners a-flutter
and petals fall in the wind,
signs of the ghostly presence of Bridal Du.

NOVICE (*comes face to face with* Bridal *as the latter exits wailing. She starts in terror.*):   Holy
sisters, hurry, hurry!

SISTER STONE, VISITING NUN (*enter in alarm*):   What's all this fuss?

NOVICE: I was hiding in the lantern shadows to see who it was, when I saw this goddess or fairy maid. She shook her sleeve and the banner fluttered, and then she vanished! I'm frightened!

SISTER STONE: What was her appearance?

NOVICE (*gesturing*):   About so tall, so thin, a pretty face, feather hair ornaments and a gold phoenix hairpin, red skirt and green jacket, jade girdle pendants all a-tinkle, must have been an Immortal come down to visit earth.

SISTER STONE: So, this is the very image of the living Miss Du. It must have been a manifestation of her spirit.

NUN: See, here on the altar, petals of apricot scattered everywhere. It is a miracle! Let us offer one more hymn to her.

ALL CELEBRANTS:

> (*TUNE: YI DUO JIAO*)
> *Breezes disperse the incense smoke*
> *moonlight floods the walks.*
> *Swift apparition of chill spirit form.*
> *Longings of love so quickly wounded*
> *on a spring night when petals fall.*
> *Speedily may you*
> *ascend to Heaven*
> *ascend to Heaven,*
> *linger no longer where you have no home.*

NUN: Of what sickness did Bridal Du perish, and what was the reason for this manifestation?

SISTER STONE:

> (*TUNE: CODA*)
> *Calm your fears*
> *do not ask for reasons.*
> *Dismantle we now altar and instruments.*

For listen, there along the walk
chill breeze still bears
cold pendants' tinkling sound.

SCENE 28: UNION IN THE SHADES

This tinkling sound of the jade pendants at Bridal's waist is not yet audible to the lovesick Liu Mengmei. All he knows of Bridal, by the opening of the great love scene at the very center of the play, scene 28, "Union in the Shades," is the self-portrait that she has painted and that he has retrieved from its burial place close to her garden tomb. When he begins his first aria with the lines

> *Where to seek fairy maid*
> *who stood before my eyes?*
> *Wavering shade*
> *as cloud-veiled moonlight*

he is recalling his literal act of worship of the portrait (which at first he took to be an image of the Bodhisattva Guanyin) in scene 26, "The Portrait Examined."

Bridal's portrait in *The Peony Pavilion* exerts something of the same kind of emblematic force as a similar artifact in another dramatic romance, the statue of Hermione in Shakespeare's *Winter's Tale*. And in fact certain parallels between the two plays are close enough for a comparative reading to deepen our understanding and enjoyment of both.

As luck will have it, historical coincidence makes comparison of the two playwrights hard to avoid. Tang Xianzu was born in 1550, fourteen years before Shakespeare, and the two men died in the same year, 1616. No doubt the differences far outweigh the similarities between the England of Elizabeth and the China of the Wanli Emperor. Yet we may point to certain common features vital to the emergence of a major form of drama. Renaissance, Reformation, and the beginnings of modern scientific thought in the West were matched by new currents of intellectual excitement in late Ming China. Bourgeois prosperity in Nanking and Soochow, no less than in London, provided both demand and support for a theater of vigor and wit. The language itself was in flux to an unusual degree, neither English nor colloquial Chinese quite settled yet into definitive patterns. Neologisms and dialect words abound in Tang Xianzu as in Shakespeare, and there is an extraordinary ease of movement between literary and colloquial diction.

Much of the text of a play will be dictated by the circumstances of its intended staging and the nature of its audience. In Ming China as in Elizabethan London, groundlings would gaze up at the actors on the platform stage above them, while gentlefolk were protected by some small distance or elevation (in the Chinese case, perhaps in a separate garden pavilion or in a gallery across the temple courtyard). There was no curtain, hence the cleared stage becomes the important marker of the break in the action and provides the formal criterion for division into scenes. There were no sets, no furnishings, but the Elizabethan theater used a rear-stage enclosure as tomb or cave, and an upper-stage edifice as battlements or as Cleopatra's monument. Since the Chinese stage seems never to have developed such devices (though it has been suggested that there must have been some kind of framework for stringing people up, from the frequency of such incidents in Yuan plays—just as Liu Mengmei is strung up for a beating in scene 53 of *The Peony Pavilion*, "Interrogation Under the Rod"), we note without too much surprise the numerous transformations that may overtake table and chair, to represent mountain top, judge's bench, boudoir, or whatever.

Winter's Tale is one of Shakespeare's last plays, belonging to the well-marked group that begins with *Pericles* and *Cymbeline* and ends with *The Tempest*. They have been categorized as romances, marked off from the tragedies, the comedies, and the chronicles by specific features. These include a pattern of action which ranges over time and space with utmost disregard for the unities; elevated personages, royal or noble or higher yet, spirits of air or oracles or gods; mixed modes, with elements of both tragic and comic, but working toward a serene final resolution beyond both of these; and the inclusion of elements of the pastoral, of song and dance and masque.[1] Northrop Frye speaks of Shakespeare's last plays as the bedrock of drama, the romantic spectacle out of which all the more specialized forms of drama, such as tragedy and social comedy, have come, and to which they recurrently return.[2]

This concept of an all-encompassing kind of drama, which not only concludes its own action with resolution and reconciliation but in itself rounds off a whole process of development in the history of the theater, is wonderfully applicable to *Peony Pavilion*. Though midway rather than late in Tang Xianzu's writing career, it is his most extensive play; and Tang himself is indeed a master-dramatist from the period of fullest flowering of the Ming *chuanqi*. More than any other Chinese play, *Peony Pavilion* exhibits the characteristics of the dramatic romance as defined for Shakespeare's last four plays.

As a final note to our listing of parallels, we should remind ourselves that both *Winter's Tale* and *Peony Pavilion* represent poetic metamorphoses of recent prose fictions. Where Shakespeare drew on Robert Greene's *Pandosto* of 1588, Tang Xianzu used a run-of-the-mill "promptbook"-type story, "Bridal Du Longing for Love Returns in Spirit Form" *(Du Liniang mu se huan hun)*. Needless to say, and fortunately for us, each playwright took the greatest liberties with his original.

To return to the intriguing emblems of Bridal Du's portrait and Hermione's statue: by electing to work in the mode of romance the playwright forswears positivism and frees himself to meditate on the intricate relations between the apparent and the real. Bridal Du really dies, Hermione only apparently (by Paulina's report—meanwhile, the audience knows no better). But is Bridal's return from the dead any more miraculous than the coming to life of Hermione's "statue"?

There's magic in thy majesty

as Leontes admits—the magic of the fine contempt for plausibility, the preposterous pretense that for sixteen years Paulina has succeeded in secreting
the queen in her "removed house," which however is evidently within walking distance of the palace:

> That she is living,
> Were it but told you, should be hooted at
> Like an old tale,

(a winter's tale?) as Paulina confesses, in one of several ironic self-parodies of
the text.

Bridal Du, to repeat, really dies and is resurrected. The playwright then
musters various available devices to justify his fable. Among them is recourse
to folk belief, which informs the trial scene (23, "Infernal Judgment," the
longest scene in the play with the exception of the grand finale). It is a scene
of purest fantasy, a trial in Hades before a grotesque, venal judge who toys
with his writing brush made of human bone and hair, and "when he is merry"
plans to

> write graffiti on the bridge
> over the River of Blood.

The chief witness for the defense is our friend the Flower Spirit, who acts as
straight man, feeding the comic judge thirty-eight flower names for him to
pun on as he sketches the course of a sexual liaison. Yet the scene ends with
due regard for proper bureaucratic procedure, as the judge checks the registers (of heartbreaks, then of marriages), and establishes Bridal's entitlement
to further years in the mortal world. Though farcically presented, the supernatural underpinnings of the scene are no more farfetched than Shakespeare's
recourse to Apollo, when the oracle reveals the truth, and Leontes by his
blasphemy in denying it instantly incurs the wrath of Heaven in the death of
his son.

Among other resources *Peony Pavilion* draws on to urge the poetic truth of
its fable is an earthy realism, never more vividly manifested than at the moment of resurrection (scene 35). As they "kneel by the stage entrance, miming the act of opening the coffin," the old Daoist nun says

> The nails are rusted through and the joins have split open. I'd say the
> young mistress has been off somewhere playing at 'clouds and rain.'

Bridal "lacks the strength to stand," and they prepare a restorative for her:

> Let me provide an extra ingredient or two,

says the lad, Scabby Turtle, and in the absence of further textual indication I
suspect he breaks wind resoundingly at this point.

But more germane to our discussion of the topos of appearance versus reality is the symbol of Bridal's portrait, which unlike Hermione's pretend-statue is an actual artifact. The portrait dominates several scenes. Scene 14, entitled "The Portrait," allows Bridal to sing a paean of praise to her own evanescent beauty as she attempts to record it by painting her own self-portrait. In the succeeding dialogue between mistress and maid, each plays with the "which is real, which an illusion" theme, and it is interesting that the maid projects a "completed" version of the portrait—perfected by the addition of a husband—which is the true destiny of Bridal, in contrast with the apparent actuality of approaching virginal death. The portrait Spring Fragrance imagines, in other words, is closer to what will actually happen than either the actual portrait or its dying author on stage.

Not until ten scenes later is the portrait disinterred, when Liu Mengmei mistakes it for an image of the Guanyin. Scene 26, "The Portrait Examined," is a solo scene in which Liu recognizes his error, reads the colophon, which riddles on his name, and falls in love with the painter-subject. This point of the play marks one of Bridal's longest absences from the stage. Her appearance at her trial in Scene 23 was very brief, with only a sprinkling of lines and no arias (scene 23 is a scene of the *zaju* type in which "Northern" music is used and the judge is sole singer). It is the portrait that carries Bridal's identity, visible to the audience and more "real" than the spirit-form, *hundan,* which appears in scene 27 in response to the mother's summons two scenes previously. Liu Mengmei's invocation of Zhen zhen is ineffectual, admittedly, at the time of utterance:

> *Till my throat bleeds I cry for Zhenzhen*
> *but does she hear?* . . .
> *I wait for her feet to move*
> *in slow swaying descent*
> *but her image stays immobile.*

In the upshot, however, the invocation in conjunction with the mother's summons does indeed call

> *the living Zhenzhen from the painted scroll,*

as Bridal herself predicted back in scene 14. The Zhenzhen motif, from the Tang story of the sylph who is induced to step out living from her portrait, is yet another device the playwright employs to fuse, or confuse, reality and illusion on the road to resurrection. It is reinforced as late as scene 30, when Bridal, surprised in Liu's chamber by the inquisitive nuns, conceals herself

> *here in the shade*
> *cast by this beauty's portrait.*

Sister Stone asks

> Surely something moved, yet there is nothing here but this beauty's portrait—has the spirit of the painting come to life?

The answer must be "yes," of course. The "living Zhenzhen" will step forth from the painting. But not yet—Bridal is still only halfway on her journey back to the mortal world.

The theatrical effect of Shakespeare's "statue" in the finale of *Winter's Tale* is again more concentrated, as Paulina draws back the curtain and Leontes apostrophizes his queen, dead to him for sixteen years:

> Does not the stone rebuke me
> For being more stone than it?

—then, in the grand climax, "Hermione comes down," sending a tingling down the spine of the most hardened cynic in the audience. But the sequence of *Peony Pavilion* scenes, from scene 26 onward, in which the ghostly form of Bridal flirts, as it were, with the painted semblance, carries with no less effectiveness the underlying theme, the power of love to conquer death and thus to attain a reality which appearances deny. (In addition to this somewhat mystical function, Bridal's self-portrait performs additional important duties in furthering the dramatic action: Liu Mengmei carries it on his mission in search of Bridal's father, Du Bao, and suffers, ironically, when this stern Confucianist takes the portrait as proof that Liu has desecrated his daughter's grave.) In a word, the artist—painter in one case, putative sculptor in the other, ingenious playwright in each—has used his powers to reconcile two whose love must triumph.

And now it is time for us to see how Liu Mengmei, having gazed at Bridal's portrait till his eyes have dazzled, succeeds at last in conjuring her spirit-form into his presence:

Scene 28: Union in the Shades

LIU MENGMEI (*enters*):

> (*TUNE: YE XING CHUAN*)
> *Where to seek fairy maid*
> *who stood before my eyes?*
> *Wavering shade*
> *as cloud-veiled moonlight.*
> *Aimlessly I pace*

silently I ponder
and already evening sun goes down.

A sunlit cloud descended from the heavens
sculptured grace, flowerlike smile:
whose brush portrayed this living presence?
Surely she gazed at me with love unspoken.

Ever since I set eyes on the beauty in the portrait I have longed for her day and night. As the evening watch draws to a close, I shall devote myself to repetition of the "pearls and jade" of her verses and to fresh contemplation of what her eyes seem to say. If only she could come to me in a dream, it would be as the spring breeze to my spirit. (*He unrolls and contemplates the portrait*) Ah, see how my lovely lady seems to speak, so clear the light from her expressive eyes! Truly,

"lone wild duck and sunset cloud
　　a single flight;
wide sky and clear autumn stream
　　one color only."

> [These lines are quoted from the Tang poet Wang Bo. Even more than other playwrights, Tang Xianzu loved to show off his vast acquaintance with the lyric tradition by the apt quote or allusion. The Peach Blossom Spring in the aria that follows is an allusion to a story of Han times, of two men named Liu Chen and Ruan Zhao who found fairy love by following such a spring into the Terrace of Heaven Mountains. Two arias later, the allusion to Green Calyx is to a fourth-century legend of an immortal who claimed that after nine hundred years of self-discipline she was able to manifest herself or to vanish at will.]

(*TUNE: XIANG BIAN MAN*)
Borne by evening breeze
a wisp of cloud from Peach Blossom Spring
discloses loveliest of mortals in flawless purity aglow
against fresh crimson gauze of sunlit window.
This one small painting I hang again,
object of all my yearnings.

Ah lady, lady, I die of longing for you!

(*TUNE: LAN HUA MEI*)
Delicately nurtured, demurely shy
modestly elegant, daughter of honored house.

Yet with what stirrings did she approach
her mirror patterned with water-chestnut flowers?
What secret thoughts prompted this portrait,
what guesses of one who, finding it, would woo her?

(TUNE: ER FAN WU TONG SHU)
As the bright moon her image floods
the sky of my sad longings.

On former nights I could sleep face to face with the moonlight, but in these past nights

so dazzling bright against dark shades
the radiance of her beauty
makes clamorous chaos of my thoughts
and there's no night, no daylight hour
I do not pine.
But that to take her portrait in my hands
could soil its delicate hues
I long to embrace her image as I lie.

Surely there must be a love affinity fated between this lady and myself? Let me recite her verses once again.

"However close the likeness
       viewed too near, too soon
from afar one would say
       a sprite borne on breeze or billow.
Union in some year to come
       with the 'courtier of the moon'
will be beneath the branches
       of apricot or willow."

(TUNE: WAN SHA XI)
These words she composed
for one who would understand,
predestined "willow" or "apricot."
From crevice in poolside mound
spring longings bore her image
like that of fair Green Calyx, fairy maid
soaring aloft, to light on this painted silk.

What I must do is perform reverences before her.
(*He does so, lighting incense*)

Agony to stare
at blushing face
clear line of brow
inscribed already in my heart;
here is your love, not lost at sky's far edge!

Here in this respite from my travels, is there no way I can bring about a moment's rendezvous with my beloved?

(TUNE: LIU BO MAO)

Could I but urge
the transformation of this solitary image
until our twin souls stood together
as on painted screen
coarse reed may accompany tree of jade!
Ah lady, those tiny ears emerging
like tip of crescent moon through cloud of hair,
do they hear one word
of all my lovelorn pleading?

(TUNE: QIU YE YUE)

How laughable
my poor attempts to joke with her!
Like a clear autumn moon
cloud-soaring over sea and sky
her gaze spans distant hills
to forest shades and misty void.
My offering should be tranquil contemplation
not ribald mockery!

(TUNE: DONG OU LING)

Then let my incantations,
my prayers of devotion
move stones to nod their heads,
the sky to rain flower petals.
Does all my piety still lack power
to bring the fairy maiden forth?
She is reluctant to step forward
for cause too light.

[In his next aria Liu compares the adored subject of the portrait with the blessed bodhisattva Guanyin, the beautiful Goddess of Mercy to whom in particular women pray in sickness, or for conception, or for ease of childbirth. Guanyin was often portrayed gazing at the insubstantiality of the world—as symbolized by the reflection of the moon on water. In keeping with this religious symbolism is the reference in the preceding aria to stones nodding their heads in agreement with the sermon of an abbot of great sanctity, to petals raining from the sky to manifest the blessed status of a Buddhist saint, and to the old fairy story of the maiden in the painting who came to life and stepped out from the scroll into the arms of her lover.]

(Sound of wind rising offstage, Liu places his hand on the scroll)

> *In mounting of damask and ivory*
> *I trust to stay my sylph from flight*
> *in wind's buffeting.*

But lest the wind tear her portrait, I should seek out some eminent painter to make a copy.

> *(TUNE: JIN LIAN ZI)*
> *Idle chatter!*
> *How can I bring to share my couch*
> *one who vies in majesty*
> *with the "Moon and Water" Guanyin herself?*
> *Yet could I find a way*
> *to meet with her in her own person*
> *surely my talk of love*
> *would bring such sweet response*
> *as portrait seems to promise?*

I'll trim the lamp and look again more closely.

(He holds the lamp closer to the portrait)

> *(TUNE: GE WEI)*
> *Should such angelic grace*
> *be encountered in mortal world*
> *surely it would prove false.*

(Sound of wind from offstage; his lamp flickers)

Suddenly a chill gust of wind. I must be careful

> *to let no lamp spark light on painted scroll.*

Enough now, I shall

> *screen my window, sleep*
> *and search for her in dream.*

(He lies down to sleep)

BRIDAL DU (*enters and recites*):
> Long my sleep, but dreamless
> in the shades below;
> ended my life, but unspent
> so many loving thoughts.
> Now beneath and moonlight
> a portrait draws my soul
> where sounds of someone sighing
> carry on the wind.

I am the ghost of Bridal Du, who died of pining after a garden dream. Before my death I painted my own portrait and buried it among the Taihu rocks. I inscribed the portrait with the lines,

> "However close the likeness
> viewed too near, too soon
> from afar one would say
> a sprite borne on breeze or billow.
> Union in some year to come
> with the 'courtier of the moon'
> will be beneath the branches
> of apricot or willow."

After several nights of spirit roaming in the grounds of this shrine, I was surprised to hear a young scholar call out from the guest room, "Gracious mistress! Lovely lady!" So plaintive was the cry, it touched my heart. Secretly I slipped into the room, to find a painted scroll hung high on the wall. Looking more closely I recognized my own portrait, and a poem in matching meter had been added. It bore the signature "Liu Mengmei of Lingnan." "Liu" for "willow," "mei" for "apricot"—surely this was predestined! Now with the consent of my infernal judges I come on this fair night to fulfill the dream I once dreamed. Ah, bitter suffering!

> (*TUNE: CHAO TIAN LAN*)
> *When scent has left the air*
> *and cold lie powder's traces*
> *and tears start by crimson gauze pane*
> *I fear return*
> *to moonlit haunt of love.*
> *Head swiftly turned in shame,*
> *hair fallen awry,*
> *hands clutch at temples.*

So, this is his room.

> *Lest I mistake the path to Peach Blossom Spring*
> *linger a moment to ensure*
> *that it is he.*

LIU (*recites in his sleep*):

> "Union in some year to come
>   with the 'courtier of the moon'
> will be beneath the branches
>   of apricot or willow."

Gracious sister!

BRIDAL (*makes a gesture of weeping as she listens*):

> *Ah, the hurt to hear his cry*
> *a tangled rain of tears*
> *word for word my broken lines of verse.*

Can he be still lying awake?

(*She peeps. He cries again.*)

> *From the screened couch*
> *his longings issue in sudden sighs!*
> *Startle him with no clamor*
> *but gently tap the bamboo window frame.*

LIU (*wakes with a start*):   Ah my mistress!

BRIDAL (*weeps*):

> *Draw near him now*
> *in form of maiden spirit.*

LIU: A sound of tapping on the bamboo frame: is someone there or is it the wind?

BRIDAL: Someone is here.

LIU: Someone at this hour, it must be Sister Stone bringing tea. You are too kind.

BRIDAL: No, not so.

LIU: Then it must be the nun who lodges here in her travels?

BRIDAL: No, not so.

LIU: Curious, curious, not the nun either. Who else could it be? I must open my door and find out. (*He does so*) Ha,

> (*TUNE: WAN XIAN DENG*)
> *of what noble family*
> *is this young maiden*
> *whose beauty startles so?*

(Bridal *smiles at him and slips into the room.* Liu *hastens to latch the door again.*)

BRIDAL (*folds her hands in her sleeves and composes herself to bow to him*):   Blessing on you, sir scholar.

LIU: May I ask whence you come, young lady, and what cause brings you here at dead of night?

BRIDAL: You must guess, sir.

> [Guessing games, especially between lovers, are enormously popular in Chinese plays, and very effective in the way they extend and emphasize moments like the present one, which represents the first meeting of Bridal and Liu outside of the dreams they have had of each other. Liu in fact has already begun the process by guessing that his visitor may be Sister Stone, and so on; in the arias that follow, the lovers bandy to and fro a whole string of popular allusions. In this first aria, the Weaving Maid is the star-love of the Herdboy: each year on the seventh night of the seventh month they meet across the River of Heaven (the Milky Way), the event celebrated on earth as the festival of lovers. Zhang Qian in a Han dynasty fairy story sailed his raft up the River of Heaven, met with the celestial lovers, and returned to tell the tale.]

LIU: Can it be

> (*TUNE: HONG NA AO*)
> *the Weaving Maid of the heavens*
> *surprised by old Zhang Qian*
> *borne by his raft along the Milky Way?*
> *Or her serving maid, Clear-as-Jade,*
> *pursued by Heaven's officers*
> *on her earthly escapade?*

BRIDAL: Those you name are celestial sylphs, what would they be doing here on earth?

LIU:

> *Then you are some mismatched mortal beauty,*
> *"phoenix fated to follow crow"?*

(Bridal *shakes her head*)

> *In some former time and place, did we*
> *"tie our steeds beneath aspen green"?*

BRIDAL: We have never met.

LIU: Have you mistaken me for

> *some hero of romance, Tao Qian*
> *or Sima Xiangru, eloping with Wenjun?*

BRIDAL: I have not mistaken you.

LIU: Is it a lantern you are seeking? The Rites prescribe

> *"maiden at night walks not without her lamp"*
> *and so you come*
> *red sleeves to share the light by my gauze window.*

BRIDAL:

> *I am no goddess*
> *come to shower petals from the air*
> *upon a bodhisattva*
> *nor seek I any lamp to weep*
> *its tears of wax through my studies.*
> *I am no consort Flying Swallow*
> *of flawed repute from former days*
> *nor willing Wenjun*
> *early widowed.*
> *But you, sir, have strayed*
> *in a butterfly dream among the blossoms.*

[Here, ghost speaking to mortal, Bridal uses the inevitable allusion to the mutability of all phenomena, the story of the Daoist philosopher Zhuang Zi, who dreamed he was a butterfly. He awoke to face the dilemma of being for evermore unsure whether he was Zhuang Zi who had dreamed of being a butterfly, or a butterfly now dreaming it was Zhuang Zi. Of the other allusions here, Tao Qian wrote an allegory about a Peach Blossom Spring and for this reason seems to have become confused or conflated with the men who followed the other such flower-bedecked watercourse to find fairy love in the Han dynasty fairy-tale. The poet Sima Xiangru and his bohemian elopement with the rich young widow Zhuo Wenjun is a romantic motif especially common in plays. Song Yu in Bridal's next aria is yet another instance of an early romantic poet who gained a reputation as something of a lady-killer.]

LIU (*ponders*):   True indeed, I did have a dream.

BRIDAL:

And so to sound of oriole pipes
I search the willow groves;
should you now seek the place of my boudoir
like Song Yu, poet of old,
"try next door or the door beyond."

LIU (*reflects*):   So that's it. In the rear garden, looking west toward the
sunset, I did see a young lady walking there.

BRIDAL: It was myself you saw.

LIU: What family do you have?

BRIDAL:

> (*TUNE: YI CHUN LING*)
> *'Mid fragrant grasses*
> *beyond setting sun*
> *I dwell with but my two parents alone.*
> *Sixteen my years,*
> *blameless bloom*
> *leaf-hidden against all breezes*
> *but moved to sighs by spring's leave-taking*
> *and by one glimpse*
> *of the elegance of your bearing.*
> *No other errand but to join you,*
> *trim lamp as wind rises,*
> *chat by evening window.*

LIU (*aside*):   Amazing loveliness in mortal form! Jewel bright as moonlight,
chance midnight meeting: how to respond to her?

> (*TO BRIDAL*):
> *Breathtaking beauty,*
> *loveliest of mortals!*
> *In lamp's glow, sudden bewitching smile!*
> *Still bright the moon—*
> *was this the night fairy raft*
> *rose to River of Heaven?*
> *Out of the dark, beauty adorned you come—*
> *or does a heavenly sylph honor my couch?*

(*He turns aside again*)

> *But who can tell*
> *child of what family*
> *she presents herself in this fashion?*

I must question her further. (*To* BRIDAL) The favor of this visit at dead of night—can this be a dream?

BRIDAL (*laughs*):   This is no dream, it is real—but, sir, I fear you cannot accept me?

LIU: I fear only that it can't be true. But, lovely lady, if I truly have your love, then this is joy beyond dreaming—how could I reject you?

BRIDAL: Then my hopes are fulfilled.

> (*TUNE: SHUA BAO LAO*)
> *From cold secluded vale*
> *a flower you bring to bloom in dark of night.*
> *Unbetrothed am I*
> *as you must surely know,*
> *cherished as daughter of good family.*
> *Tenderness*
> *at peony pavilion,*
> *bashfulness*
> *by rocky path,*
> *rustling of breeze*
> *by study window.*
> *Sharing this lovely night*
> *how precious we shall find*
> *cool breeze and brilliant moon!*

> [Wind and moon, *fengyue*, combine to form the commonest metaphor for romance, just as clouds and rain betoken the sexual act. The closing lines of Bridal's aria here constitute her direct invitation to Liu.]

LIU:

> (*TUNE: DI DI JIN*)
> *Soul starts as if in dream*
> *but wakes to find moon*
> *still coolly gleaming.*
> *This sudden splendor—*
> *do we dream now on Witch's Mount?*

Now, lady, my gratitude to you for

> *never fearing*
> *to walk in flower-patterned shade,*
> *never stumbling*
> *crossing the cool green moss,*
> *never trembling*

to think your parents deceived,
never doubting
that I am your true love.
See Dipper slant,
petals fold
as flowers sleep in deep of night.
We shall laugh,
sing for joy,
never wind and moon so fair.
Wilfully I bend to me
your pliant, fragrant softness,
bringing you distress
but for one passing instant.

BRIDAL: Forgive me, sir, I have one thing only to entreat you.

LIU: (*smiles*): Say it, whatever it is, my dearest.

BRIDAL: This body, "a thousand gold pieces," I offer you without hesitation. Do not disdain my love. My life's desire is fulfilled if I may share your pillow night by night.

LIU (*laughs*): You give me your love, my dearest: how could I dismiss you from my heart?

BRIDAL: One thing more: let me leave before cockcrow, and do not see me off but guard yourself against the chill dawn wind.

LIU: I shall do as you ask. But may I know your honored name?

BRIDAL (*sighs*):

> (*TUNE: YI BU JIN*)
> *Flower has root*
> *and jade its bed of origin*
> *but once revealed, the storm may rage too fierce.*

LIU: I hope you will come to me each night, my dearest, from now on.

BRIDAL: Sir, it is for you

> *the spring breeze opens this first bloom.*

SCENE 32: SPECTRAL VOWS

In *The Peony Pavilion* the sexual longings of Bridal Du, whose strength carries her through dream and ghostly states to triumphant union with her lover, are courageously celebrated as manifestations of *qing*, passion, and ranged solidly on the side of spontaneity and innocence. Guile is the mark of the elders, Du Bao and his "shadow," Tutor Chen. Du Bao sacrifices his daughter's marital prospects to family ambition, cannot conceive of passion as the source of her distress and cause of her death, and refuses, in his blind rationalism, to accept the mysterious truth of her resurrection. Tutor Chen, in early comic scenes, is portrayed as a bumbling old pedant who makes ridiculous glosses on love-poems he doesn't recognize as such, and who is completely blind to the beauty of the spring, which is setting Bridal's heart aflame.

Bridal's innocent *qing* or passion is diametrically opposed to the *li*, rationality, of Du Bao and Tutor Chen. It is conveyed with compelling power in love scenes with Liu Mengmei which hold the kind of place in the Chinese theatergoer's regard that is occupied in the West by the balcony scene of *Romeo and Juliet:* scene 10, "The Interrupted Dream," is the best-known scene in all of Kunqu opera, a tour de force of erotic lyricism. It is a prime example of what Richard Strassberg has usefully defined as the "lyric capsule": "an enclosed realm located at the heart of the drama, a place where the conventional spatial, temporal and social relationships of the outside are suspended. It is presented less in terms of fixed, concrete phenomena than of images reflecting the psychological states of its inhabitants."[3]

The "enclosed realm" of "The Interrupted Dream" is the garden, whose imagery constitutes the entire stuff of the scene, and the suspension of the "relationships of the outside" is achieved by the dream origin of the lovers' encounter. At the same time, the scene is the goal toward which all narrative elements of the preceding scenes have tended, in their establishment of aspiring young hero and cloistered maiden, with Du Bao's family ambition as obstacle to their love.

Viewed in this light, the celebrated idyll of the sheep-shearing in Bohemia, which occupies the central place in the structure of *The Winter's Tale,* may be seen as a protracted "lyric capsule." Because *Peony Pavilion* is much more centrally dedicated to its young lovers, however, and because the *chuanqi* genre itself imposes demands of great length and elaboration, the play contains not one lyric capsule but several. Scene 30, "Disrupted Joy" (the title aptly recalls the earlier "Interrupted Dream") marks the progress of the lovers from dream union to spirit union, with a visit by Bridal in ghostly form to the waking Liu Mengmei. Images of fruition now succeed the opening blossoms of the earlier scene (Bridal brings her lover wine, flowers, and fruit):

LIU MENGMEI: How kind of you. What fruits are these?

BRIDAL: Green apricots.

LIU: And the flowers?

BRIDAL: "Lovely lady" plantains.

LIU: Then the apricots will be sour as my own unfulfilled ambitions, while the flowers will glow pink as my lady's lovely cheeks. Let us drink a loving cup.

(*They drink from the same cup*)

BRIDAL:

> (*TUNE: BAI LIAN XU*)
> Into a cup
> shaped of lotus leaves
> pour the sweet wine.

LIU:

> Nectar you have brewed
> to stir hearts to spring:
> cheeks flush
> as flowerbuds the east wind brings
> to reddest glow in leafy bower.

BRIDAL:

> Then seek to pick
> no rarer fruit nor bloom
> for in this apricot, sir, you must know
> all graces gather
> while this fair plantain flower
> flowers for you.

The rules of *chuanqi* require that virtually every step of the story must be presented in onstage action. If a man leaves home for the examinations in the capital, we must have a parting scene, a travel scene, and an examination scene. If a rebellion breaks out, we must hear the rebels boasting and watch the fighting as they meet their fate. And as love progresses we must watch it grow: hence the whole sequence of *Peony Pavilion* love scenes, culminating in the wonderful moment when Liu Mengmei, unflinching before the revelation that his beloved is no living woman but a ghost, undertakes (so to speak) to restore her to the world of light. We end our visit to the *Peony Pavilion* with this climactic event of the middle section of the play:

Scene 32: Spectral Vows

LIU MENGMEI (*enters*):

> (*TUNE: YUE YUN GAO*)
> Clouds at dusk over gilded cloister
> prayer flags flap in gentle breeze;
> as bell's reverberation fades

already heart grows warm.
Sweet as orchid or musk
comes love to musty bookworm.

Too early yet.

Flower shadows tremble
patching the moonlight.

(*He trims the lamp*)

Shield a scene so lovely
from too fierce a flame.

(*He laughs*)

"Too soon we reach the end
of an intriguing book
but the enchanting mistress
watched for, never comes."

When my fair one visited the other night we were surprised and disturbed by the nuns. Tonight I plan to use this time of waiting to chat with the Abbess in the lecture hall and allay her suspicions.

(*He mimes half-closing the door, and leaves*)

Door ajar awaits my visitor
but oh, what heart have I
for the call I now must pay? (*Exit*)

BRIDAL DU (*enters*):

Lone spirit, timid lest night breeze
stir my belt ornaments.

(*She starts in alarm*)

A shadow moved—is someone there?
No, only a cloud
steals light from the moon.

Here is Master Liu's study, but ah, where is he?

Lamplight sends shadows flickering
through dimness of studio.
May its light reveal
the beauty of this spirit form
for lamp's flame is one with flame
of my own loving thoughts. (*She sighs*)

My rendezvous with Master Liu is hidden only from mortals; it is known to all in the shades. (*She weeps*)

However deep the temple hides
in bamboo shade

how can wind's rustling be kept from men's ears?
And how can man and wife withstand the miles
of winding road through yellow springs of Hell?

Wishing to speak, but no sound comes
threatening to frown, but brows remain clear.
Clinging still to vows beneath blossoming branch
yet fearful that this self lives only in dream.

Although my name is entered in the ghostly registers, the mortal body of
Bridal Du remains incorrupt. My days in the shades are numbered, I am
to return to the world of light. On that day long past it was for Master
Liu I died, today it is for Master Liu I return to life. Our destiny as man
and wife is clear to my mind. But if I do not speak out tonight, how long
can we continue this masquerade between mortal and ghost? Still I fear
my story cannot fail to startle Master Liu. Truly,

> words of a night
> 　　between man and shade
> a hundred years
> 　　of connubial joy.

LIU (*reenters*):

> (*TUNE: LAN HUA MEI*)
> *Bamboos lean on the breeze*
> *across painted balustrades.*

(*Offstage sound of bird calling; he starts*)

> *A startled crow alights again*
> *by the kiosk where petals fall.*

Ha, the door is wide open now.

> *Jade Maiden from the skies descended*
> *her car a purple cloud.*

BRIDAL (*mimes emerging from his study to greet him*):　Welcome, Master Liu.
LIU (*bows*):　Welcome, my love.
BRIDAL:

> *I trimmed the lamp*
> *awaiting my beloved.*

LIU:

> *Dear one so constant*
> *so true to me.*

BRIDAL:　While I waited I composed a pastiche of lines from Tang poets.
LIU:　Please let me hear it.

BRIDAL:

> "Matchmakers I'd engage
>   yet stand uncertain
> so cold the moon
>   on hills as moonlight pale.
> Whose voice that sings
>   this dirge of spring's passing?
> Specter returned to enchant
>   the amorous Ruan Zhao."

LIU: You have an excellent talent, my dear.

> [Though this line is placed in the mouth of Liu Mengmei and addressed to Bridal we may see it as a sly piece of self-advertisement on the playwright's part. Tang Xianzu seems to have had voluminous knowledge and total recall of the corpus of Tang poetry, and was a champion player of the popular game of piecing together new rhyming stanzas, which would make some sort of sense, from unrelated individual lines by assorted Tang poets. (Since only a handful of metric types of line were in use, the supply was almost unlimited.) Tang enjoyed the exercise of this skill so much that he concluded all but one of the fifty-five scenes of *The Peony Pavilion* with a "Tang pastiche" appropriate to the situation at the time.]

BRIDAL: What visit were you making, sir, so late in the night?

LIU: Last night the nuns disturbed us, so tonight while waiting to welcome your arrival I visited the Abbess to make sure she was safely in her cell. I did not expect you so early.

BRIDAL: I could not wait for moonrise.

LIU:

> (*TUNE: TAI SHI YIN*)
> *How could poor student earn such bliss,*
> *hand of celestial being*
> *more true, more loving than mortal woman.*
> *Gentle is she, smiles flowering in her eyes*
> *as I, like one whose bite*
> *inch by inch encroaches on heart of sugarcane,*
> *I enter by degrees the realm of sweetness.*

But those nuns the other night,

> *a senseless storm cut short our spring*
> *and you, my dearest*

your tortuous night visit wasted
your timid spirit jangled by these alarms——
yet instead of showing anger
you come to retrace our path of joy.

BRIDAL:

(*TUNE: SUO HAN CHUANG*)
All unprepared for their rude irruption
my senses scattered in fright.

> [In fact, during the incident they are speaking of, when
> the gossipy, inquisitive nuns interrupted their nocturnal
> lovemaking in scene 30, Bridal was much more calm and
> collected than Liu himself, but here she is obviously laying
> claim to the timidity expected of a decorous young lady.]

As moon dimmed behind surging cloud
I hid in shadow of portrait scroll;
then, startled, stumbled
among the rocks by the path.
Wild escapade
for one so delicately nurtured!
Risking too
should rumor breathe as far as my father's house
the torrent of my mother's angry words.

LIU: What distress I have caused you, my dear. How can I be worthy of
such love?

BRIDAL: You are distinguished above all men.

LIU: May I ask whether arrangements have been made for your betrothal?

BRIDAL:

(*TUNE: TAI SHI YIN*)
No red-wrapped pledge in return
for horoscope of bride-to-be
did my parents yet receive.

LIU: What kind of husband do you wish for?

BRIDAL:

A young scholar whose devotion
would match my own.

LIU: I am such a one, full of love for you.

BRIDAL:

Your youth, your loving heart

> *captured my slumbering soul*
> *which can find rest no longer.*

LIU: Then be my wife, my dearest.

BRIDAL:

> *Since your home*
> *is in far Lingnan*
> *who knows but that you intend me*
> *to serve you as concubine?*

LIU: Not as concubine, but as wife, for I am as yet unmarried.

BRIDAL (*smiles*):

> *Is there no other house*
> *of venerable lineage intertwined*
> *that yours should accept the graft*
> *of plant from place unknown?*

Please tell me, do your parents still live?

LIU: My late father was an officer of the court, my late mother held the rank of First Lady of the County.

BRIDAL: Then you are the scion of an official house. How is it you remain so long unmarried?

LIU:

> (*TUNE: SUO HAN CHUANG*)
> *Orphaned I drifted from year to year*
> *finding in beauty's common run*
> *none to command my devotion.*
> *Who would ride with me*
> *as with Xiangru in scented carriage*
> *or how could I like Xiao Shi*
> *ascend to Heaven in faery love*
> *with daughter of ducal house?*

> [The poet Sima Xiangru was the romantic lover of Zhuo Wenjun in the allusion we saw in Scene 28; Xiao Shi's beloved was the beautiful fairy Nongyu, "Fondle Jade."]

> *So lightly you dispense your smiling graces—*
> *I tell you true*
> *were you less perfect*
> *in talent and youthful beauty*
> *still could I never bear to see our union*
> *short-lived as drying dew.*

BRIDAL: Since this is your desire, sir, then let a matchmaker be found for our engagement, so that I need no longer suffer such fears and alarms on your account.

LIU: Tomorrow morning I shall present myself at your residence to pay my respects to your honored parents and ask your hand in marriage.

BRIDAL: If you come to my house, ask to see only myself: it is early yet for you to meet my father and mother.

LIU: So you are truly of distinguished family!

(Bridal *laughs*)

What is behind this?

> (*TUNE: HONG SHAN ER*)
> *Purity so abstracted*
> *of beauty sweet as incense, clear as jade*
> *banishes thought of mortal origin.*

BRIDAL: If not mortal, must I then be some celestial creature?

LIU:

> *But why these lone night journeys*
> *no handmaid in attendance?*

Please let me know your name.

(Bridal *sighs,* Liu *turns aside*)

> *Fearful of disclosure*
> *like Flying Garnet of the poet's dream.*

> [Xu Hun of Tang times dreamed of meeting a fairy maiden in the magical Kunlun Mountains. He included her name in a poem, and in a subsequent dream received a scolding for such an indiscretion.]

If you are so unwilling to reveal your name, I can only believe you to be some celestial nymph, with whom a poor student like myself dare hold no further tryst:

> *though fairy maid bestow her love on me*
> *how could I hope to escape*
> *the wrath of those who hold celestial courts?*

BRIDAL:

> *Rank my poor self with heavenly spirits*
> *and you declare my premature death.*

LIU: But if not a creature of Heaven, how can you be mere mortal?

BRIDAL:

> *What harm in speaking out*
> *in the close secrecy of our elopement?*

LIU: If not mortal, then you must be some sprite of flowers and moonlight, some demon of romance.

BRIDAL:

> *Then in search of truth*
> *uproot the flower, but do not wait*
> *for rise of dawn and moon's decline!*

LIU: Come, tell me your story.

BRIDAL (*starts to speak, then hesitates again*):

> *My secrecy*
> *threatens this joyful rendezvous*
> *yet words rise to my lips*
> *only to sink again.*

LIU: My dear,

> this way you will not say
> that way you will not say.
> Who'll be the one to learn your secret
> if not your student lover?

BRIDAL:

> Try to tell—
> how to tell?
> This is my fear, sir scholar:
> "betrothal makes wife,
> elopement only concubine."
> I will tell my story
> when incense smoke has sealed our wedding pact.

LIU: If this is your wish, let us light incense and I will take you as proper wife with formal vows.

LIU, BRIDAL (*after formal prostrations*):

> (*TUNE: DI LIU ZI*)
> *Spirits of Heaven, spirits of Heaven*
> *accept the incense of this pact.*
> *Liu Mengmei, Liu Mengmei*
> *sojourner in Nan'an*
> *met with this maiden's favor*
> *takes her for his wife.*
> *In life one room*
> *in death one tomb;*
> *should heart prove false to word*

then death be the reward
swift as this incense melts away.

(Bridal *weeps*)

LIU: Why do you weep?

BRIDAL: I weep without wishing to, so deeply does your devotion move my heart.

> (*TUNE: NAO FAN LOU*)
> *Wandering scholar committing*
> *your love to me alone,*
> *surely this is no casual oath*
> *lightly to be unsaid.*
> *Still my history sticks in my throat*
> *as though tongue were cut out.*
> *Heed now my Lord of Spring,*
> *hold calm your spirit;*
> *I who so long have hesitated*
> *still fear my words*
> *will send you tumbling to the ground.*

LIU: What do you have to tell me?

BRIDAL: Sir, where did you find this portrait here?

LIU: Within a mound of Taihu rocks.

BRIDAL: Am I as pretty?

LIU (*looks at the two together, and starts in surprise*):   Why, it is the very image of you!

BRIDAL: Do you understand now? I am the girl in the portrait.

LIU (*offers thanks to the portrait, shaking his folded hands*):   I did not burn incense in vain. Please, my dear, explain how this can be.

BRIDAL:

> (*TUNE: ZHUO MU FAN*)
> *Master Liu*
> *now hear my history.*
> *The sometime Prefect of Nan'an,*
> *Du Bao, is my own father.*

LIU: But His Excellency Du Bao was transferred from here to the Commissionership at Yangzhou: why should he leave his daughter behind?

BRIDAL: Trim the lamp.

(Liu *does so*)

> *As brighter burns the lamp*
> *so shall hidden truths be clarified.*

LIU: Will you tell me your gracious name, lady, and the years of your age?

BRIDAL:

> Hear now the marriage pledge of Bridal Du
> of years sixteen
> fitted for matrimony.

LIU: So my darling is Bridal Du!

BRIDAL: But sir, not yet your mortal darling.

LIU: Not mortal? What then, a ghost?

BRIDAL: A ghost.

LIU (*in alarm*):   Oh, terror, terror!

BRIDAL:

> Stand back, sir,
> listen closely to my story.
> And I have asked you not to fear
> for already I am at the midpoint
> between ghost and living woman.

LIU: My dear, how have you been permitted to keep me company here in the world of light?

BRIDAL:

> Relegated to the courts of Hades
> I found pity there for my gentle birth,
> descendant of Prefect Du of Nan'an.
> The Lady Registrar I entreated
> for permit to return to life,
> the Mistress of Reincarnations granted
> fulfillment of my remaining span,
> which you, sir, are foreordained to share.
> Your solemn vow to take me as your wife
> fills my cold bones with new warmth.

LIU: Now that you are my wife I shall have no more fears. But how am I to secure your return? How can the moon be scooped from the water's surface, or flowers plucked from the void?

BRIDAL:

> (*TUNE: SAN DUAN ZI*)
> Sun, moon, and stars still light me,
> I walk my way though ghost in form
> for still my spirit endures,
> years that remain to me
> I am permitted to take up again.

Sir, are you not versed in the canonical texts?

My heart is one
whether mortal my being or no:
who is to tell illusion from reality?
Though seemingly you must
pluck flowers from the void
you are not called on to retrieve
moon from lake's surface.

LIU: Since you are to return to life from death, may I know the place of your untimely burial?

BRIDAL: It is beneath the flowering apricot tree that stands by the Taihu rocks

there in my beloved garden
where lonely dreams
beneath the apricot's shade
ripened bittersweet as ripening fruit.

LIU: What if you should run from me to some other goal?

BRIDAL:

In faithfulness as pure
as incense in secluded vale
moonlit at dusk
I'll stay with you, though road
lead far as the nine springs of Hades.

LIU: So cold you must have been!

BRIDAL:

Frozen body and soul
in coldest chastity.

LIU: What if I should cause your soul to start in terror?

BRIDAL:

(TUNE: DOU SHUANG JI)
Through caverns dug by spreading roots
leads path to mortal world
and my cold flesh already
you have caressed to warmth.
Fear not to start my spirit
winging away in terror
for at sight of you my body and soul
must reunite imperishable.

LIU: There is so much to tell.

BRIDAL:

> Truly, "one night of wedded union
> one hundred nights of bliss"
> but the tale we tell is of a love
> three incarnations long.

LIU: I'll question you no more. But it will be difficult for me to secure your return single-handed.

BRIDAL: Sister Stone will help you.

LIU: Not knowing how deep you lie, I can't be sure how soon we can get through to you.

BRIDAL:

> (TUNE: DENG XIAO LOU)
> Ha, a man shows his worth
> by "going through to the end."
> Though three feet round
> the rocks piled on my coffin
> take tempered spade and dig your way to me
> where shades' cold breath disperses
> so close to light of day.

(Sound of cockcrow offstage)

> (TUNE: BAO LAO CUI)
> After my endless sleep of endless nights
> now cockcrow takes me from your pillow:
> untimely cry, banishing dreams of home
> of sleeper beyond the frontier
> so far from mortal world.
> Waning moon
> cannot withstand the cuckoo's call
> borne on dim-lit breeze of dawn;
> and yet I have told
> but one part in three of my story.

> (TUNE: SHUA BAO LAO)
> Halting words
> so slow to leave this clove-scented tongue.
> Yet you untied my clove-perfumed girdle,
> to you belonged my clove-fragrant chastity.
> Be swift to act now,
> do not delay,
> my love is too deep for many words.

(Sound of wind rising offstage)

Ghostly garments swirl in the wind: I go.

(She hastens offstage)

LIU *(filled with alarm and doubt)*:   Uncanny! Liu Mengmei, son-in-law to Prefect Du: surely this was a dream? But let me try to recall: her name Bridal, her age sixteen years, and buried beneath the flowering apricot in the rear garden. Ah no, it was flesh and blood I held in my arms, we loved as mortals love. What perversity makes Miss Du proclaim herself a ghost?

BRIDAL *(reenters)*:   You are still here, sir.

LIU: Why are you back so soon?

BRIDAL: I have one last instruction for you. Now that you have taken me as your wife you must look to this at once and not delay. For if you hesitate, my story is already revealed and I can come to you no more. Put all your mind to this and let nothing go wrong. For if I do not return to the living, then I can only follow you with hatred from the nine springs of Hades below.

(She kneels to him)

> *(TUNE: CODA)*
>
> Master Liu, you alone
> are the lord of my rebirth.

(He kneels in his turn to raise her to her feet)

> Have pity on me

—do not make me hate you from the yellow springs below, while you

> revile me as an importunate ghost!

(She exits with a ghostly wailing, and pausing to look back at him)

LIU *(softly, to himself)*:   So it is a ghost who possesses Liu Mengmei. She has told me her story so openly, and with such troubled grief. Whatever the truth, I can do nothing but follow her instructions. The first thing then is to consult with the old Abbess.

(He ends the scene by reciting a pastiche of lines from four different Tang poets):

> Waking from dream, where now
> > the clouds that wrapped my love?
> The troubling recollection
> > a skirt patterned with golden butterflies.
> I'd seek the lonely grave—
> > but who will guide me?
> Let messengers summon
> > the Lord of Purple Light.

WU BING'S

The Green Peony

The funniest single scene in Wu Bing's witty satire *The Green Peony* (*Lümudan*)[1] is scene 18, "The Alcove Quiz," in which the delectable heroine, Jonquil Che, administers a literary examination to Liu Wuliu, the boorish clown who vainly aspires to her hand. At the end of this chapter I provide a complete translation of this "Alcove Quiz" scene, but to bring out as much as possible of its comic flavor we need to take a look at *The Green Peony* as a whole. As we move through my description of the play I will dip into a number of different scenes, translating short extracts that will help to define the exact nature of the wit that is the prime and central value of the world of Wu Bing's stylish lovers.

The Green Peony reflects a society in which skills of a scholarly and especially literary kind defined a young man's potential for success in the most exalted career possible, which was service in the imperial bureaucracy. In consequence, no quality could more commend itself to an eligible young woman, or more importantly to her father, than wit. The ability to handle words became the prime certification of the prospective son-in-law. And since Wu Bing dreamed romantically of a high compatibility between hero and heroine, he demanded wit not only of the masculine but of the feminine partner also: the matching of wits becomes, then, the paradigm for the pairing of lovers.

The best-known example from the English tradition of a romance deter-

The Green Peony: Gu Can and Liu Wuliu (seated) wait while Che Shanggong makes his excuses before the examiner Shen Zhong.

mined by the matching of wits is surely *Much Ado About Nothing*, and in my discussion of *The Green Peony* I will draw some obvious parallels between these two great comedies. Even so, we shall see that the terms of the amorous contests differ between the two plays in fundamental ways. For what makes *Green Peony* so quintessentially Chinese is its preoccupation with the traditional Chinese system of examinations for the bureaucracy. Before crossing verbal swords with Beatrice, after all, Benedick has fought with cold steel on the battlefield. Wu Bing's lovers, in contrast, enter the lists for their fair ladies not by wielding swords but by plying their writing-brushes in supervised literary composition.

The thirty scenes of *The Green Peony* trace a fairly complicated plot line, and for convenience of reference I begin with a brief synopsis. This is based on the entry describing the play in the drama volume of the excellent new *Chinese Encyclopedia (Zhongguo da baike quanshu)*, which began publication in Beijing in the 1980s. To help keep the dramatis personae straight in our minds, I include in parenthesis the role-type of each of the characters, as follows:

> Shen Zhong (Father), scholar of the Hanlin Academy, forms a literary club in order to select a husband for his daughter Winsome (Companion).[2] In a club meeting held in the format of a literary examination, each member composes a quatrain on the set topic of the green peony. Liu Wuliu (Villain) deputes his resident tutor, the poor student Xie Ying (Hero), to supply the required poem for him, while Che Shanggong (Clown) asks his sister Jonquil (Heroine) to ghostwrite his; only Gu Can (Friend) composes his own poem. Hero and Heroine fall in love upon reading each other's poems, but for much of the action Heroine confuses the identities of Hero and Villain. Later, after viva voce examination, the machinations of Villain and Clown are exposed. Hero and Friend pass high on the list of the official examinations, and in the finale a double wedding ceremony joins Hero with Heroine and Friend with Companion.

This simple synopsis shows us seven principals. If we exclude the Father (the Chinese term for the role-type is *wai*, "extra"), we are left with six young people who, in the course of the action, perform an elaborate minuet of groupings. There are, first of all, three pairings in terms of the traditional role-types of Chinese opera. Hero (juvenile lead) and Friend (secondary male character) are *sheng* and *xiaosheng;* Heroine and Companion are *dan* and *xiaodan;* and Villain and Clown are *jing* and *chou*. In each of these pairs the first-listed takes the leading position. Hero must mate ultimately with Heroine, Friend with Companion; and in the machinations of the negative characters the initiative is taken always by Villain, while Clown plays the sidekick part. In this way we get two new pairings, of the marital kind, while the Villain–Clown combination remains unchanged and unloved through to the end of the play, which finds them appropriately dishonored and discomfited.

The six young people form also, it will readily be seen, two triangles. The Villain, as chief negative character, after an unsuccessful wooing of the Companion, has set his sights on the female lead or Heroine, so that we have a triangle of Hero–Heroine–Villain. The Clown, since the Heroine is his own sister, must center his desires on the secondary female figure, the heroine's Companion, which gives us a second triangle of Friend–Companion–Clown.

At this point we may look more closely at the boy-girl pairings. The matches of the lovers are made on the basis of the quality of their wit, as displayed in poetic composition. Significantly, their status as wits, and therefore as lovers, is exactly the reverse of the social position they occupy at the beginning of the play. Hero Xie Ying might in fact be described as a refugee, the scion of a family displaced from the Northern Song capital of Bianjing (modern Kaifeng) by the "crossing to the south" when the dynasty retreated to Lin'an (Hangzhou), yielding up most of the lands north of the Yangzi River to the Jin dynasty of the Jurchen invaders. Xie Ying now occupies the unenviable position of a poor dependent tutor in the household of the rich wastrel Liu Wuliu (Villain). Our Hero is thus on a distinctly inferior social level to that of his Friend, Gu Can. This young literatus is associated with Xie Ying only by virtue of shared interest in fine writing, but he is an old family friend of the distinguished courtier Shen Zhong. This gentleman (Father in our schema above) is a scholar of the Hanlin Academy, the distinguished group of metropolitan savants who were the supreme arbiters for the imperial court in matters of literary composition and documentation.

As with the men, so with the young women. Heroine Jonquil Che is presented to us merely as the improbably talented sister of the Clown, the dimwitted Che Shanggong. (Though the brother's stupidity might seem more plausible if we bear in mind the possibility that he is the son of a concubine and thus only half-brother to the brilliant Jonquil.) Their parents are deceased, and although Che Shanggong is evidently rich enough to keep up with Liu Wuliu, his crony, in the classic pursuits of drinking, gambling, and whoring, Liu himself reflects (in a monologue early in scene 16) that Jonquil would not compare with her Companion, Winsome Shen, as a marital catch. Again, the supreme social ranking is that of Father Shen Zhong. Like the Hero, our Heroine Jonquil Che also must rely on superior literary skill rather than social status to justify her leading part in the action of the play.

SCENE 2: COMPOSITION UNDER PRESSURE

The first (and decisive) contest of skills is between three of our four young lovers. Winsome Shen (Companion, the secondary female character) is not included in the competition proper, but in fact can be said to be the inspiration for it. At her Father's suggestion during an idle stroll, she has composed a poem on the eponymous green peony, the rarest bloom in their garden.[3] The Father, Shen Zhong, who is so impressed with the poem that he later tries to pass it off as his own, conceives from it the notion of a poetry contest on the same topic, the prize to be the hand of his own daughter Winsome. The contest will be conducted by the rules already formulated for the literary club which Xie Ying and his friends have established in scene 2, "Composition Under Pressure," as follows:

XIE YING: These are, in order, our strict rules and penalties: Item: meetings scheduled for the third, sixth, and ninth months; members to assemble on time; no postponements for wind or rain; unexcused failure to attend subject to fine.

> (*TUNE: ZAOLUOPAO*)
> *No false claims of prior business, feigned sickness,*
> *pretexts, or prevarications accepted.*

LIU WULIU (*shakes his head*):   Too harsh!

XIU: Item: absolutely no provision of candles; failure to complete composition during daylight subject to fine. Item: composition to be conducted via profound thought and silent contemplation; idle chat or random change of place subject to fine.

> *Boast of "finishing before the candle burns down to the notch"—and you lose.*
> *No strolling to copy from donor of crabapple tree.*

> [Time limits could be set by cutting notches on candles, but here the contest must end in daylight, no candles permitted. The second allusion is to a Tang prince who was placed in charge of court literary activities in return for presenting the Emperor with a crabapple tree (*linqin*) with particolored blossoms.]

CHE SHANGGONG (*sticks out his tongue in amazement*):   Even harsher!

XIE: These are all old regulations, but we have some new ones that are important also.

LIU, CHE: What are they?

XIE: Item: Plagiarizing existing works subject to fine. Item: passing
material from hand to hand subject to fine.

> *No sneaking someone else's jewel*
> *to replace your own weird fish-eye;*
> *and forswear the wildgoose's leg*
> *that bears the secret missive!*

> [After the celebrated envoy from the Han emperor to the
> Hun barbarians, Su Wu, had survived many years of cap-
> tivity the Han court claimed it had shot down a wildgoose
> that bore a silken missive from him on its leg. By this ruse
> they discredited the Huns' false claim that Su Wu had
> died.]

LIU, CHE: This is harsher than ever! Can't these be eased up a little?
XIE:

> *Speak not of favor if you would join as friend!*

SCENE 3: AN ODE IN THE XIE MANNER

Winsome Shen's initial composition on the subject of the green peony is
the substance of scene 3, "An Ode in the Xie Manner." The scene constitutes an early poetic climax in the text and consequently the poem itself takes
on unusual importance. It will be worth our while to look at it in some detail.

Following the perfunctory prologue scene and the predominant comic dialogue of scene 2, Winsome's arias in scene 3 demonstrate the characteristic
elegance of the spring garden theme, reminiscent of Tang Xianzu's *Peony Pavilion,* but are marked by no great originality. They are content rather to play
with such well-known tropes as those of the Yu baodu aria in the following
passage, with its dust collecting on inkstone in token of the maiden's springtime lassitude, and the inescapable allusion to the Shu king Wangdi reincarnated as a bloody-breasted hawk-cuckoo mourning the spring.

In contrast, Winsome's "topical ode" (*yong wu*), a poem celebrating the
green peony, ingeniously fulfills the generic requirements of wit and originality by fusing the personae of poet and subject. A cardinal principle of the
topical ode is that its subject must not be overtly specified other than in the
title, so that the poem functions in fact as a sort of riddle: the more thoroughly the topic can be disguised, the better. A flower, for example, becomes a
young woman in a lyric on the topic of "White Lotus," by the philosopher-

poet Wang Fuzhi, who was a generation younger than Wu Bing and was also a
Ming loyalist, though not a martyr:

> Slender moon-sliver plunged in autumn shadows,
> Flickering reflection close on silver pool.
> Freshly powdered against soft clouds of hair,
> Dew sprinkled clear as jade, and a fragrance self-aware.
> Against the wind from the reeds, and the cold of the autumn
>   waves
> She guards her rust-gold heart, with a glance in the mirror of
>   dawn.
> When the time comes we will ask where her spirit wanders
> Between green waters and cloudless skies in the long, pure night.

In this kind of esoteric literary game, one would obviously be regarded as
having cheated if one were to look at the title before guessing that the topic is
the lotus and not some fairy maiden.

Let us see now how scene 3 introduces Winsome's quatrain (Phoenix,
Winsome's maid, has just listed the names of over a score of varieties of red,
yellow, and white peonies):

WINSOME: Isn't there one more?

PHOENIX: I don't know.

WINSOME: Daddy, what is the name of this variety?

SHEN ZHONG: This is the green peony, which is not listed in the old
catalogues. It was the master horticulturist of the Tang dynasty, Song
Zhongru, who developed this color by means of his magical skills and
passed it down to us. One bush is worth a hundred ounces of gold.

WINSOME: "The stormy petrel feels for it . . . butterflies and bees long to
be its friends . . . ." Li Bai's lyric "by the pool named Rising Joy" fails to
do it justice; Xu Yanqiong's high price in the garden called Splendor
Proclaimed was paid in vain. Truly a beautiful flower!

> [Winsome flaunts her erudition here by citing a whole
> string of classical poems and stories centering on peonies,
> and what is more by phrasing her allusions in "four-six
> syllable" balanced prose. The great poet Li Bai wrote his
> lyrics on the peony, upon imperial command, for the de-
> lectation of the beautiful Yang Guifei. Xu Yanqiong's "high
> price" was paid for a rare peony he transplanted a thou-
> sand miles to embellish his Sichuan garden.]

SHEN ZHONG: Since you are so enamored of it, why not dash off a little
verse, in the manner of Xie Daoyun hymning the snow?

WINSOME:

>*(TUNE: YU BAODU)*
>Dust gathers on brush and inkstone
>lax for so long to prepare silk for writing.

(*Aside*):

>Concerned lest verse composed at this moment of spring's approach
>should tease my idle heart to the brink of sorrow;

yet how today should both remain silent,

>fair bloom and seductive maid, no word from either?

Then must I perforce

>study the hawk-cuckoo and bewail the spring!

SHEN ZHONG:　Have you finished your poem?

WINSOME (*recites her composition*):

A sip of wine among the flowers,
　　choice lines press their claim,
But impatience yields to shame, to lack
　　the poetic gift of Miss Xie.
Springtime blouse declines
　　to compete with flowers' finery
Green sleeves henceforth
　　will show a special cut.

> [As is normal in Chinese verse, no pronoun whether "it" or "she" appears in Winsome's quatrain. Obviously the first couplet relates to the poet herself, it is she who is drinking and she who laments the inferiority of her own talent to that of the third-century woman poet Xie Daoyun (the Xie of the scene's title, Xie yong, "Ode in the Xie Manner"). It is part of the playwright's feminist ploy that the Hero Xie Ying shares the surname of the most celebrated woman poet in China's history. But the light spring blouse with its green sleeves, of lines three and four, is both the dress Winsome herself is wearing or will wear, and a metonymy for the peony that is her subject. The woman who is composing the poem becomes the green peony itself, which cannot match the reds and yellows for gorgeousness but has its own "special cut."]

SHEN ZHONG:　Distinction in the aspect of the flower, distinction in the feeling of the verse; no verse but this could match this flower, no flower but this could inspire this verse. Delightful! Phoenix, another cup of wine!

SCENE 6: CLANDESTINE CRITIQUE

Though not quite the equal of the supremely talented Heroine Jonquil Che, Winsome Shen in the poem we have just read demonstrates a happy gift for versification, just as later in scene 6, "Clandestine Critique," she shows herself a discerning judge of poetry. It is this latter scene that sets before the audience the hard evidence for ranking Hero Xie Ying and Heroine Jonquil Che as the prime pair of lovers, with Friend Gu Can and Companion Winsome Shen herself subordinate to them. The contest has taken place, the ghostwriters have made their contributions, and Father Shen Zhong has ranked the three entries. Now Winsome Shen reads out the poems of the three contestants, which she has found on her father's desk:

WINSOME (*reads out* Liu Wuliu's *poem [which is actually the work of Xie Ying]*):

> Profusion of blooms from the hands of Yao and Wei
> 　　vie to be first to open,
> But this is sought in vain
> 　　in the Temple of Mercy gardens.
> Roll up the blind when the rain stops
> 　　to enjoy the clearing sky—
> Surely it is the freshness of moss
> 　　reflected in this flower!

> [Several varieties of peony took their names from their cultivators, the Yao and Wei families of the city of Luoyang, which was famous for its flowers. The Temple of Mercy, Ci'ensi, was founded in the Tang capital of Chang'an. Though its gardens contained both the earliest and the latest-blooming varieties, the green peony, as the poem indicates, was not to be found there.]

This is the most wonderful verse-making in the world, no wonder my father ranked it number one.

(*She reads out* Che Shanggong's *poem [which is actually the work of Che's sister Jonquil]*):

> If not the scion of prized blooms
> 　　that grow on Tianpeng Mountain
> Would it challenge the red and purple
> 　　in contests of the fragrant?
> In vase of slender neck
> 　　the color of rain-washed sky
> A single stem might well suit
> 　　a coiffure of "green clouds."

No less charming than the previous piece, can only be placed second.
(*She reads out* Gu Can's *poem*):

> Jade-green as the light sea-swell,
>   emerald as mountain mist,
> A flower that wears so fair a face
>   must know how it is loved,
> As if the name it bears
>   should still be remembered
> Though Li Bai, the "Green Lotus Master"
>   chose the wrong hues to praise!

> [Syntactic inversion in the fourth line does not make this poem any easier to read. Gu Can alludes to the same story already cited by Winsome Shen in scene 3, quoted above, of Li Bai's composition on imperial command. Li's verses praised red, purple, and white peonies but missed the green, even though his own cognomen was "Master of Green Lotus."]

Powerful in concept, evidently an expert literary talent, an injustice to relegate him to third place . . . .

> (*TUNE: YI CHUN LE*)
> *Making clandestine judgment*
> *Silently I ponder:*

The line about the "freshness of the moss reflecting in the flower" seems to soar in such a natural way—how could I ever match that?

> *Women, you must graciously accept defeat!*

The line in my own poem, "Green sleeves henceforth will show a special cut," is authentically feminine; but the line in the second-placed poem, "A single stem that well might suit a 'coiffure of green clouds' "—this too smacks a little of paint and powder!

> *If not a dweller in maiden's chamber*
> *how came so subtle a conceit to tease this poet?*
> *First the image of emerald sleeves' new mode*
> *and then, to match, "green clouds" of woman's hair!*

(*She laughs:*)

> *Smart scholar,*
> *filching a line from the boudoir*
> *for his own skillful use.*

And I do not think the third-placed poet is in any way less gifted than the other two!

(TUNE: XUESHI JIE CHENG)
A scatter of bright pearls flung in the face—
no easy task to find a match!

The first two answers

by chance won favor with my connoisseur father—
yet you should not be bringing up the rear!
Willing to be placed third
when ranking is so difficult
you'll stay for now in lowly state.

We have reached only the sixth of the thirty scenes of the play, not one of the four young people has yet set eyes on his or her future partner, and yet the love affinities are already crystal clear. What our playwright has done is to establish each of his characters by means of the poem he or she has composed. The four quatrains on the topic of the green peony are the lovers' emblems, they "carry" the identities of the young people, standing in for them when they cannot physically meet. For we must remember that the young people are not of the peasant class, they are not free to intermingle prior to the conclusion of marital arrangements. The young man may take the liberty of his sex to associate, when away from home, with female entertainers of one sort or another; for the young woman, needless to say, there can be no question of contact with any male person other than family member, servant, or perhaps some wandering monk or a priest during a festival temple visit. In particular, a view of her intended spouse is a most improbable hope. But— what need to see face and form when the verses composed by the beloved reveal in such delightful detail the all-important soul itself?

For convenience I repeat at this point the three poems read out by Winsome Shen in scene 6, plus Winsome's own poem from scene 3. We list them now under the names of their actual authors, not those of the clown-examinees who (in the first two cases) have submitted them:
Hero Xie Ying's quatrain:

Profusion of blooms from the hands of Yao and Wei
        vie to be first to open,
but this is sought in vain
        in the Temple of Mercy gardens.
Roll up the blind when rain stops
        to enjoy the clearing sky—
Surely it is the freshness of moss
        reflected in this flower!

Heroine Jonquil Che's quatrain:

> If not the scion of prized blooms
>> that grow on Tianpeng Mountain
> Would it challenge red and purple
>> in contests of the fragrant?
> In vase of slender neck
>> the color of rain-washed sky
> A single stem that well might suit
>> a coiffure of "green clouds."

Friend Gu Can's quatrain:

> Jade-green as the light sea-swell,
>> emerald as mountain mist,
> A flower that wears so fair a face
>> must know how it is loved,
> As if the name it bears
>> should still be remembered
> Though Li Bai, the "Green Lotus Master"
>> chose the wrong hues to praise!

Companion Winsome Shen's quatrain:

> A sip of wine among the flowers,
>> choice lines press their claim,
> But impatience yields to shame, to lack
>> the poetic gift of Miss Xie.
> Springtime blouse declines
>> to complete with flowers' finery
> Green sleeves henceforth
>> will show a special cut.

Two facts strike us at once. First, no matter who claims to have authored the poems (we will come later to the business of the ghostwriting) two of the four are obviously of feminine origin. When in scene 7 the academician Shen Zhong claims his daughter Winsome's quatrain as his own work, Gu Can immediately protests that the author must be female—and young. The self-comparison with the poet Xie Daoyun and the self-identification with flower in green-sleeved blouse make the case clear. Turning to the second of the three poems recited in scene 6, there is a feminine air to the phrase "contests of the fragrant" (which could refer to competition between pretty women as well as flowers), and boudoir touches in the images of the slender-necked vase and the cloud-styled coiffure (each suggestive of the allure of the poet herself).

The second obvious fact is the close affinity between the first and second poems of scene 6, which are indeed the quatrains by Hero and Heroine respectively. Each of the two quatrains opens with a couplet proclaiming the rare quality of its subject, the green peony not to be found even in the gardens, famous for their peony collection, of the Temple of Mercy in Chang'an, but surely descended from the green variety listed by the Song poet Lu Yu in his catalogue of peonies at Tianpeng Mountain in the southwestern province of Sichuan. By this time we should be receptive to the notion that in each poem the flower that is the topic stands for the poet's own self, put forward as a rare prize in the marital stakes.

But the truly remarkable correspondence between the first- and second-ranked poems is in the identical comparison of the flower's color with the pale turquoise-green of the sky after rain. Though the color is the same, the two poets use different phrasing to define it and pursue different associations from it. The male poet, the Hero Xie Ying, looks upward and outward from his study window to "enjoy the clearing sky": his action and attitudes are evidently symbolic of his aspirations for his career, which in the old cliché will place his feet above the clouds once examination success has secured a place for him in the official world. The woman who composes the second poem, the Heroine Jonquil Che, in contrast looks downward and inward to the vase in her boudoir. She in her imagination sees the flower as cut, placed in a vase or at the temple of a beautiful woman, an indoor bloom: hers is the claustrophobic feminine view, not the sweep of vision which in the brilliantly original figure of the first poem sees the moss of the path reflected from the sky upon the petals of the green peony, the subject image which unifies the whole quatrain.

In fact Xie Ying composes not one but two quatrains on the topic of the green peony. The first is the one we have just considered, the poem Xie writes as surrogate for the pompous ass Liu Wuliu. Much later in the play, in scene 22 in response to a suggestion from Nurse Qian, Xie Ying wittily encodes a message to his beloved Jonquil Che in the form of a second quatrain on the same topic:

> Color of leaf, color of petal,
> > hard to tell apart
> But a fragrant breath
> > pervades the galleried hall.
> Close discrimination
> > under misty moon

Not to be misled
>   by the black peony of Mr. Liu!

—the force of the message lying in the allusion in the last line to the story of a rich man who, on a flower-viewing expedition, claimed that the water-buffaloes in his rice-paddies were the "black peonies" of his estate. The surnames of this man and of Liu Wuliu are homophonous though not identical, and Xie is of course pleading with Jonquil not to confuse him with Liu Wuliu, his dumb ox of an employer, for whom Nurse Qian earlier mistook him.

The one poem we have not yet considered, the quatrain by the Friend Gu Can, which is placed third in the ranking in scene 6, is more contrived than the first two, more far-fetched and, at the same time, less original in its imagery. The images are undoubtedly appropriate to a male poet, outdoor visions of sea waves and mountain mists, and the poet's aspiration is daring enough as he summons up the revered figure of Li Bai in the last line. Gu Can, like the two women poets, personifies the flower as a beautiful woman in his second line, but he does not identify himself with it: rather, he may be seen as delicately suggesting his own readiness to attach his affections to the flowerlike author of the poem originally set as model for the contest, the work of the Companion Winsome Shen, who will be his choice as bride.

To complete our consideration of quatrains composed throughout the play by the principal characters, we must turn briefly to scene 17, "Trick Draft," to listen to the Hero Xie Ying as he engineers the exposure of his rival, Liu Wuliu, by ghosting at this second time of asking not a serious quatrain on the perennial "green peony" topic but an absurd piece of doggerel. He soliloquizes on the subject of Liu's inadequacy:

XIE YING: Ah, Liu Wuliu, what kind of an opinion do you have of yourself
that you dare dream of my beloved Miss Che?
>   (*TUNE: JIN LUOSUO*)
>   *The humble rail perches on a single branch*
>   *and since when could a fieldmouse boast of its talents?*
>   *The student of strategy must learn*
>   *to know both the enemy's strength and his own—*

why waste your fantasies on the distant sky?
This idiot cur—
can a flock of chickens fly with a phoenix?
No betrothal gifts of lamb or goose,
but lean on me to parade as bridegroom in your stead!

All very well to get me to do your cheating for you—but when it comes to cheating my own Miss Che!

A real novelty
to borrow a man's betrothal gifts
and then to steal his bride!

But even though you can ask me for a poem, you can't do much about your appearance—

just think it over,
for someone who looks like a son-in-law
you'd better have me take your place!

> [Commentators give high praise to skillful use of allusions in this aria. The profusion of animal images is generally aimed at comparing the midget capacities of Liu Wuliu with the soaring talents of the singer, Xie Ying, himself; the central image is from the Daoist text *Zhuangzi,* where ignorant sparrows chattering in brambles are compared with the mighty roc with its vision of the universe. The importance of knowing both the enemy's strength and one's own is from the celebrated manual of strategy known as *Sunzi.*]

(He glances at the topic)
So, the topic is still the green peony.
(He composes aloud)

> This peony flower
>   has a color all its own
> Not red or purple,
>   not yellow or white.
> A green-haired turtle
>   crawled up the stem,
> But I guess the young lady
>   can't tell what it is.

(He laughs)
The turtle in the poem is meant for him, but he'll never realize it—he's sure to go straight ahead and copy it out.

We have discussed our pair of aspiring young scholars, Xie Ying and Gu Can, and our talented young ladies, Jonquil Che and Winsome Shen. We have seen how the poems of these four carry the identities of their respective authors into a kind of marital quadrille, forming pairs by the use of the single criterion of wit. The parallel with *Much Ado About Nothing* is quite close, as we have suggested. Gu Can and Winsome Shen, more elevated in social standing but with distinctly inferior poetic gifts, parallel the rather colorless couple of Claudio and Hero, while Jonquil Che and Xie Ying are the Beatrice and Benedick of *The Green Peony*. This is why Jonquil and Xie Ying fill the role-types of heroine and hero in *Green Peony,* dominating the action in just such a manner as Beatrice and Benedick dominate *Much Ado* (which has at times, indeed, been known by their names rather than by the title Shakespeare gave it).

Jonquil and Xie Ying cannot, under the roles of propriety obtaining in Ming China, engage each other directly in conversation of any kind, let alone the kind of witty badinage traded by Shakespeare's pair; but once the reading of the other's poem has inspired love in the breast of each, the two show impressive resourcefulness in the pursuit of their romance. Jonquil Che, employing Nurse Qian as go-between, exercises the skills of a detective to distinguish the true identity of Xie Ying. He, in turn, as we have just seen, exercises ingenuity in his scheme to bring about the downfall of his rival, his stupid and unscrupulous employer Liu Wuliu (though we must wait until scene 18, "The Alcove Quiz," with which I end my description of the play, to see Xie Ying's scheme take its effect).

SCENE 5: CLUB MEETING

The major comic scenes of *The Green Peony* revolve, naturally enough, around the pair of principals whom we have not yet seen in action, Liu Wuliu and Che Shanggong, Villain and Clown in terms of their role-types. As we follow these two through the scenes in which they predominate we become more and more aware of correspondences in the comic structure of the two plays, *Green Peony* and *Much Ado About Nothing*. Liu and Che, negative characters, in their fruitless pursuit of the gifted and beautiful young ladies, must present themselves as scholarly men of outstanding merit. The means they choose to perpetrate this swindle are the classic devices of comedy: we are in the world of mistaken identities, impostures, and deliberate falsifications familiar to us from *Much Ado* and the whole tradition of Italian comedy from which it stems. We may list in short order some very noticeable parallels:

- both plays being comedies of wit, the negative characters among their dramatis personae will by definition include specimens of witlessness to offset the principals. In *Much Ado* these include those celebrated manglers of words, the pre-Malaprop perpetuators of malapropisms, Dogberry and Verges; in *Green Peony,* the negative characters Liu Wuliu and Che Shanggong are themselves the prize ignoramuses, whose first display of verbal incompetence is the gross misreading of the topic set for the poetry contest (in scene 2);
- as for impersonation, in scene 9, "Seeking the Handsome One," the go-between Nurse Qian puts some pointed questions to Xie Ying under the misapprehension that he is Liu Wuliu. Xie, amused by the woman's evident matchmaking intent, for no apparent reason allows the error to stand, which of course leads to further complications. Similarly in *Much Ado,* Don Pedro's undertaking to impersonate Claudio is weakly motivated in terms of rationale, but useful to the dramatist for comic plotting purposes; again, where Shakespeare inserts a masked ball into his action to facilitate a whole series of mistaken identities, Wu Bing has his characters attach false names to their literary compositions, and in this way, so to speak, mask their own true capacities, with similar consequences in terms of comic misunderstanding;
- one result of such misunderstandings is the kind of talk at cross-purposes which runs all through the masked ball scene, and is found in *Green Peony* in scene 18 when, as we shall see below, Liu Wuliu insists that he is truly the author of the atrocious doggerel that Xie Ying has cooked up for him;
- as examples of deliberate misinformation, we could cite from *Much Ado* the Friar's plan to announce the death of Hero, and from *Green Peony* the false report of examination results engineered by Liu and Che in scene 29.

But when we look more closely at Liu and Che we see them as quite different in kind from the negative characters, Don John and Borrachio and the others, of *Much Ado.* Though we have used the term "villain" for Liu Wuliu we must stress that this is only a coarse, general translation for the role-type *jing,* which more precisely indicates something like "leading character of the pair *jing-chou,* often negative, possibly violent, occasionally villainous." Liu Wuliu is certainly not a villain in the sense of Don John, the very type of the Shakespearean bastard consumed with envy of those more fairly favored. Liu and Che are more fools than knaves. Nothing in *Green Peony* comes close to melodrama, there is no parallel to the vile traducement of Hero, the threat of Hero's death, or the order Beatrice gives Benedick to assassinate his friend.

For now we must stress the fundamental difference in intent of Wu Bing's comedy *The Green Peony.* Wu Bing is not writing of love threatened by spiteful envy, nor of love denied by scornful wits who by the end of the play will have their eyes opened even as their pride is humbled. For Wu Bing's characters, love means the recognition and reward of talent; but the real purpose of his writing is not so much to celebrate love as to castigate the self-love of foolish impostors. Where, for Shakespeare, satire constitutes merely one element, the substance of the Beatrice and Benedick subplot, for Wu Bing satire is the fundamental justification of his play. The primary and specific target of the satire is the abuse of the examination system by shallow men with deep pockets, men who could afford to bribe examiners, to pay surrogates, to buy their way into the ranks of the scholar-officials who ran the country and monopolized social prestige.

Even the briefest consideration of Wu Bing's life-history will explain this concern. He is honored by Chinese scholars as a Ming loyalist. He was styled Wu Shiqu, "Stone Gully," and used the pen name Canhua zhuren, "Bright Flower Master." He was born in Yixing in the east coast province of Jiangsu in 1595, developed poetic skills as a boy, and passed the third degree examination of *jinshi* at the age of twenty-four. For twenty-five years he served as a Ming official, rising at one time to the important position of superintendent of schools for Jiangxi province—evidently, his knowledge of examination procedures and their abuse was the fruit of years of experience. He wrote five major plays, of which the best-known is not *The Green Peony* but a romantic comedy, *The West Garden (Xiyuanji),* whose ghostly lovers owe much to Tang Xianzu's *Peony Pavilion.* When Wu Bing was close to fifty, in 1644, the Manchu invasion reduced the Ming dynasty to abortive attempts at revival in the south and west of the country. Wu Bing continued his service to the dynasty at the court of the prince Yongming in the south, taking the rank of Secretary of the Board of War and Scholar of the Eastern Cabinet. He was taken prisoner in a mop-up operation by the Manchus in 1647, and the following year died of starvation, thought to have been self-inflicted in demonstration of his unshaken loyalty to the native dynasty.

It is a far cry from the light satirical comedy of *Green Peony* to the loyalist martyr's suicide, and we should do wrong to take Wu Bing's "villains" too seriously. Still, it is clear that for much of his life Wu Bing watched his beloved Ming imperial order being undermined by worthless and corrupt place-seekers and pseudo-scholars until it was shaky enough to collapse at a push from the new Manchu power. In *The Green Peony* he works his revenge on a breed of rich idlers with absurd pretensions to learning and taste. As models for such men he establishes Liu Wuliu and Che Shanggong as his *jing-chou* or villain-clown combination.

Of these two, Liu is the more cunning rogue, Che the slow-witted hanger-on; both are vain, self-indulgent, and fundamentally stupid. They dominate the major comic scenes, which follow their adventures as candidates for examination in pursuit of the hand of the heiress Winsome Shen. I conclude my description of *The Green Peony* with a look at three scenes, strategically placed throughout the play, which are basic to the characterization of Liu and Che and, in this way, central to Wu Bing's satiric purpose.

All are examination scenes. Ostensibly they depict friendly literary contests held under club rules in a domestic setting; in fact the audience is perfectly aware of the parallel with the official halls of examination, in the provincial or national capital, where the prize will be not the hand of a local beauty but entrance into the imperial bureaucracy with its open avenues to wealth and fame. Scene 5, "Club Meeting," sets the pattern for the chicanery of Liu Wuliu and Che Shanggong, and I translate below some two-thirds of the whole. Scene 25, "Examination by the Rules," is something of a repeat performance, with the difference that on this occasion the rules against leaving the room or communicating with outsiders are strictly enforced. I quote from this scene only a brief extract in which the final discomfiture of the two clowns is most clearly demonstrated. Scene 18, "Alcove Quiz," is the central major comic scene in which the essential stupidity of Liu and Che is exposed, and I close my account of *Green Peony* with a translation of this scene in its entirety.

Scene 5 is ideally suited to Wu Bing's satirical purpose. The playwright allows his clownish pair of contestants to succeed, initially at least, in substituting the work of others for their own. Paying a more gifted substitute to take a test in one's place has been practiced, no doubt, since competitive examinations were first invented; here the process is presented vividly and dramatically, with every trick of the trade exposed as the candidates have their servants smuggle in cribs in lunchboxes or make clandestine communications during phony trips to the toilet. The serious candidate, Gu Can, provides an excellent foil to the pair of clowns, as the dignity of his exchanges with the examiner Shen Zhong contrasts with the earthy dialogue of Liu and Che.

Scene 5: Club Meeting

SHEN ZHONG: The purpose of our examination today is to select the worthiest competitor. Seating according to assigned number, token to be obtained before leaving one's place. Each of you to observe faithfully the society's regulations; no chatting, no socializing. As for such abuses as concealing cribs or submitting the work of others as one's own . . . . (Liu *and* Che *start in alarm)* . . . these are not the actions of honest men, no need for me to worry over such things.

LIU, CHE: Anyone who would do something like that is worth less than a pig or a dog!

SHEN ZHONG: One more word I have to say to you: in presuming to read your papers, I shall be totally impartial; there is no prior assumption as to who will prove superior or inferior on this particular occasion. He who is ranked last should raise no groundless objections, nor should he who stands first suffer himself to put on airs. An association which begins free of offense will be certain long to endure.

LIU, CHE, GU: Your students will faithfully observe these your instructions.

(They take their assigned seats: Liu *in the first seat, "heaven,"* Che *in the second, "earth,"* Gu *in the third, "dark")*

LIU: May we have the assignment please.

SHEN ZHONG *(hands out assignment):*   The assignment for each of you is to compose a quatrain on the subject of the green peony.

LIU: Why haven't my brush and inkstone arrived yet?

SERVANT *(enters bearing writing-case):*   This is His Honor Shen's house. Uncle, my master is inside there taking an examination, have they given out the topic yet?

GATEKEEPER: They have.

SERVANT: I have his brush and inkstone here, may I take them in? *(Hands the writing-case to Liu)*

LIU *(surreptitiously handing him the assignment):*   I'd like my lunch a bit earlier today.

(servant acknowledges order and exits)

GU: Alas, I can make no attempt at the "Greater Elegantiae," but to my great good fortune I am in "the very presence of refinement." Deign to bestow a word of wisdom, a spring breeze to offer hope of a swift reviving shower!

LIU: Good for him, he's gone up to discuss the topic, to ask for some hints, let's all listen.

SHEN ZHONG: In the composition of poetry, the art lies not in piling up allusions, nor yet in plagiarizing the work of others for extravagant phrases, but in contemplating the topic from beyond the topic's confines and in seizing the brush before the brush makes mark:

(TUNE: LIANGZHOU XINLANG)

To make orioles weep by portraying sadness,
to wake the flowers by singing of delights,
these are the natural gifts of the poet
who scratches his head, pleading with blue heaven

> *to grant the boon of a dazzling line.*
> *"Spring grasses sprout by pool's edge,"*
> *"desolate the maples by the river,"*
> *classic lines, the toast of their day.*
> *Though you gentlemen are but three*
> *you are the pick of your peers:*
> *old songs of the West Garden are yours to revive.*

GU: We are most grateful for your instruction.

GU, LIU, CHE:

> *Lines to be chosen,*
> *thoughts pursued to the end,*
> *urged on by the lash of our predecessors' skill.*
> *Let joy in this choice gathering*
> *inspire to high achievement.*

CHE: Request permission to leave the room.

> [The text gives no "exit" direction for Che at this point, presumably because he does not leave the stage, but merely opens the imaginary door of the examination room to step "outside" where Nurse Qian will meet him.]

SHEN ZHONG: My continued presence here might prove constraining or disturbing to you, and so I shall take my leave:

> Dawn is the time for the sharpest effort;
> to stave off lassitude, a noontime nap.

(*He exits, followed by* Attendant)

NURSE QIAN (*enters*):   "Entrusted with a task, it's only right to complete it." I'll wait here for the question. Why hasn't the master come out with it yet?

CHE (*greets her*):   Here's the question, Nurse Qian. Bring the answer as soon as your mistress has finished it. I'll see you here after noon, and don't be late!

NURSE: I understand.

(Nurse Qian *exits*, Che *hands in the toilet token*)

GU: I have never seen a green peony, it must surely be a rare variety!

LIU, CHE: You're right, and it surely is a bothersome question!

GU:

> *No flowerlike tint,*
> *leaf and bloom like shadows, not to be told apart*
> *but visualized beside some path of mystery.*

What value now, the precious name
"A Pinch of Red," bestowed in the Aloe Pavilion!

> [In this place one of the most glamorous women in Chinese history, the Tang Emperor Minghuang's favorite Yang Guifei, left a trace of rouge from her fingernail on the petal of a peony. In subsequent years the variety bore a red marking and so was given the name "A Pinch of Red."]

I imagine it

compassionate of other blooms
bedewed with shining tears
of a chill purity bestowed by Heaven.
Green tunic, cast your glow upon my sleeve,
sprinkle your willowsap to clear my vision!

> [A willow sprite once sprinkled the sleeve of a poor scholar with sap, the efficacy of which resulted in his placing first in the palace examination. Gu gracefully imputes the same magic powers to the green peony, imploring it—or her, since he has personified the flower—to act as his muse, empowering his eyes to envision her (with a hint also that she increase the perspicacity of his examination answer).]

GU, LIU, CHE:

Lines to be chosen,
thoughts pursued to the end,
urged on by the lash of our predecessors' skill.
Let joy in this choice gathering
inspire to high achievement.

LIU:　"Peony" was the topic assigned in my study the other day—what a pity I didn't do it!

CHE:　Think you're the only one didn't do it? I'm lost too!

LIU:　Why hasn't my man brought lunch yet? The sun's directly overhead and I'm starving!

> *Cock crows yet again by noontide wall*
> *crane cranes his neck in vain before springtime hall.*

(*He lowers his voice*): Don't tell me he hasn't finished it yet?

> *"Idly tapping as midnight lamp burns low."*

> [Liu here adapts a line in which the poet Zhao Shixiu describes himself as impatiently tapping the chess pieces he

has set out to await a belated friend. Commentators point out several cases of this kind, in which the dramatist displays his own poetic wit, but only at the cost of attributing to the clownish Liu Wuliu an erudition completely out of character.]

SERVANT (*enters, bearing lunchbox, and gapes about him*):   Good, his honor Shen isn't in his place. Your lunch, sir. (*Surreptitiously passes the written answer to* Liu)

LIU: Waiting till this time before you brought my lunch, you scared me half to death!

(*He steals a glance at the paper. As he does so,* Gu *rises from his seat.* Servant *coughs and* Liu *hastily hides the paper.*)

I suppose, friend Gu, you're thinking I've had the answer smuggled in? Here's my lunchbox for anyone to search!

GU: I merely stood up, why do you think I would bother to be watching you?

LIU:

A few scraps of garlic
some spinach, a drop of soup—
that's all the evidence of wrongdoing!

GU (*laughs*):   So you didn't smuggle anything in—that's fine, who needs all these protestations?

LIU (*to* Servant):   Home with you now at once, my man, and don't come back again, otherwise people will start viewing me with suspicion.

(Servant *exits,* Liu *surreptitiously copies out the answer*)

Brush weighing ten tons suddenly feels light
as stolen gourd is faithfully reproduced.

GU, LIU, CHE:

Lines to be chosen,
thoughts pursued to the end,
urged on by the lash of our predecessors' skill.
Let joy in this choice gathering
inspire to high achievement.

CHE (*whispers aside*):   Brother Liu looked as if he were up to something just now, but my little tranquilizer hasn't appeared yet, I'll have to request another toilet token so that I can wait outside for Nurse Qian.

LIU: How come you are off to the toilet again?

CHE: I've had a problem with my bowels for the past few days. Friend Gu is here too, if you suspect me of some sort of hanky-panky when I leave the room you can follow me to the privy and check whether there's any manservant from my house comes anywhere near.

GU: Another one full of protestations!

CHE (*leaves the room and looks about*):   How come Nurse Qian isn't here yet?

> *Ah the blushes I suffered when I gave her her orders—*
> *was she only pretending to agree to what I asked?*

My sister is usually a very slow-moving person.

> *It's not right, in humble cottage*
> *to be doing your morning makeup at high noon!*

Oh good, here she comes.

NURSE QIAN (*enters*):   And here you are waiting for me, sir. (*She delivers the written answer to* Che)

CHE: Oh thank you so much, sister, you've actually taken the trouble to write in regular formal script. Now if only I could

> *borrow also your "Bronze Bird Terrace" inkstone*
> *for characters as choice as those that won*
> *a gift of fine geese for the famous Wang Xizhi—*
> *I need the magic brush of your calligraphy as well!*

NURSE QIAN: You copy it out nicely now, sir, and I'll be off. It's like they say, "in heaven or on earth, a good turn's number one."

CHE (*returns the toilet token and surreptitiously copies out the answer*):

> *Whoever could have guessed*
> *the marvel of the poetry contest*
> *is the work of the fairer sex,*
> *recopy the piece—still you may find*
> *the text gives off a fragrance.*

GU, LIU, CHE:

> *Lines to be chosen,*
> *thoughts pursued to the end,*
> *urged on by the lash of our predecessors' skill.*
> *Let joy in this choice gathering*
> *inspire to high achievement.*

(*All the contestants finish writing*)

ATTENDANT (*enters*):   His honor asks that each of you gentlemen witness in person the sealing of the answers. (*He "seals" the answers*)

> [He would do this in the approved manner of the officials supervising the state examinations, by substituting a cipher—actually a character from a prescribed sequence—for each candidate's name, to conceal the identities of the writers in order to prevent fraud]

GU, LIU, CHE:

> (*TUNE: JIEJIE GAO*)
> Documents so light beneath the paperweight.
> Each renumbered,
> no loophole here for personal plea to pass through!

CHE: Satisfied with your performance, brother Liu?

LIU: I'm

> *full of happiness.*

You seem quite satisfied too, brother Che?

CHE: I'm

> *brimming with success.*

LIU (*aside to* Che): But see how unhappy young Gu looks, of the three of us he's the one who's

> *a picture of distress.*

CHE: Thanks to our protectors,

> *mediocre talents have a fighting chance.*

LIU: I'm sorry to say

> *our famous scholar may well prove unlucky!*

GU, LIU, CHE:

> *What happy fate today translates*
> *each humble fish to dragon?*
> *Like peach and plum his pupils bloom*
> *before the tutor's gate!*

> [Scholars successful in the examinations were said to have turned into dragons just as did the carp that successfully leaped the rapids at "Dragon's Gate"; an honored teacher was said in a poem by Bai Juyi to have no need of flowers before his gate since he had pupils like peaches and plums in bloom throughout the land.]

SCENE 18: THE ALCOVE QUIZ

Before introducing this scene we will look ahead just for a moment at one of the last of the scenes of farcical discomfiture of the villain-clown pair. This is scene 25, "Examination by the Rules."

In scene 5 there are no impediments to prevent the two impostors Liu and

Che from leaving the room at will, passing out the topic to the surrogates who will write the answers for them, and receiving in due course the smuggled answers to submit as their own work. By scene 25 Shen Zhong has come to a fairly clear understanding of what has been going on, and this time takes the necessary precautions, supplying both food and toilet facilities within the examination room itself, just as would be the case in the government examination halls in the capital. The hapless clowns Liu and Che are carefully watched by Shen in person and their servants and surrogates are refused admission and driven away. Reduced to desperation, the two give up their attempt to win recognition as scholars and feign sickness as the only possible face-saving escape from their dilemma.

LIU WULIU (*leaves his seat under pretext of illness*):   I must have caught a cold overnight, my head's aching and there are spots in front of my eyes! I've finished thinking out my answer, I just can't get it written down. I'll write a few extra pieces next time to make up for it.

SHEN ZHONG (*smiles*):   Please don't force yourself if you are not feeling well, do return home now.

(Che Shanggong *leans over his desk and yells that he has a stomachache*)
   Why are you shouting like this?

CHE: It's my old colic, I'm having another attack!

SHEN ZHONG: Help him out.

(Liu *and* Che *leave the room, whereupon each announces that he has recovered from his sickness*)

ATTENDANT: Why were you gentlemen pretending to be sick?

LIU, CHE: We were really sick to start with, but we just got better.

ATTENDANT: Now that you've recovered, why not go back in and finish your essays?

LIU, CHE: That way it will break out again!

(*They exit with renewed protestations of sickness*)

We have already seen how in scene 17 Xie Ying sets up Liu Wuliu for exposure by composing an absurd doggerel for Liu to submit in his upcoming oral examination by the heroine, Jonquil Che. The joke is that the poet identifies himself this time not with the flower, which is the topic, but with a fuzzy green turtle crawling up its stem in allusion to the peony's rare color. Liu in other words, when he claims authorship of the poem, is calling himself a turtle. Not so bad, perhaps, in English. But long ago an imaginative Chinese eye saw in the shrinking neck of the turtle the unmistakeable look of a wizened penis, and "turtle" has been a synonym for "cuckold" ever since.

   Scene 18, "The Alcove Quiz," turns poor Liu Wuliu inside out. He is onstage throughout, most of the time seated at his examination desk, where he shows every sign of embarrassment and discomfort. He is a rich idler, overfed and overdressed, ill-fitted to the confines of the scholar's desk. Being totally incapable of literary composition he can only stretch and yawn, drum his fingers, and pretend to be humming his lines over: in fact he is dividing his time between waiting for his crony to bring him the answer Xie has promised to write for him, and trying to crane his neck round the curtain to catch a glimpse of the delectable Jonquil Che, his examiner and intended bride.

Behind the curtain Miss Che is accompanied by her old nurse. Miss Che, as is only proper, never leaves the privacy of her alcove, but the nurse emerges from time to time to bully poor Liu, especially at the point where he is strutting and mincing round his half of the stage in the absurd attempt to impress the young lady with his elephantine "elegance." The comings and goings from the alcove to the "examination hall" proper are complicated also by Miss Che's brother, Che Shanggong, the clown who is Liu's crony. He serves as a sort of go-between in this scene, smuggling in the crib to the hapless examinee, skulking onstage and off in the attempt to avoid detection, and finally entering the alcove to plead, in vain, the virtues of Liu's ghosted poem before his sister. By the end of the scene even Che Shanggong has given up on Liu, who is left alone on stage completely discomfited. All in all, the construction of the "alcove" scene is a fine example of Chinese dramaturgy, where in the absence of sets and scenery of any kind beyond a couple of poles supporting a simple curtain, the groupings and movements on stage are skillfully orchestrated for maximum comic effect:

Scene 18: The Alcove Quiz

(An examination desk is set up onstage)
LIU WULIU *(enters)*:
   "Were't not for bone-piercing cold
   How could the plum's scent reach our senses?"

> [Some varieties of plum, or more properly Chinese apricot, bloom so early in the year that snow may still cover the branches. Such a scene, with its suggestion of triumph over hardship, soon became a very popular subject for painters. The lines Liu is quoting are from the final scene of the classic southern play *The Lute*.]

Poor Liu Wuliu, nothing I can do but submit myself for examination if I plan to wed Miss Che. She has set "green peony" as topic, and I've passed this on to my servant with instructions to get the answer from my tutor, young Xie Ying. I'm only afraid that Miss Che's a sharp one, nothing to stop those sparkling clear-as-autumn-stream eyes of hers from looking round the curtain, not like the last time when the old boy was in charge and I could fool around as I wished. If I try to have my man smuggle in the answer again, won't that just blow the whole thing? Best to ask brother Che to do it for me this time, his sister will never suspect him. Good scheme, good scheme! (*He shouts:*) Brother Che!

CHE SHANGGONG (*enters in response*):
> If whoever wants to marry has to face an oral quiz
> I'm happy to live a bachelor, thank you very much!

Why don't you just write your piece, what are you calling me for?

LIU: Something I want you to do. Very shortly my man will be along with a paper, and I'd like you to pass it to me on the quiet.

CHE (*laughs*):   Smuggling in the answer, eh?

LIU: Not so loud, your sister will hear!

CHE: She isn't here yet.

LIU: I've no alternative, I must ask you to do this for me, but if we can bring it off I swear I'll give up my engagement to Miss Shen in your favor!

CHE (*laughs*):   Well all right then, I'll back you up just this once.

LIU (*peers across*):   Some shadow moved behind the curtain, I think your sister's here.

(Che *scuttles offstage*)

JONQUIL CHE (*enters followed by* Nurse Qian):   A novel phenomenon today—

    (*TUNE: NORTHERN XINSHUILING*)

> [The musical structure of this scene is unusual and effective. "Northern" and "southern" tunes alternate, which is not in itself so uncommon; what is special to this scene is that the more virile and vigorous northern melodies are given to the heroine, who is performing a strictly male function as examiner, whilst the man in the scene, the absurd fop Liu Wuliu, is given the more languorous, flute-accompanied southern music, presumably to accentuate his wimpy nature, until his final comic ditty of the scene.]

raise the crimson curtain on a woman examiner
seated in high hall, gilt hair ornaments aquiver.

Young lady placed in charge
old nurse must serve as proctor.
Here where lowered curtain sways
you see our Halls of Examination, blossom-bowered.

LIU: Oh, with her

(TUNE: SOUTHERN BUBUJIAO)

pearls and feathers and wisps of scent
here so close beside me—
puts me beside myself—what can I do?

(*He takes a peek around the curtain*)

She's stealing glances beneath her fan!

(*He rises to his feet*)

I'll take an elegant pace or two

with mincing gait and twisting waist
how debonair can one get!

NURSE QIAN (*steps out from behind the curtain and bawls at him*):   Hey, mister scholar!
Leaving your seat like this, wandering off for a little stroll, aren't you
afraid the lookout will grab you for breaking the rules?

LIU (*rushes back to his seat*):   Here! Here I am—

would I dare disregard the rules?
Please, honored tutor,
lenient treatment for a first offense!

NURSE QIAN: Pay attention to your composition, sir.

LIU: I will.

(*As Nurse Qian retires behind the curtain again, Liu sets himself to intoning in a loud mumble*)

JONQUIL:

(TUNE: NORTHERN ZHEGUILING)

Buzzing his misbegotten lines like a swarm of mosquitoes at dusk—

(*She laughs*): Nurse, look there at his shadow in the sunlight,

sun shines on fuzzy whiskers
as his shadow dances.

NURSE QIAN (*laughs*):   He really is a funny sight, just like a sheep munching
grass.

(*Liu rubs his eyes, pummels his waist, strokes his belly and shows every sign of weariness*)

JONQUIL: Why does he

thrust his knuckles deep into his eyes
pretend his waistband is a winnowing sieve
lightly pat his tremendous paunch?

NURSE QIAN: From the looks of it, he's ready for a snooze.

JONQUIL:

> *Don't think to win a bride by lying abed—*
> *nothing for you but a dream of anthills!*

>> [Two well-known allusions here, the first to the story of a young man who succeeded as suitor because of the nonchalance he displayed by taking a nap in the east room or guest-room, which gave the origin to the expression "eastern bed" for son-in-law; the second to the famous "dream of Nanke," in which a man found a microcosm of the world with all its successes and failures in the busy affairs of an anthill.]

(Liu *falls asleep and begins to snore.*)

> *What is this sound of heavy breathing?*
> *Can young Jiang's magic writing-brush*
> *be furnished him in his dream?*

>> [Allusion to the story of a youth who dreamed that the poet Guo Pu bestowed a multicolored brush on him in his dream. On waking he was able to compose fine lines, but inspiration deserted him later in life, after Guo Pu in a second dream visit retrieved his magic brush.]

(Nurse Qian *comes out again and pounds on* Liu's *desk*)

LIU (*waking with a start*): Servant, has Mr. Xie finished that crib yet?

NURSE QIAN (*in a loud shout*): Mr. Liu, no more sleeping, wake up and write your piece!

LIU: I wasn't asleep, I was meditating on the inner significance of the topic!

> (*TUNE: SOUTHERN JIANGERSHUI*)
> *Propped at table, lost in pursuit of thought,*
> *d'you think I had pillowed my head to lure the demon slumber?*

I tell you, ma'am, it's not that my

> *inspiration's flagging for the moment,*

it's more like

> *palpitation of a lover's heart—*

how can I be sure to understand when her

> *lute's vibration sounds a secret message?*

>> [Allusion to the ancient lovers Sima Xiangru and Zhuo Wenjun, who communicated via the cryptic "language of

the lute." Each of these three lines of the aria uses the word *xin*, "heart / mind," in the sense of "thoughts" in the phrases "literary thoughts," "spring (i.e., lascivious) thoughts," and "lute(-borne) thoughts."]

NURSE QIAN: Hurry up and finish!

LIU: Oh, I'll be sure to

> *hand in my today's exercise*
> *at clang of warning gong*
> *to save you the bother of pressing me for it.*

SERVANT (*enters*):

Answer composed, we hasten its transcription
but keep transaction secret from maiden in alcove.

I've solicited the answer from Master Xie, and now I have to pass it in to the examination room.

NURSE QIAN: Orders to the gatekeeper: no one admitted without authorization. (*She disappears behind the curtain again*).

SERVANT: What to do?

CHE SHANGGONG (*enters and beckons to* Servant):   Over here! Your master and I have settled it, I'm to pass the answer to him.

SERVANT: That's the best way. The author says to tell you that no matter how they interrogate my master, he must insist that this is his own work. (*He passes the poem to* Che).

"Eyes see banner of victory,
ears hear tidings of joy." (*Exit*)

CHE (*comes down to* Liu's *desk*):   Feeling satisfied, brother Liu?

LIU: I've got it all composed here in my belly, I just haven't written it down yet.

(*They exchange knowing winks*)

JONQUIL:

> (*TUNE: NORTHERN YAN'ERLUO WITH DESHENGLING*)
> *Why these meaning glances?*

(Liu *and* Che *whisper in each other's ears*)

> *Why this juncture of lip and ear?*

(Che *stands by* Liu's *side and slips the crib to him*)

> *Why this interest so intense he's leaning on him?*

(Liu, *as he takes the crib, looks in the direction of the alcove*)

> *And why this sudden concern about me?*

CHE (*stands away from* Liu *and pretends to study a draft answer*):   What a marvelous beginning, the very first word of this draft.

(Liu *makes gestures of modest deprecation*)

JONQUIL: Nurse, the way those two are mumbling to each other, I suspect a crib is being smuggled in.

NURSE QIAN (*draws aside the curtain and yells*):   The young lady says someone is smuggling a crib!

(Che *scurries offstage.*)

LIU: Who could that be? That was your young master just now, coming to read my composition.

NURSE QIAN: Miss, you don't think it could be the young master passing a crib to him.

JONQUIL:

> It's not my own brother worries me
> but the thought that he's working for someone else.

Nurse, I'd like you to go out there and search him—but please don't think me

> an overcautious overseer:

it's just that I can't stand

> tricks played in front of my very face,
> so don't imagine, slippery sir
> you can slide so smoothly through the needle's eye.

NURSE QIAN: How can I be so bold as to search him?

JONQUIL:

> Now, nurse,
> no muttering, or
> reluctance to inspect puts you at fault,
> reluctance to inspect puts you at fault!

NURSE QIAN (*emerges from behind the curtain*):   Master Liu, it really did look as though there was some cheating going on just then.

LIU: If you think I was cheating, why don't you search me?

(*He makes a show of displaying an empty sleeve and opening the front of his gown*)

NURSE QIAN: I can't see there's anything there. (*She reports back at the top of her voice.*): Search completed, no one's cheated. (*She returns to the alcove*)

JONQUIL: It was perfectly obvious there was cheating going on, but since we found nothing when we searched him, let's have a look at his poem. If it really is a good one, we'll have to examine him some more.

LIU (*sings to himself as he surreptitiously copies out the poem*):

> (*TUNE: SOUTHERN JIAOJIAOLING*)
> Let the man of honor strive as he will
> the crafty trickster gets the better of him—
> and how to convict when no loot is found?

See how fast

> *my writing brush 'scatters a thousand troops'*
> *my writing brush 'scatters a thousand troops'*.

(*He finishes writing and yells*):

Candidate submits answer!

CHE SHANGGONG (*enters*):   Have you finished your distinguished composition?

(*He reads it and expresses admiration*)

LIU (*complacently*):   I myself feel that I haven't completely disgraced my-self this time, but I fear it is unworthy of your honored sister's pe-rusal.

CHE: Let me take it in and show her.

LIU: With reverently folded hands I await her disposition.

(Che *presents the poem to* Jonquil, *who reads it and bursts out laughing*)

JONQUIL:

> (*TUNE: NORTHERN SHOU JIANGNAN*)
> *Oh dear! Now I see how exquisite it is,*
> *such a display of skill was worth the lengthy wait!*

CHE: It took a lot of effort.

JONQUIL:

> *And to his credit*
> *so beautifully copied, not a word wrongly written!*

CHE: Nicely copied, really.

JONQUIL:

> *Compared with last time*
> *a far superior composition.*

CHE: He placed first last time—this time there should be a special category.

JONQUIL: But good as it is, I'm only afraid it isn't his own work.

CHE: You supervised the examination yourself, sister—did you see anyone smuggle anything in to him?

JONQUIL:

> *Ask him the truth*
> *ask him the truth—*
> *who was it ghosted this doggerel for him?*

CHE (*emerges from behind the curtain*):   All my sister did when she read your poem was laugh out loud.

LIU: She must have enjoyed it. Did she say it was good?

CHE: She laughed, and then she said, it was even better than the last time.

LIU: So she really likes it?

CHE: The only thing is, she suspects you got someone else to write it.

LIU: With a talent like mine, it's bad enough that other people don't ask me to write things for them, but that I should ask others to write for me . . . !

JONQUIL (*laughs*): He believes I really meant to praise it and insists that it's his own work! Nurse, go out again and ask him about it.

NURSE (*emerges from alcove*): Master Liu, if you didn't write it yourself you should come right out and say so.

LIU: Three of you standing there, six eyes watching me, you've even searched me, are you telling me a composition could fly in here out of thin air?

CHE: If you didn't cheat, why not swear an oath?

LIU: I'll swear. (*He lowers his heads and raises his folded hands in a gesture of oath-taking*). Ha, I know what's happening!

> (*TUNE: SOUTHERN YUANLIN HAO*)
> *False accusation, blame without cause*
> *groundless excuse to back out of the betrothal!*

I'll tell you this, ma'am, you're not going to break off this marriage agreement!

NURSE QIAN: Master Liu, you mustn't get so upset.

LIU: I didn't offer myself for examination, it was your young mistress invited me. If the poem's no good, that's an end of it, but

> *since my modest offering has been accepted,*

why now do you

> *use it to drag me into all this fuss,*
> *use it to drag me into all this fuss?*

CHE: I'll go in again and plead your case. (*With Nurse Qian, he returns behind the curtain*)

NURSE QIAN: Did you hear how he was acting up?

JONQUIL (*laughs*):

> (*TUNE: NORTHERN GU MEIJIU WITH TAIPING LING*)
> *Convinced his lines are precious gold*
> *his scale's too wobbly to weigh their worth.*
> *Mixing up his words absurd*
> *he reduces all present to helpless hoots—*
> *has he really no clue what his poem means?*

CHE: From what you say it can't be very good. What is it really like, sister?

JONQUIL (*laughs*):   His ghostwriter has been playing tricks on him—

> *making him hop like a monkey on a string*
> *puppet-master working him at every chance.*

The victim of the trick

> *too foolish to show any judgment;*

the perpetrator

> *too clever by half to escape all blame!*

NURSE QIAN: If you merely tell him it's all a joke, miss, I'm afraid he won't accept that. Best to explain what's behind the joke to our young master so that he can go respond to him.

JONQUIL (*recites the poem, laughing as she does so*):

> "This peony flower
>   has a color all its own. . . ."

CHE: That's good and clear.

JONQUIL:

> "Not red or purple,
>   not yellow or white . . ."

CHE: It's neither red nor purple nor is it yellow or white, precisely because it's green. On the mark, on the mark!

JONQUIL: The last two lines are the funniest of all, they go

> "A green-haired turtle
>   crawled up the stem,
> But I guess the young lady
>   can't tell what it is"—

obviously this means he's calling himself a turtle!

(Che *and* Nurse Qian *join in her laughter*)

> *True or false*
> *he says it himself!*
> *Better for him, if he'd only think,*
> *to admit he had someone else write it!*

(Jonquil *and* Nurse Qian *exit, and* Che Shanggong *comes out from behind the curtain again*)

LIU: I suppose your sister didn't have much to say about it?

CHE (*laughs*):   Just let me ask you—how do you interpret the meaning of this poem?

LIU: There's no disputing it's a superb work, what's the need for interpretation?

CHE: My sister says you've been made a fool of, being called a turtle right there in the poem.

LIU: How can that be?

CHE: Just now I listened to my sister reading it aloud and so I still have some notion of it. Let's try reading it together.

(*They read it aloud together, and* Che *bursts out laughing*)

From now on I'll just call you Turtle Liu! This paper is your own handwritten admission, I'm going to keep it right here.

(Liu *grabs the paper and tears it up*)

I've wasted a lot of thought and effort on this marriage agreement, acting as go-between for you, and then helping you out today by smuggling in the answer for you, I thought we had it made. Who told you to go copying out this poem and wreck your own chances? It's not just you who have lost face, I've lost face as well. Excuse me, I'm off! Like they say, "bring me every drop of water the West River holds, it can't wash clean the shame I feel today." (*He exits*)

LIU: That beast young Xie, eats my rice, takes my fees, then turns right around and tricks me! I'll send him packing on the spot! I was so full of beans when I presented myself for this quiz this morning, and now I feel so flat, how can I just turn round and go back home? Let's have a song, cheer things up a bit:

(*TUNE: NORTHERN QINGJIANG YIN*)

Pretty maid claims to judge poesy

quizzing a single examinee;

boasts of discrimination, nice as can be,

puts on an act of authority—

but what a mistake to flunk a beau like me!

RUAN DACHENG'S COMIC MASTERPIECE,
The Swallow Letter

The fame of Ruan Dacheng (1587–1646) was at least equal to that of Wu Bing, author of *The Green Peony,* as a major dramatist of the Linchuan school founded by the illustrious Tang Xianzu. But whereas Wu Bing left a "fragrant name" in the histories of the period as a patriot who remained loyal to the Ming dynasty he served, Ruan was widely reviled as a treacherous, opportunistic politician whose death, like Wu Bing's, may have been self-inflicted, but if so was perhaps occasioned by well-justified shame, since at the time he was serving as guide and adviser to the invading Manchu troops. Only a couple of years earlier, in the fateful year 1644, the Manchus had founded in Beijing their Qing dynasty, which was to endure into the twentieth century. Remnants of the Ming court had fled to Nanjing, where Ruan Dacheng was among those who crowned Prince Fu emperor in the attempt to restore the fortunes of the Ming. The attempt failed within months and Ruan Dacheng, by surrendering to the Manchus, ensured that his name would be forever execrated in the Ming dynastic history under the category of "traitorous ministers."

One of four plays which survive from the eleven that Ruan Dacheng wrote in the last decade of the Ming dynasty is *The Swallow Letter.*[1] A light romantic

The Swallow Letter: In their portrait-hung reception hall, the parents-in-law of Huo Duliang urge him to make peace with his two wives, while Mama Meng looks on and Governor Jia arrives bearing the imperial proclamation of investiture for all—the classic comic grand finale.

comedy, it became widely and wildly popular, and it was presented at the southern court in Nanjing in 1644 as part of the festivities for the coronation of Prince Fu.

Half a century after the founding of the Qing the learned Kong Shangren wrote his great historical drama *The Peach Blossom Fan* (*Taohuashan*), a threnody for the fallen Ming dynasty and a moving tribute to the loyalists who served it to the bitter end. Ruan Dacheng appears as a character in this tragedy, a negative character whose political opportunism is at the opposite pole from the stalwart integrity of the hero Hou Fangyu and his staunch bride Fragrant Princess (it is her fan, splashed with the blood she has shed in defense of her honor, that supplies the emblematic title of the play as a skillful painter converts the bloodstains into peach blossoms). In the fourth scene of *Peach Blossom Fan* Ruan Dacheng is depicted as comically alternating between gratification and furious indignation as his servants report the reactions of a mandarin audience to a performance of his *Swallow Letter*. For even while singing the praises of Ruan's play itself as a piece of versification sublime enough to make them forget their wine-cups, his critics pass harsh judgment on his shameless political maneuvering. An allusion in the very last lines of *Peach Blossom Fan,* sung by offstage voices as the last character exits, contemptuously contrasts Ruan (represented by his play) with the heroic owner of the fan:

> *Fisherman and woodcutter*
> *Chatting of the past,*
> *Each to each recalling*
> *Dreams that did not last:*
> *Scorn for the swallow letter*
> *Praise for the painted fan,*
> *Sighs for old companions*
> *Ere grief befell Jiangnan. . .*

Scorn seems certainly to have been an appropriate reaction when one spoke of Ruan Dacheng's political activities. The standard biographical dictionary for those years, Arthur Hummel's *Eminent Chinese of the Ch'ing Period,* describes him as the descendant of a family "of influence, but of corrupt and unsavory reputation."[2] This is no idle comment, for his great-grandfather, Ruan E, governor of Fukien, belonged to the clique of no less a villain than Yan Song, one of the most universally reviled monsters from real life in all of Ming fiction and drama. One of the characteristic accusations lodged against Yan Song was that as President of the Board of War, when troops under his command suffered defeat at the hands of frontier tribes, Yan at once ordered the massacre of an entire Chinese village and had the villagers' ears submitted to court as enemy trophies, claiming his troops' campaign as a glorious victory.

Ruan Dacheng himself in the 1620s was active at court as a toady of the notorious eunuch Wei Zhongxian. No man outside of the imperial family, not even a member of the Privy Council or the Chief Minister himself, was allowed within the domestic precincts of the palace. But the eunuchs who performed the most intimate of palace functions posed no threat, and enjoyed in consequence virtually unlimited access to the emperor and his womenfolk. From this privilege they derived great power, and despite their general lack of education and their vast ignorance of the outside world, the most successful members of the eunuch tribe could manage to manipulate wide and corrupt networks of wealth and influence. By late Ming times the numbers and strength of the eunuchs had grown to disastrous proportions. Statesmen of integrity fell foul of palace eunuchs and paid with their lives; crafty politicians built their careers with the assistance of these creatures, and with enough skill and luck in the skein of palace intrigues managed to die in their beds.

Ruan Dacheng, with the backing of the eunuch Wei Zhongxian, rose to the rank of Grandee of the Imperial Household, in which capacity he could indulge his love of theater by helping to oversee the provision of entertainment for a pleasure-loving court. But the eunuch Wei overstepped even the generous bounds of late Ming politics. In 1627 he fell into disgrace, and soon afterward Ruan Dacheng, deprived of his leading backer, was himself impeached and retired from court to private life in the south, in the cultural mecca of Nanjing. He continued nonetheless to enjoy considerable wealth, in a spreading mansion with a complement of servants large enough to staff a private theatrical troupe. Ruan wrote his plays in this decade of the 1630s, and his household troupe gave performances that were the admiration of the connoisseurs of the city.

On his return to political life in 1644, when Prince Fu set up his court in Nanjing, Ruan Dacheng used his friendship with the powerful Grand Secretary Ma Shiying to lever himself up to the position of President of the Board of War. In this office he seems to have busied himself mostly with attempts at revenge on the many contemporaries who at one time or another had insulted him. (On one occasion, one hundred and forty prominent citizens had signed a denunciation of Ruan that was then publicly posted in Nanjing.) In the words of Hummel's *Eminent Chinese* again, Ruan's "bribery, avarice and political intrigue became notorious, but all attempts to remove him failed. When the Ming emperor fled in 1645 Ruan escaped to Jinhua, Zhejiang, where the gentry refused to receive him. Later he surrendered to the Manchus and punished the helpless city by leading Qing troops to destroy it."

To the present day the reputation of Ruan's dramatic oeuvre has suffered from his categorization as a "traitorous minister" (*jian chen*) in the Ming dynastic history. We may accept the views of the modern editor of *The Swallow Letter*, Liu Yihe, as a summary of the critical consensus of today. Liu justly praises the characterizations, especially the unusually realistic portrait of the old medicine woman, Mama Meng. He admires the hero of the play for his fidelity to a courtesan. He concludes, however, that *The Swallow Letter* should not be assigned to the first rank of plays. In his judgment its one-husband–two-wives theme is too conventional, too commonplace a feature of the "beauty meets genius" type of romance; the thought-content of the play is shallow; the contest between the two wives in the final scene is vulgar, reflecting Ruan Dacheng's own vulgar ambitiousness; and the plot as a whole is marred by excessive reliance on coincidence.[3]

Taking Liu Yihe's judgments one by one, and accepting a certain inevitable Marxist coloration in a Shanghai publication of the 1980s, I find them reasonable enough. Mama Meng is certainly a splendidly convincing portrait of a woman whose class background alone would elicit strong Marxist interest. She is a medicine woman, skilled in herbal lore and folk traditions of healing, in demand for the treatment of women's ailments in an age when prudishness prohibited the male doctor from setting eyes on a woman patient. Having such easy access to her clients' homes she is also of course a tale-carrier, gossip, and most importantly, a go-between. She has an important part to play in facilitating the union of the lovers in our play, and we shall see her in richly comic action in the final scene, when she forces compliance with her orders by the time-honored technique of shaming her hosts—lying down on the floor, wailing and beating her breast, until the two rival wives agree to make up their differences and live in harmony together.

As a Marxist, the critic Liu Yihe naturally relishes attention to a working-class woman; by the same token, he admires the hero, Huo Duliang, for his constancy to a lowly courtesan. But it is hard to accept his strictures on the "shallow" thought-content of the play, or on the excessive reliance on coincidence in the plot. Why must we look at all for profundity in a light, witty domestic comedy? And how many romances would ever be written, if chance reunions, fortuitous resemblances, or mistaken identities were banned from the stage? Above all, the contest between the two wives in the final scene is not to be dismissed as merely "vulgar." It is a triumph of comedy, a fitting culmination to the elaborate patterning of the action, a formalized, highly structured design which still manages to project convincingly live, flesh-and-blood characters both in Mama Meng and in the group of young people whose tangled affairs she sorts out. To inject a degree of realism into such a stylized dramatic finale is an achievement of high order, and the final scene of *The Swallow Letter* is truly a high-water mark of Ming comedy.

We shall not follow every twist and turn of the plot of *The Swallow Letter*. A few brief explanatory comments should suffice to introduce the three scenes I have translated. In the standard fashion of the late Ming romance, the center of the action of the play is occupied by Huo Duliang, the young scholar-hero, of the *sheng* role-type, and Flying Cloud, the heroine of the *dan* role-type, who will end the play as his marital partner. The first scenes we present from the play form a matched pair. In scene 11, "Writing the Note," the heroine falls in love with the portrait of Huo Duliang, whom she has never seen, and (being a talented young lady) writes a poem to ease her amorous promptings. In the following scene, "The Note Retrieved," the hero comes into possession of this poem by an author whose identity he can only guess at, and responds with instant passion to the message of love it conveys.

But we should have a short and thin entertainment if there were no complicating factor to this romance. The complication is that the painting at which we see Flying Cloud gazing so longingly in scene 11 shows not only an elegant young man but also a young woman of great beauty, who in fact closely resembles Flying Cloud herself. This girl is the secondary female lead, the *xiaodan,* a courtesan named Wandering Cloud. From the very beginning of the play we have witnessed the domestic bliss she enjoys with the hero Huo Duliang. Enchanted by the beauty, Huo has painted a portrait of Wandering Cloud attended by birds and butterflies amid blossoming tress, and then in response to her request he has added his own self-portrait to the scene. And this is the painting that has thrown Flying Cloud's thoughts into such a turmoil. For a switch has taken place, a mix-up that springs the action of the play. The portrait of Huo Duliang and Wandering Cloud has been sent to a scroll-maker for mounting, but so has another painting, a portrait of the Bodhissattva Guanyin that belongs to Flying Cloud. The two paintings have inadvertently been switched in the scroll-maker's shop, and the double portrait delivered by mistake to Flying Cloud.

And so now in scene 11 we watch Flying Cloud as she drowsily succumbs to the beauty of a spring day in her garden court. The scene opens with two dancers graced with fluttering wings as butterflies, who tease the love-struck girl as they flirt with the blossoming trees. And not only with the blossoms— their antennae play with her skirt, she recalls a suggestive dream of catching her skirt on a rose thorn, and her maidservant is not slow to catch the inference. The maid brings in the painting that has captured the springtime longings of her young mistress. She brings also a mirror, and Flying Cloud is intrigued to note how closely the girl in the double portrait resembles her own reflection.

Mistress and maid speculate on the couple in the painting—man and wife? Or "wild ducks that couple on a flooded pond"—a courtesan and her client in a house of the pleasure quarter? Whatever the answer, the young man has captured Flying Cloud's heart, and the urge to compose in verse becomes too strong to resist. As she writes she sings an aria to the tune Tiying'er, in which she alludes to two famous messages of love from past ages. The poet Su Hui expressed her longing for her absent husband in an ingenious palindrome of eight hundred and forty characters; Yu You and a palace maiden, in the second allusion, according to a Tang dynasty tale exchanged messages by writing poems on fallen leaves and floating them in and out of the palace along the rain-channels. The girl was eventually released from palace service and became Yu You's wife.

In the poem she writes, which she reads aloud to herself (and the audience), Flying Cloud speaks of blossoms that perish, in transparent allusion to her own youthful beauty going to waste in her solitary languor, of the two lovers in the portrait and the suggestive dancing of butterfly and oriole, of her "pain," evidently of lovesickness, and of the astonishing resemblance between herself and the "partner fair" in the painting.

The poem is intended purely as an exercise in self-expression, but Flying Cloud has not reckoned with the mischievous swallow that swoops down and flies off with the sheet of pink notepaper held in its beak. When the maid has left her alone on the stage Flying Cloud continues to sing the praises (in the aria Siji hua) of the youth in the painting. She suspects that he is somewhere near at hand and wonders, in the next aria, where her stolen poem will end up—evidently she cherishes hopes, though unspoken, that Heaven will direct the swallow to deliver her message to the dream lover who has inspired it.

Scene 11: Writing the Note

(*A pair of butterflies enter, flying, and dance*)

FLYING CLOUD LI (*enters slowly, and sings*):

    (*TUNE: BUBU JIAO*)

    What wind has strewn the petals all about?

Look——

a pair of butterflies, now seen, now gone!

How prettily the butterflies dance, fluttering here right on to my dress!
But oh, why do you

touch my cheek, brush against my hair?

Now off again to the flowering trees to search the blossoms,
'mid branches tipped with pink and purple
lovingly lingering.

(She mimes the action of staring up into the blossoms, then returns stage center)

My! Now they are hovering about my skirt!

Trying to leave, borne back again
feelers probing the folds of my skirt!

(The butterflies fly about the table, she slaps at them but hits only the tabletop, then sits dozing while they dance overhead)

MAIDSERVANT *(enters)*: "Silently tiptoe into the boudoir; still she dreams of
Witch's Mount." Dear me, miss, only just finished your toilet, how can
you be asleep again right here at your dressing-stand? —— Let me wake
her gently to begin her needlework. *(She coughs lightly and calls to her mistress)*

FLYING CLOUD *(Slowly raises her head, and sings)*:

(TUNE: FENGMA'ER)
Drowsy, unraveling strands of dream
by fretted noontime window:
hopelessly tangled
the desires of my heart.

(She sits up)

Little Plum-blossom, what is that sound beneath the eaves?

MAID:

Wind-chimes, dangling for lack of breeze
set to tinkling by birds pecking the blossoms.

FLYING CLOUD *(recites in verse)*:

Spring slowly ages
but orioles ignore us and our pain;
a thin rain wets the window gauze;
by daybreak, almond blossom for sale in the lane.

MAID:

Brow drawn by thoughts
of a youth in a painting, skin clear as jade!

> Stand a while beneath the eaves,
> see swallow home before you lower the shade.

FLYING CLOUD: For a day or two now I have felt quite upset, Plumblossom, and just now I seem dimly to remember a dream of standing between blossoming trees, slapping at those butterflies, and then my skirt caught on a rose thorn and when I tried to pull free I woke up.

MAID: I know just what it is, it's that painting that was delivered to us by mistake the other day, it showed just such a scene, and once you set eyes on it you could think of nothing else, and that's why you had this dream. And was that young man in the red tunic with you in your dream, I wonder?

FLYING CLOUD: Don't talk such nonsense! But go fetch that painting, let me study it a little more closely.

MAID: Very good. (*She brings the painting*) Here it is, miss.

FLYING CLOUD (*unrolls the painting and studies it*):

> (*TUNE: HUANGYING'ER*)
> No other cause of heart's unease
> than this fine brush that stirs spring longings.

Ha!

> No telling, from speechless painting,
> whether imaginary or real!
> May well be mere chance—
> but how can the likeness be so close?

Plumblossom, the mirror!

(Maid *brings the mirror,* Flying Cloud *stares into the mirror, then at the painting, and laughs*)

The girl in this painting really is exactly like me, except for just this pink birthmark on her cheek. The only difference

> tiny peach petal on pale rose cheek;
> and if I should, out of fondness
> breathe life into her painted form
> she might fly down
> to stand beside me, my twin!

MAID: See how lifelike, the painted oriole and the two white butterflies!

> (*TUNE: YING TI XU*)
> Oriole seems to twitter by one's ear
> and a soft fragrance fans from butterfly wings.
> And such a youth to enter budding grove
> with cheek as fair and gown as sweetly smelling!

But miss, this couple in the painting, are they man and wife, or is it a scene of "buying smiles in the house of joy"? If these are respectable people, surely they shouldn't be got up so gorgeously, yet if theirs is just a casual encounter, how could they appear so familiar with each other?

> *If not a wedded pair*
> *then why no trace of bashfulness?*
> *Or can they be*
> *wild ducks that couple on a flooded pond?*

Oh miss, this young gentleman in the painting! In his

> *(TUNE: JI XIANBIN)*
> *tunic red as almond blossom, black silk cap*
> *standing beside her, smiling beneath the boughs*
> *fit to rival Pan Yue, girls throwing gifts*
> *of fruit into his scented carriage as he rode along!*

FLYING CLOUD: And yet

> *how much at home this woman seems*
> *pictured there large as life*
> *caught in a lovers' tryst!*

The signature reads "Huo Duliang" and the brush-strokes seem freshly made, this person must be somewhere about! As I

> *turn it in my mind*
> *it's clear this Master Huo exists*
> *painting his cloud-coiffed beauties.*

This painting seems half real, half made-up, it seems now to mean something, now not, truly I find it hard to puzzle out. As it happens here are the "four treasures of the studio" ready to hand on this table, I shall compose a poem in lyric meter to give voice to my secret discontent.

(She grinds ink on inkstone, takes paper and brush, and begins to write)

> *(TUNE: TI YING'ER)*
> *Notepaper black-ruled, flecked with gold*
> *for spring-tormented heart*
> *not to embroider palindrome like Su Hui*
> *nor inscribe lines to Yu You*
> *on autumn leaf floated down palace gutter,*
> *but simply fill a page*
> *with foolish brush-strokes laying out my cares*

to clear the mist from my eyes
and win a moment's calm.
Languid and ailing (she looks up)
I hear among the rafters springtime swallows
endlessly nitter-natter.

(*Her poem completed, she reads it aloud to herself*):

"Where blossoms perish in the wind and rain
In the spring boudoir dreams grow chill again.
        Languid against the balustrade
I search the painted scene to ease my pain:
        Green Sleeves in pride
        By Red Tunic's side
While butterfly and oriole dance at will;
        But myself, double of his partner fair—
When shall I meet with him on Witch's Hill?

—Flying Cloud of Weiqu, author."—And I believe my poem is a match for the painting!

(*She places it on the table*)

MAID (*looks up at the eaves and down again*):   How odd! Why is this swallow from the eaves flying back and forth like this before your dressing-table? It's never done this before! (*She slaps at it*) And it has spattered your toilet-case all over with mud! Oh my—now it has flown off with your poem in its beak! (*She calls after the swallow*) Swallow, come back, come back! Give my young mistress her poem back!

FLYING CLOUD (*laughs*):   Silly child! How can a swallow understand human speech? We shall simply have to let it go.

        (*TUNE: MAO'ER ZHUI*)
        Fly away, fly away swallow
        wearing your forked tail like a hairclasp
        and in your beak a passionate missive—
        on whom now will your sweet mud-spatters fall?

MAID:

        Ah Heaven, Heaven!
        Surely a Purple Swallow go-between
        to join two hearts as spokes to hub!
        (*TUNE: CODA*)
        Pear-blossom hides the little court—

(*She points to a nest*)

        Oh swallow, swallow—

        come you must back to your nest—

and then I'll tether you with scarlet thread
and take back that pretty note.

Let me clear away the writing things and go in first, Miss, then you may go to your room and rest. Truly, "red beans scattered by parrot's beak, frothing tea from speckled bowl." (*Exit*)

FLYING CLOUD (*turns to watch until* Maid *is safely indoors*):   Oh dear, when that little wretch was about I could hardly give vent to my feelings! (*She laughs*) But this young Master Red Tunic in the painting really is adorable!

> (*TUNE: SIJI HUA*)
> *An immortal, met in a painting,*
> *at the corner of his brow*
> *by the dimple in his cheek*
> *such style, such elegance!*
> *So natural*
> *in light silk tunic of almond-blossom red,*
> *and at his fragrant shoulder*
> *this woman leaning,*
> *gazes interlocked*
> *a thousand passionate gleams.*
> *Brocaded wings of butterflies*
> *oriole call in verdant haze*
> *wisps of willow-floss drift*
> *to touch her phoenix hairclasps—*
> *such splendor before their eyes.*
> *Signs of clouds gathering over love's terrace!*
> *Though far the mountains*
> *far the waters*
> *far the loved one*
> *not far off is the painting!*
>
> (*TUNE: HUAN XI SHA*)
> *Mix the "unicorn-marrow" ink*
> *smooth the frost-tipped hairs*
> *charge brush—but draft no sooner finished*
> *than saucy swallow swoops from nest*
> *snatches it in his beak*
> *and in a flash is half way up the heavens!*
> *And Heaven, Heaven*
> *may do me no good turn*
> *but drop it over stream or muddy ditch!*
> *Then "autumn leaf" sailing down palace gutter*

into the mists of spring
will end like drifting floss or floating weed.
(TUNE: NAIZIHUA)
Twice thirty drawn-out days, the months of spring
in ordinary times
languid enough——how now
when hopeless longings tug at the heart!
How long before I see the youth in the painting?
For not till then
can I tell him——everything!

SCENE 12: THE NOTE RETRIEVED

Among Flying Cloud's last thoughts in scene 11 is the fear that Heaven may do her "no good turn," but may allow the swallow-messenger to drop her poem "over stream or muddy ditch." Evidently her hope is that the message of love-longing she has written will not fall by the wayside but will find its way to its implicit object, the young scholar Huo Duliang whom she knows only as painter of the self-portrait she so admires.

And this, as we might have guessed, is exactly what happens in scene 12, "The Note Retrieved." Our young hero, Huo Duliang, is alone on stage for the first two-thirds of the scene. His opening aria metaphorically expresses his ambition: peach and plum, as carefully cultivated fruits, are standard metonymy for students, who in turn are the "humble fish" who by leaping the rapids of the state examinations may transmute into dragons, lords of the river.

Huo Duliang is whiling away the time with a stroll in one of the beauty spots of the capital, the Serpentine River of Chang'an. But his thoughts seem to be less of the coming examinations than of his mistress or common-law wife, the courtesan Wandering Cloud. He sees her as another Wenjun, who with her poet-husband Sima Xiangru became the classic model of romantic elopement and marriage for love. The images of his arias suggest amorous dalliance in general: the "east wind's discontents" (i.e., thoughts of love); the fanciful notion that Wandering Cloud, whose portrait has been lost, has in fact been spirited away to Yang Terrace, home of a legendary goddess who daily transforms into "clouds and rain" (metonymy for lovemaking). In the aria to the tune Zaoluopao, all the images are of nature in the guise of a beautiful woman.

The swallow drops Flying Cloud's poem at his feet, and Huo instantly understands that its author is a young woman of gentle birth: verse of this quality could come only from the educated daughter of a good family or from a specially trained courtesan, and the words "boudoir" and "balustrade" indicate the former rather than the latter. Equally instantaneously, he falls in love with her. He is now passionately involved with two women, his "crazy bouts of lovesickness redouble," as he longs to possess not only Wandering Cloud, who is already his mistress, and to whom he will soon (in scene 19) swear to be a faithful husband, but also this unknown poet Flying Cloud, who has accidentally become the owner of his painting. He returns to the love-nest he shares with Wandering Cloud, who seems to accept with some equanimity the idea of a rival for Huo's affections. She describes the swallow as "a go-between to shame bee or butterfly," sees Heaven's hand in this and advises Huo to keep the swallow-message safe while he prepares for the examinations. We do, however, catch a certain note of envy in Wandering Cloud's comment that Huo's painting, "not my good fortune to appreciate," has "found its way into an opulent home"—this envy of the courtesan for the daughter of good family will find its full expression in the quarrel of the comic finale of the play.

Scene 12: The Note Retrieved

HUO DULIANG (*enters*):

> (*TUNE: FAN BU SUAN*)
> *Peach and plum as Serpentine warmer flows*
> *herald the spring examination season*
> *when humble fish transmute to lordly dragons!*
> *Miss the time, and lose the chance to display*
> *the skill of Yang Xiong with his "Sweetwater Ode"—*
> *and so I stroll here to relax a moment.*

> > [Yang Xiong (53 B.C.–A.D. 18) presented this ode to the throne after he had been recommended for court appointment as a poet comparable with the great Sima Xiangru.]

(*He recites*):

> Powerless to stop the petals' fall
> Crossing the bridge where no one cares to climb:
> Vernal breezes through six score of days
> Orioles grieve as each flower meets its time.

> Outlines of far hills, green and clear
> Fit image for the curving of a brow.

> A cloudless sky, the scents of flowering plants
> And butterflies are extra busy now.

The other day I sketched a portrait of the two of us for Wandering Cloud, and was delighted with the way it turned out. But who would have guessed, when we sent it to be mounted, that the idiot of a scroll-maker would return it to someone else by mistake and leave us with a painting of the Bodhisattva. It's a genuine Wu Daozi, in fact. Well, my painting skills may be no match for a Wu Daozi, but I hold that Wandering Cloud's looks are not too different from the Bodhisattva herself, the Moon-on-Water Guanyin of the Southern Seas! — An absurd affair, but where to start looking for my painting? Let it go. — It's still some time before the examinations begin and I'm at a loose end away from home, best thing is a quiet stroll here on the Serpentine embankment.

> *(TUNE: BUBU JIAO)*
> *Not all these strands of willow-floss*
> *suffice to bind the east wind's discontents.*
> *Dew on orchids like weeping eyes*
> *screened by blue-black swallowtail fronds.*
> *A jug of amber wine*
> *swansdown robe laid aside*
> *step softly through the Serpentine mists*
> *to see the drifts of falling petals*
> *a farewell banquet for the spring.*

I have been thinking how that painting of Wandering Cloud is such an exact likeness that no matter whoever it was delivered to me by mistake, they couldn't possibly have such a beauty about and so they couldn't have any use for it, it would be pointless for them to keep it. Still, what luck that the painting that was wrongly returned to me was nothing less than a portrait of the Guanyin. She is hanging in my chamber at this moment and I take pleasure in burning incense and making offerings before her.

> *(TUNE: ZUI FU GUI)*
> *With utmost skill I sketched the lovely form*
> *of my devoted Wenjun, Wandering Cloud,*
> *but carelessly that ne'er-do-well mislaid it.*

Surely it must have been

> *her natural grace had such appeal*
> *that she was spirited off, transformed to cloud and rain*
> *in love-games by Yang Terrace.*

I lost the lovely face, peach petal in spring breeze
but gained a manifestation from Potlaka
the Moon-on-Water Guanyin Bodhisattva!

Here I am on the bank of the Serpentine. Just clearing after a shower—
what an enchanting scene!

(TUNE: ZAOLUOPAO)
Blossom at Weiqu like a lovely face
the rouge more lustrous after rain
tresses of water-plants tugged by the breeze.
When will hooves trample the almond-scented mist
and moth-antenna brows be painted new
on skin hibiscus-smooth?

(He looks up at the sky)

Odd how this swallow keeps swooping back and forth above my head,
almost as though it were claiming acquaintance!

Fly on, fly on swallow
to and fro, breeze-borne
pink bodice and perky tail
flirting with the willow catkins
but why this red petal, dropped on a flurry of air?

(His gaze travels down to ground level)

Why has it shed this tuft of pink feathers now?

(Picks up the note and examines it)

No, not feathers, it's a note, no bigger than an autumn leaf and covered
with tiny characters the size of flies' heads, let me see what it says.

(He reads Flying Cloud's *poem aloud)*

"Where blossoms perish in the wind and rain
In the spring boudoir dreams grow chill again.
Languid against the balustrade
I search the painted scene to ease my pain:
    Green Sleeves in pride
    By Red Tunic's side
While butterfly and oriole dance at will;
    But myself, double of his partner fair—
When shall I meet with him on Witch's Hill?

—Flying Cloud of Weiqu, author." Ha, if I read this carefully, it must
surely have been composed by the person to whom my portrait was
delivered. But how is it that the diction, the calligraphy are so refined in
every detail? Evidently the work of a young lady!

(TUNE: HAO JIEJIE)
Roseate note
composed in maiden's chamber
clearly reveals the whereabouts of my painting.
Such skill, such choice of phrase
no whit behind the fair Ban Zhao herself.

[Ban Zhao assisted her brother Ban Gu in the compilation
of the *Hanshu* (*History of the Former Han Dynasty*).]

To think, I was just doubting whether another such beauty as Wandering
Cloud could exist on this earth, and here is such a one, right here! (*Points
to the note*) This last phrase, "double of his partner fair"—written
evidence! Oh Huo Duliang, Huo Duliang, you'll find it hard to distract
yourself now!

Hard to find distraction
when passion's fever strikes so swift
and crazy bouts of lovesickness redouble!

But wait, yesterday Wandering Cloud was in such distress over the loss
of that portrait, she was still worrying this morning. I must hurry back
now and tell her what has happened to it, to set her mind at rest.
(*He takes a turn about the stage*)
Truly

"treading the spring" one dallies without thinking,
fragrance in one's robe draws the butterflies to one's home.

(*He knocks at the gate*)
Open up, open up!
WANDERING CLOUD (*enters*):

(TUNE: MATIHUA)
His knock, a bird pecking at blossoms
tells me my lord and master's here.

(*She mimes opening the gate,* Huo Duliang *enters and greets her*)
Master Huo! You left so early today, where have you been spending your
time?
HUO: Upon rising this morning I went for a stroll on the Serpentine
embankment.

(TUNE: JIANG'ER SHUI)
Lone seeker of spring's traces
among sweet-smelling herbs.

WANDERING CLOUD: What was it like by the Serpentine?

HUO: A lovely scene!

> *A swallow, dark-robed aristocrat*
> *skimming peacefully over the water*
> *twittering of spring's unrest*
> *seemed to expect my coming . . .*

WANDERING CLOUD: And what happened with the swallow?

HUO:

> *As it pecked at the blossoms*
> *it shed——no petals but a flowered paper.*

This note came fluttering down. Read the poem it contains and you will see that it is obviously by the person who by mistake took delivery of your portrait. Don't worry, we will make enquiries at our leisure and get it back. And she is another "Cloud," a Miss Flying Cloud!

> *Savor this love lyric to the full*
> *and find another "Cloud"*
> *with fresh spring looks the image of your own!*

WANDERING CLOUD:

> (*TUNE: CHUAN BO ZHAO*)
> *Your skillful painting*
> *not my good fortune to enjoy*
> *for it found its way into an opulent home,*
> *found its way into an opulent home.*

Just think, that swallow——

> *a go-between to shame bee or butterfly——*
> *more than mere chance guides Heaven's plan in this!*
> *Keep the note safe*
> *don't treat it lightly.*

This is no casual matter, dear husband. Put the note safely away, and then when the examinations are over you can enquire at your leisure into the whereabouts of our portrait.

SERVANT (*enters*): "Prepared for breaking of cassia bough, summon the prize-winning picker of flowers." Master Huo, a message from Master Xianyu just now: today the Board of Rites announced that the examinations open tomorrow at daybreak, and he requests that you start out at the fifth watch.

> ["Picker of flowers" (*tan hua*) was the sobriquet for the man who placed third in the *jinshi* examinations; "breaking the cassia bough" was a metaphor for such success.]

HUO: Very good (Servant *exits*) Why so sudden a start to the examinations? I caught a chill from the morning breeze and feel a little out of sorts, I shall take a short rest now in my chamber. Let me ask you to put these writing materials in order for me.

> (*TUNE: CODA*)
> Gates open to examination hall
> where the most precious coins will be your words.
> Hone skill of hand to "steal the perfume"
> be first to break the cassia bough
> and stroll the Almond Orchard in spring triumph!

SCENE 42: INVESTITURE COMPLETED

By scene 42, the final scene of the play, the Li family has taken in both Wandering Cloud as adopted daughter and Huo Duliang himself as husband to the actual daughter of the house, Flying Cloud. It is a situation symbolized by the stage-setting, in which we see the reception hall of the Li family graced by the two paintings that have figured so prominently in the action of the play, the portrait of the Bodhisattva Guanyin, which was owned by Flying Cloud, and the double portrait Huo Duliang painted of himself and Wandering Cloud.

Our hero Huo Duliang has succeeded in taking possession of both his loves: the only remaining problem is that of precedence, since each woman insists she is the proper first wife and no mere concubine. The solution to the problem, as we shall see, is appropriately ingenious and provides an ending of charming neatness. Huo Duliang's achievements have been in two realms, the realms civil and military into which all government divides—just as all plays do. In the civil realm he has won examination distinction as Prize Candidate, while in military service he has contributed an ingenious stratagem for the defeat of the rebel An Lushan. Each of the two wives can thus receive high honor, and in fact the only way to distinguish them in rank remains the purely unavoidable theatrical one. A play can have only one heroine proper (*zhengdan*), and this is Flying Cloud; Wandering Cloud is the other member of the usual pair as *xiaodan*. Flying Cloud then comes out on top as Governor's Lady, but in any case she is obviously the social superior to Wandering Cloud and must take precedence. Apart from this, with Wandering Cloud declared Partner of the Prize Candidate we have a judiciously balanced arrangement to effect a thoroughly bigamous ménage à trois.

One detail of this scene requires explanation: Wandering Cloud in advancing her claim to wifely status seeks recognition of her achievement in discovering a forgery of examination numbers. Code words rather than names were assigned to examination papers to prevent abuses, but the villain of the play, the ignorant young wastrel Xianyu Ji, gets around this inconvenience by bribing an usher to switch his cypher with that of the brilliant hero. Wandering Cloud discovers the trick when by chance, in the house of Li Andao who is the examiner, she catches a glimpse of the paper the villain is claiming as his own. Months of devoted service as the hero's amanuensis (in one aria she refers to herself as "old companion by the stove," in yet another allusion to the Sima Xiangru story) enable her to recognize the calligraphy as Huo's and to expose the deception.

Scene 42: Investiture Completed

(Portrait of the Bodhisattva Guanyin hangs center-stage; double portrait of Huo Duliang and Wandering Cloud hangs stage right)

FLYING CLOUD *(enters dressed in everyday wear)*

(TUNE: LAN HUA MEI)

Lightly settle star-shaped flakes
on hair fresh-coiffed before the mirror;
against snow-silent air
clink of jade bridle-studs from Jianzhang Palace;
bracelets and pendants tinkling
she emerges from scented boudoir.

See, here is the Guanyin portrait that used to be mine, hung now in this place: I must pay my respects to the Bodhisattva, *(she bows before the portrait)*

to offer in prayer
where Mount Potlaka seems to soar above this roof
a lotus petal of holy incense.

WANDERING CLOUD *(enters, also in everyday dress)*:

(SAME TUNE)

Once more, dreams of King Xiang on Witch's Mount—
but an interloper has stolen the perfume for Han Shou
and I, domestic chick, suddenly find myself
a duckling from a love-nest in the wild!

> [A fourth-century young lady, enamoured of the handsome Han Shou (whom she eventually married), stole for presentation to him the rare perfume her father had received as a gift from the emperor himself.]

See, here are the Bodhisattva image and the double portrait, let me just pay my respects to the Bodhisattva before I have another look at our portrait.

> homage to Guanyin, then inspect
> the portrait of the "partner of porridge days."

(*She bows, then looks from the double portrait to* Flying Cloud *and back again*)

Truly

> the same features, the one portrayed
> and the one who took the painting by mistake!

(Wandering Cloud *and* Flying Cloud *bow to each other*)

HUO DULIANG (*enters, still in the formal dress he wore to the banquets to celebrate his successes*):

> (*SAME TUNE*)
> Prize Candidate feasted in Unicorn Chamber
> now tipsy treads a path of plum blossoms
> fragrant and gleaming white as jade.

(*He salutes the Bodhisattva portrait, bows to* Flying Cloud *and* Wandering Cloud, *then studies the double portrait*)

See how I am just a single person, yet put the two of you together with the lady in the portrait, and there are three as closely alike as if printed from one and the same block. (*He laughs*): Together with her,

> the portrait makes Three Graces here assembled:
> Now to place bridal headdress
> on raven clouds of hair
> for a monopoly of pride
> in high estate and high romance alike.

WANDERING CLOUD (*questions* Huo): These bridal head adornments you speak of, my lord—how many sets are there?

HUO: Only one set—how could there be more?

WANDERING CLOUD: Both of us can claim a likeness to the girl in the portrait—I wonder then, can both of us lay claim to this headdress?

HUO (*laughs*): How could you both wear it? . . . This is rather awkward for me! (*He points to* Flying Cloud) Let Flying . . .

WANDERING CLOUD: Flying what?

HUO: Let sister Flying Cloud wear it for the moment.

FLYING CLOUD: My lord, this is a serious matter, how can you speak of "for the moment"?

WANDERING CLOUD: Indeed, not even for the moment!

FLYING CLOUD: Ridiculous!

> (*SAME TUNE*)
> One horse, one saddle, that's the proper thing—
> how could this "Cloud" come "Wandering" out of nowhere
> to dream of amorous tryst with the King of Chu?

WANDERING CLOUD (*points to Guanyin portrait*):   My lord, do you recognize which
of the bodhisattvas this is?

HUO: It is Guanyin.

WANDERING CLOUD: There you are—

> *Incense from Mount Potlaka burned as we made our pact*
> *lotus flowers stood witness our vows were no lies:*
> *from which strange peak comes this "Cloud" "Flying" now*
> *to steal my place as Goddess?*

HUO (*laughs*):   Each of you has a point—you put me in a difficult position.

(Flying Cloud *and* Wandering Cloud *turn their backs on each other. Pipes and cymbals strike up.*)

LI ANDAO, MADAM LI (*enter in formal dress*):

> (*TUNE: WAN XIANDENG*)
>
> *Swallows rejoice beneath painted eaves*
> *mid swelling sounds of pipe and song.*

(Huo *bows to them, but the two young women remain with backs turned to each other and do not
move*)

LI (*startled*):   This is a day for feasting in brocaded hall, there should be
nothing but joy on every hand. What reason can there be for these two
girls to be at odds like this?

FLYING CLOUD (*steps forward and kneels before them*):   I appeal to you, my parents.

LI: Rise, child.

FLYING CLOUD: Your daughter has lived in seclusion in the women's
apartments since childhood days, and now that she is grown, she has
entered into marital bliss. When Master Huo and I drank the nuptial cup
our match was made by the Military Governor of the province, it was no
casual encounter. Yet today here is Miss Wandering Cloud Hua, trying to
seize your daughter's title of investiture by force. This is contrary to all
reason, truly an absurd notion.

LI: Child, today is a day of celebration, if there have been words between
you why not yield a little and compromise?

FLYING CLOUD: Other things may be compromised, but how can one
compromise in the receipt of imperial favor? (*She drags* Huo *forward*)

> (*TUNE: JIE SANXING*)
>
> *Daughter of eminent family, "pearl in palm of hand"*
> *I do not covet pomp of fancy title!*
> *But you, in house of joy bewitched by other brows*
> *of one long skilled in arts of "cloud and rain"*
> *how can you let her vie for your favor,*
> *this drifting willow catkin,*

> *while I, plum blossom pure*
> *am left to my own devices?*

(*She makes a deep bow toward the back of* Wandering Cloud)

> *Gladly I yield—*

I ask only permission to take back the Guanyin image that was mine, for I will abstain year-round from meat, worship the Buddha, and live at home as a homeless nun—

> *gladly I yield:*
> *return to me the image of white-robed saint*
> *the bronze chimes and the burning incense!*

(*She moves to take down the Guanyin scroll, but* Madam Li *restrains her*)

MADAM LI: Child, why so hot-tempered? Amicable discussion is best, whatever the problem!

WANDERING CLOUD (*kneels*):   I appeal to you, my parents.

LI: Please rise also.

WANDERING CLOUD: Fitness for marriage should depend not on whether one's family is high or low in status, but on whether one's betrothal came first or later in time! Master Huo and I burned incense and swore oaths before the Buddha, vowing to be man and wife and never to forget one another. Moreover, if it had not been for my discovery of the forged examination numbers, the Prize Candidacy would have gone to a scoundrel. Master Huo today is the honored husband—why should I not equally be the esteemed wife? This is why I wish to remind Master Huo of our former union—only for this, and not to give offense to Elder Sister!

LI: Something in what you say also!

FLYING CLOUD: Father, if you say she is in the right, then I must be in the wrong!

WANDERING CLOUD: Are you saying that only you are in the right, and what our father says is wrong?

(*She weeps, then drags* Huo *forward to stand center stage*)

> (*SAME TUNE*)
> *Poor blossom by humble wall*
> *how could I aspire to share*
> *glory of spring in royal park?*
> *Yet though my lord be drawn*
> *in triumph by four noble steeds*
> *could he forget his old companion by the stove*
> *sharing the secret melodies of the lute?*

Now as you light the imperial "lotus-bud" candles
say no more of "the drinking of old
in the chamber where the lovely one
played her brocade-clad zither."

(*She makes a deep bow toward the back of* Flying Cloud)

Gladly I yield—

for my part I ask permission only to take back this double portrait from the old days, and then willingly, in skirt of coarse cloth and with a thorn for hairpin, I shall keep my lonely room. I do not believe the gentleman in this portrait will prove fickle-minded—I shall take him for my companion!—

gladly I yield
to tie the nuptial knot
with the young scholar in this painting.

(*She moves to take down the double portrait, but* Huo *restrains her*)

HUO: A hot-tempered one over there, another hot-tempered one here, how can we settle this?

MAMA MENG (*enters*):   "At word of family feast, we hurry to painted hall." Your old servant kowtows!

LI, MADAM LI: Please rise.

MENG: Congratulations, sir, congratulations, madam.

MADAM LI: Mama Meng, you're here at just the right moment. Our two young ladies have been having words over the matter of the title of investiture. Please try to get them to see reason.

MAMA MENG: I'll try. (*She takes a long look at* Flying Cloud, *then a long look at* Wandering Cloud) Oh dear, oh dear! Why such a pother at such a time on such a day of rejoicing? Don't you know, Miss Flying Cloud, it's a commonplace thing for a person who becomes an official to take two or three secondary wives?

(*SAME TUNE*)

Nothing excessive in just two or three—

FLYING CLOUD: You don't understand, Mama Meng, why should I worry about some "two or three"? But in the beginning, when Master Huo was in the military service and was taken in as son-in-law, it was Governor Jia who oversaw our wedding, and you yourself were the go-between.

MAMA MENG: Quite right, quite right.

FLYING CLOUD: Ours was no casual union, I was no secondary wife, so how today can this Miss Wandering Cloud Hua come up with a demand for the title of investiture?

MAMA MENG: Miss, it's true what they say, "want best for all, let great act small."

FLYING CLOUD: What do you know about it, what is this "let great act small"?

(*She gives* Mama Meng *a shove.* Mama Meng *turns to address* Wandering Cloud.)

MAMA MENG: Tell me, Wandering Cloud, there have been many cases of mistress made wife, but when was there ever one with your luck, no sooner a wife than wife of the Prize Candidate himself! And His Excellency and Madam Li treating you like their own flesh and blood, it ought to be enough for you, you should try not to cause so much trouble—

> *for when was there ever*
> *promotion like yours?*

WANDERING CLOUD: Mama Meng, what is this talk of "mistress made wife?" It was in my home that Master Huo did his studying and passed his examination, and that time when you came to treat him when he was sick, you saw it with your own eyes, we lived as man and wife. Then later I suffered through all those complications brought about by that note he found with the poem in it. So why is it, now he's become an official, I can't ask for the title of investiture?

MAMA MENG: You mustn't be offended, Wandering Cloud, but she is the great one, you are the lesser one, you will have to give in to her a little.

WANDERING CLOUD: Ridiculous! What is this "great one, lesser one"?

(*She gives* Mama Meng *a shove.* Mama Meng *stares at her.*)

MAMA MENG: What a temper! Prize Candidate Huo, you will need to mediate matters between these two, or jealousy will get the better of them and it will not look good.

> *Shield each with your favor*
> *be their support as solid as the hills:*
> *equitable solution must come from you.*

HUO: This is a difficult question to deal with. And you are being stupid, Mama Meng—why do you have to bring up the idea of jealousy?

MAMA MENG: If it isn't jealousy that's caused this, what is it?

HUO: It's merely that there is only one title of investiture, and both of them are competing for it, that's what makes it difficult.

(*He gives* Mama Meng *a shove*)

MAMA MENG: Enough, enough! All on account of you people, this poor old body has been through so many adventures, but that won't satisfy you. Today when you've got what you wanted, you forget all that and just treat me as a balloon you can kick to and fro between you. Miss Flying Cloud,

I stood as your companion
amid a thousand troops, a myriad steeds;

and Wandering Cloud, on account of that poem-letter,

how did I survive
a hundred knocks, a thousand blows?

(*She bursts out wailing*)

O how could you treat me like this—

all yelling at me
all yelling at me
till I must risk my feeble life
here on the floor of this noble hall!

(*She throws herself to the floor, where she lies beating her breast with both fists*)

HUO, FLYING CLOUD, WANDERING CLOUD: Please get up, Mama Meng!

MAMA MENG: I'll never get up, not till you've shown me you're all friends with each other, then I'll get up.

FLYING CLOUD, WANDERING CLOUD: We promise to do as Mama says.

MAMA MENG: Promising is not enough. You must all three bow to each other. (*They do so*) Still not good enough—you must all give each other a smile. (*The three of them smile at each other*)

MADAM LI: We truly owe it all to you, Mama Meng, from start to finish. Now you mustn't go away again, but stay here in this house to be supported for the rest of your life.

(Mama Meng *expresses her gratitude. Enter an Official bearing the imperial proclamation of investiture, followed by* Governor Jia Nanzhong *with two* Attendants *bearing elaborately decorated headdresses*)

JIA NANZHONG:

(*TUNE: WAN XIANDENG*)
Illumination streams from purple Edict
and coronets display the latest style.

The deed of investiture has been prepared. Give ear, kneeling, to the reading of this proclamation:

(*He reads out the imperial edict as all kneel*)

"WE understand that OUR court has proper standards for the appreciation of civil merit and the encouragement of military valor. However, in the nurturing of the nation and the government of the state, the gift of talents both civil and military is seldom enjoyed by a single individual. Were an officer of outstanding virtue to stand forth, he should receive praise and reward as encouragement to renewed vigor. Now Huo Duliang, Captain in the Imperial Guard, has demonstrated the skill to compose 'while leaning against his horse's flank'; he comes to OUR aid as the happy omen of a dream of bears. He forsook his

writing-brush to join in the service of the war-chariots; he donned the official robe to assist the display of OUR virtue. The call to arms brought terror to the soul of the Wolf of Heaven; next heard was the phoenix-like voice of the Hanlin scholar. Now WE observe with pleasure that the glow of the common people's cooking fires has replaced the glare of signal beacons from the frontier watchtowers. Accordingly, WE appoint Huo Duliang Scholar of the Office of Resplendent Letters, to serve concurrently as Governor of Helong, with the insignia of red carp and gold pouch. All matters of protocol relating to the investiture of Scholar Huo's parents and wife, to honor his contributions whether civil or military, to be determined conjointly by the Board of Rites and the Privy Council and put into practice accordingly. By decree!"
Give thanks for the imperial favor!

(*ALL shout "Give thanks for the imperial favor."* Jia Nanzhong *and* Huo Duliang *exchange bows.*)

LI (*to* Jia):   I was on the point of inviting my old comrade to visit, to mediate a problem for us, when lo and behold you arrive with the imperial proclamation.

JIA: How can I help?

LI: Just now our two young ladies were exchanging words on the subject of the title of investiture, and I could think of no solution to their dispute. But now by imperial order you and I are to determine the protocol for Master Huo's parents and wives. What do you think, old friend, how should these matters be determined?

JIA: Though these are matters of state, yet they are also matters within your own household. I will abide by your decision, whatever disposition you feel is best.

LI: In my humble opinion, the unique qualities of Master Huo's late father and mother should be acknowledged by investiture in the first rank. The problem lies with the title of wife. At the time of his success as Prize Candidate, he was living in the home of Wandering Cloud, so that the title of Partner of the Prize Candidate should indeed go to Wandering Cloud; but when subsequently he served as aide to the forces under your command, it was my daughter who accompanied him, and thus the title of Governor's Lady should go to Flying Cloud. What is your view?

JIA: A most satisfactory disposition! (*To* Flying Cloud *and* Wandering Cloud): Please don your accoutrements at once, without further ado. (*To* Li): Tomorrow, old comrade, we will report our determinations to the court.

(Flying Cloud *and* Wandering Cloud *express their gratitude to* Li Andao *and* Jia Nanzhong)

ALL:

> (*TUNE: QINGJIANG YIN*)
> Vermilion wax of royal seal

settles the fate of mandarin ducks:
now cease the wrangling on either side!
Flowered coronets of equal height
rose-colored capes cut to one measure:
two "Clouds" have merged to one desire!

(*A swallow flies across the stage*)

MAMA MENG (*points to the swallow*):   Look, the swallow has come back!

(SAME TUNE)

Fine-curving tail in raven black
amorous creature flying showily back and forth;
a single missive carried in your beak
has settled this love-match of three lifetimes
past, present and to come!

From now on let all lovers

cherish together purple swallow
with cacatua, born in paradise!

(*ALL exit except* Huo, Flying Cloud, *and* Wandering Cloud, *who all three bow to the swallow*)

HUO, FLYING CLOUD, WANDERING CLOUD: Swallow, swallow, our thanks for the good turn. But from now on we shall keep a firm hold of our poems—you shall not carry off another one!

(*They exit to cymbals and drums*)

In the scene in Kong Shangren's *Peach Blossom Fan*, which shows our politician-playwright Ruan Dacheng reacting with indignation to his critics, we hear him put the plaintive question, "What have politics to do with art?" Perhaps the answer is only this: that it would be a waste of our time to look for signs of progressive thinking in Ruan's comedies, lively and brilliant though they may be. In diction and style he was an important follower of the great Tang Xianzu, whose *Peony Pavilion* is hailed, deservedly, as a profound expression of enlightened late Ming thinking about women and the family, about love and duty and social relations, a true vindication of "the holiness of the heart's affections." But in his social as well as in his political philosophy, Ruan was no Tang Xianzu. Ruan's hero Huo Duliang throughout *The Swallow Letter* has no nobler thought in mind than to possess the favors of each of two young beauties without sacrificing the exclusive devotion of either, and we can only lament the amorality or immorality of this self-serving Don Juan, even as we enjoy the ingenuity and stylish wit that lead him to his coveted goal.

A judgment of this kind may seem unduly harsh, or at least unhistorical. It was obviously possible for a man to end up with two wives in a Chinese novel or play, as in real life—not just a wife and concubine, which was not unusual, but two actual wives. The trio rather than the pair of lovers is a feature of many novels and plays of the "genius meets beauty" genre to which *The Swallow Letter* belongs. But almost always the acquisition of two wives is the result of some extraordinary set of circumstances, some wondrous spin of fortune's wheel. It is only rarely that the hero sets out virtually from the beginning of the action to pursue two separate loves. And it is hard to think of another case in which he makes the reservation, as Huo Duliang does more than once in *The Swallow Letter,* while he is swearing fidelity to one love, to offer his heart to a second also once she has been identified.

The foremost of all romantic heroes in Chinese fiction is Jia Baoyu, chief protagonist of the great eighteenth-century novel *Dream of the Red Chamber,* which David Hawkes and John Minford have translated (superbly) under their preferred title *The Story of the Stone.* Jia Baoyu is a profoundly sympathetic figure, but there is no question of his dedicating his love to one woman alone. He is instructed in the arts of love in a dream by a woman whose name, Jianmei, translates as "Conjoined Perfection," and "conjoined perfection" certainly seems a fitting representation of the two girls, Baochai and Daiyu, who together constitute Baoyu's dream love, his ideal woman. So what is the difference between these two beautiful cousins who share Baoyu's heart, and the two "clouds," Wandering Cloud and Flying Cloud, who in Ruan Dacheng's play end up as joint wives of Huo Duliang?

The answer is, all the difference in the world. Baoyu craves the love of both his cousins (though in differing fashion) because they are totally complementary in their qualities and have the defects of their virtues. Baochai is too square, Daiyu too prickly, but put them together and you create the utterly ideal companion-lover-wife. Now when we turn to the objects of Huo Duliang's desires, we find virtually no difference between them at all. Physically they are so alike that the mother of Flying Cloud at one point mistakes Wandering Cloud for her own daughter. Both are talented, beautiful, and sharp-eyed in looking out for their own interests.

What makes Huo Duliang desire both of these women is nothing more admirable or sympathetic than simple sexual acquisitiveness. The only real difference between Flying Cloud and Wandering Cloud is the difference in social status between daughter of good family and courtesan, that is to say, a difference in availability. Flying Cloud, daughter of scholar Li Andao of the imperial academy, is unattainable before marriage; Wandering Cloud, courtesan of the pleasure quarter, is unretainable after marriage for a man who aspires to court employment. And Huo Duliang wants whatever is available, he wants fulfillment both premarital and conjugal, he wants entertainer and social asset, whore and wife, love profane and sacred. He wants, in short, to have it all, and the entire action of the play is dedicated to seeing that he gets it. One need be no ardent feminist to point out that if Huo Duliang had been female he would have received the kind of treatment meted out to Madame Bovary, and not the ultimate honors of Prize Candidate, imperial favor, and twin-brided grand finale.

The Swallow Letter is great entertainment. It is also truly decadent, the overripe fruit of the Linchuan (Tang Xianzu) tradition of elegance. Fortunately we do not have to admire either Ruan Dacheng's politics or his social views to enjoy the wit of his most celebrated comedy.

NOTES

Introduction

1. L. Carrington Goodrich and Chaoying Fang, eds., *Dictionary of Ming Biography, 1368–1644* (2 vols.; New York: Columbia University Press, 1976), 1:241.

2. See W. L. Idema, *The Dramatic Oeuvre of Chu Yu-tun, 1379–1439* (Leiden: E. J. Brill, 1985).

3. Described in Zhao Jingshen et al., "Mingdai yan ju zhuangkuang-de kaocha," in *Xiju yishu,* nos. 3–4 (1979):180.

4. Zeng Yongyi, "Zhongguo gudian xiju-de tezhi," in *Zhongguo gudian wenxue luncong* (Taipei: Zhong-wai wenxue yuekan she, 1976), 2:371.

5. See Barbara E. Ward, "Readers and Audiences: An Exploration of the Spread of Traditional Chinese Culture," in Ravindra K. Jain, ed., *Text and Context: The Social Anthropology of Tradition* (Philadelphia: Institute for the Study of Human Issues, 1977).

6. Lu Eting, *Kunju yanchu shigao* (Shanghai: Wenyi Press, 1980), 232.

7. Basic materials for Tang Xianzu's life are in his collected works, *Tang Xianzu ji* (Shanghai: Classics Press, 1973), the chronology by Xu Shuofang, *Tang Xianzu nianpu* (Shanghai: Classics Press, 1980), and the collection of materials edited by Mao Xiaotong, *Tang Xianzu yanjiu ziliao huibian* (Shanghai: Classics Press, 1986), which includes a biography by Zou Diguang, *Tang Yireng Xiansheng zhuan.*

8. This is the subject of an "eight-legged essay" translated and analyzed by C. I. T'u in an informative article, "The Chinese Examination Essay: Some Literary Considerations," in *Monumenta Serica* 31 (1974–75):393–406.

9. Charles Rosen, "Too Much Opera?" *New York Review of Books* 26, no. 9 (May 31, 1979):14–20.

10. In Wm. Theodore de Bary, ed., *Self and Society in Ming Thought* (New York: Columbia University Press, 1970).

11. Wei Hua, "The Search for Great Harmony: A Study of Tang Xianzu's Dramatic Art," Ph.D. dissertation, University of California, Berkeley, 1991.

12. Jean Mulligan, *The Lute: Kao Ming's P'i-p'a-chi* (New York: Columbia University Press, 1980).

13. Gu Qiyuan, *Kezuo quyu,* quoted in Richard Strassberg, "The Authentic Self in Seventeenth-Century Drama," *Tamkang Review* 8, no. 2 (October 1977):71.

The White Rabbit *Plays*

For the benefit of the specialist, the following are the more readily accessible editions of *Baituji*.

Chenghua edition: *Ming Chenghua shuochang cihua congkan shiliuzhong, fu Baituji chuanqi yizhong.* Shanghai Museum, 1973. Edited reprint of play only under the title *Chenghua xinbian Liu Zhiyuan huan xiang Baituji.* Yangzhou: Classics Press, 1980.

Sixty Plays edition: *Baituji,* in Mao Jin, ed, *Liushizhong qu.* Nanjing: Jiguge, c. 1630; reprinted Taipei: Kaiming Book Co., 1970.

Xie Tianyou edition: *Liu Zhiyuan Baituji.* Beijing: Fuchuntang, late-Ming; reproduced in *Guben xiqu congkan chuji.* Shanghai: Commercial Press, 1954; reprinted Yangzhou: Classics Press, 1980.

White Fur Robe scenes: *Zhuibaiqiu,* preface dated 1770, reprinted Taipei: Zhonghua Book Company, 1967.

1. Milena Dolezelova-Velingerova and J. I. Crump, Jr., *Ballad of the Hidden Dragon* (Oxford: Oxford University Press, 1971).

2. J. I. Crump, Jr., "Liu Chih-yuan in the Chinese 'Epic,' Ballad and Drama," *Literature East and West* 14, no. 2 (1970):154–71.

3. Anne E. McLaren, "The Discovery of Chinese Chantefable Narratives from the Fifteenth Century: A Reassessment of Their Likely Audience," *Ming Studies* 29 (Spring 1990):1–29.

4. My study of the *White Rabbit* plays owes more to Dr. Sun Chongtao than to anyone else. Some of his principal articles on different aspects of the subject are as follows: "Chenghua ben 'Baituji' yu 'Yuan chuanqi' 'Liu Zhiyuan,'" *Wenshi* 20 (1983):211–21; "Chenghua ben 'Baituji' kanxing beijing yu kanben-de xingzhi wenti," *Xiqu yanjiu* 11 (1984):163–75; "Mingdai xiwen-de qudiao tizhi: Chenghua ben 'Baituji' yishu xingtai tansuo-zhi yi," *Yinyue yanjiu* 3 (1984); "Chenghua ben 'Baituji'-de paichang jiegou: Chenghua ben 'Baituji' yishu xingtai tansuo-zhi er," *Difangxi yishu* 2 (1986).

5. Wilt Idema, "The Wen-ching yuan-yang hui and the chia-men of Yuan-Ming Ch'uan-ch'i," *T'oung Pao* 67, nos. 1–2 (1981).

6. Qi Biaojia, *Qupin,* in Zhu Shangwen, ed., *Ming qupin jupin* (Taipei: Yenwen Press, 1960):73.

7. Luo Jintang, *Mingdai juzuojia kaolue* (Hong Kong: Longmen Book Company, 1966):103.

8. See the 1983 article by Sun Chongtao listed in note 4 above.

9. Wang Jisi, "Liu Zhiyuan gushi-de yanhua," *Song-Yuan-Ming-Qing juqu yanjiu luncong* (Hong Kong: Dadong Book Company, 1979), 4:4—8.

10. These fictional instances were pointed out to me by Zhao Yiheng in a Berkeley seminar.

11. Ye Kaiyuan, "'Baituji'-de banben wenti," *Lanzhou daxue xuebao* (shehui kexue ban) (1983), 1:81—91; 2:76—84.

The Girl Washing Silk

1. Xu Wei, quoted in K. C. Leung, "Balance and Symmetry in the Huan Sha Chi," in *Tsing Hua Journal of Chinese Studies,* n.s. 16, nos. 1 and 2 (December 1984):179—201.

2. This is a stage direction in a version of the scene included in the mid seventeenth-century collection published by the Laifengguan. See Chu Jiaofeng, "*Huanshaji* jiaoji," *Guoli Beiping tushuguan guankan* 10, 2 (1962):124.

3. This is the reconstruction by Zeng Yongyi, "Xi Shi gushi zhiyi," in *Xiandai Wenxue* 44 (1971):84—90. Legend blends with historical fact in English-language retellings of the story, such as those in Eloise Talcott Hibbert, *Embroidered Gauze* (London: Kegan Paul, Trench and Trubner, 1938), and Bernard Llewellyn, *China's Courts and Concubines* (London: George Allen and Unwin, 1956). The accounts in both these books are in turn based on Wu Shu-ch'iung, *Hsi Shih, Beauty of Beauties* (Shanghai: Kelly and Walsh, 1931).

4. E. H. Schafer, *The Vermilion Bird: T'ang Images of the South* (Berkeley: University of California Press, 1967), 82—83.

5. Stephen Owen, *The Great Age of Chinese Poetry: The High T'ang* (New Haven: Yale University Press, 1980), 121.

6. Hans Frankel, *The Flowering Plum and the Palace Lady* (New Haven: Yale University Press, 1976), 21.

7. Zeng Yongyi, "Xi Shi gushi zhiyi."

8. Bo Jianshi, "Guanyu Huanshaji-de yixie wenti," *Yuan-Ming-Qing xiqu yanjiu lunwen ji* (Beijing: Peoples Literature Press, 1959), 2:266—81.

9. Shih-hsiang Chen and Harold Acton, tr., *The Peach Blossom Fan* (Berkeley: University of California Press, 1976), 20—21.

10. K. C. Leung, "Balance and Symmetry in the Huan Sha Chi."

11. Zhai Bo, "Jinguo burang xumei—ji Kunju xiaosheng Shi Xiaomei," in *Peoples Daily,* June 18, 1986; courtesy of Professor Wu Xiaoling.

12. Zhang Dai (1597—1684?), *Taoan mengyi,* quoted in Lu Eting, *Kunju yanchu shigao,* 161.

13. Zhang Dai, quoted in Lu Eting, 49.

The Plantain Kerchief

1. Qi Biaojia, *Qupin,* 4.

2. Translation by A. C. Graham of a line by the Tang poet Li Shangyin. The horn is of rhinoceros and is traditionally supposed to possess healing as well as aphrodisiac powers.

3. Lu Eting, *Kunju yanchu shigao,* 90.

4. Ibid., 330–36.

5. Wang Jilie (b. 1873), *Yinlu qutan* (reprinted Taipei: Commercial Press, 1971), *juan* 2, 26b.

6. Ling Mengchu, *Tan qu zazha,* quoted Jin Menghua, *Jiguge liushi zhong qu xulu* (Taipei: Jiani Cement Company Cultural Foundation, 1969), 234.

The Peony Pavilion

1. Frank Kermode, *William Shakespeare: The Final Plays* (London: Longmans, Green, 1965) offers a more detailed list:

First, they all seem to be affected by a new disregard for psychological and narrative plausibility, by a metrical freedom which goes beyond anything in the earlier plays, and finally—to quote the most notorious of their detractors, Lytton Strachey—by a failure of "concentrated artistic determination and purpose." Secondly, there are more positive resemblances. All the Romances treat of the recovery of lost royal children, usually princesses of great, indeed semi-divine, virtue and beauty; they all bring important characters near to death, and sometimes feature almost miraculous resurrections; they all end with the healing, after many years of repentance and suffering, of some disastrous breach in the lives and happiness of princes, and this final reconciliation is usually brought about by the agency of beautiful young people; they all contain material of a pastoral character or otherwise celebrate natural beauty and its renewal. (pp. 7–8)

2. Northrop Frye, *Anatomy of Criticism* (Princeton: Princeton University Press, 1957), 117.

3. Richard Strassberg, "The Authentic Self in Seventeenth-Century Drama," *Tamkang Review* 8, no. 2 (October 1977):61–100.

The Green Peony

1. An edition of this play annotated by Luo Sining is included in the *Gudai xiqu congshu* series: Wu Bing, *Lümudan* (Shanghai: Classics Press, 1985).

2. "Winsome" translates the first syllable of the personal name, Wan'e, of Shen Zhong's daughter. "Jonquil," the name I have invented for Che Shanggong's sister, suggests the "secluded fragrance" which would be the literal translation of her personal name Jingfang. Here as elsewhere I am following the convention established long ago by Chi-chen Wang of translating the names of female characters in order to distinguish them from the males, whose names are merely transliterated. The intention is to reduce confusion for the reader who does not have the Chinese characters to help with gender distinction.

3. The green tree-peony is indeed such a rarity that I was unsure of its actual existence until my student Wang Tian, traveling in China, sent me a color photograph of one.

The Swallow Letter

1. This play also appears in the *Gudai xiqu congshu* series, in an edition by Liu Yihe and Zhang Anquan: Ruan Dacheng, *Yanzijian* (Shanghai: Classics Press, 1986).

2. Arthur W. Hummel, ed., *Eminent Chinese of the Ch'ing Period, 1644–1912* (2 vols.; Washington, D.C.: Library of Congress, 1943), 1:398.

3. Liu Yihe, ed., *Yanzijian,* Introduction, 5.

SUGGESTED READINGS

Translations

Hung Sheng, *The Palace of Eternal Youth,* tr. Yang Xianyi and Gladys Yang. Beijing: Foreign Languages Press, 1955, 1980.

K'ung Shang-jen. *The Peach Blossom Fan,* tr. Chen Shih-hsiang and Harold Acton, with the collaboration of Cyril Birch. Berkeley: University of California Press, 1976.

Mulligan, Jean. *The Lute:* Kao Ming's *P'i-p'a chi.* New York: Columbia University Press, 1980.

Tang Xianzu. *The Peony Pavilion.* tr. Cyril Birch. Bloomington: Indiana University Press, 1980; paperback ed. Boston: Cheng and Tsui, 1994.

Studies

Dolby, William. *A History of Chinese drama.* London: Elek Books, 1976.

Hanan, Patrick. *The Invention of Li Yu.* Cambridge: Harvard University Press, 1988.

Henry, Eric P. *Chinese Amusement: The Lively Plays of Li Yu.* Hamden, Conn.: Archon Books, 1980.

Hung, Josephine Huang. *Ming Drama.* Taipei: Heritage Press, 1966.

Strassberg, Richard E. *The World of K'ung Shang-jen.* New York: Columbia University Press, 1983.

OTHER WORKS IN THE COLUMBIA
ASIAN STUDIES SERIES

Translations from the Asian Classics

Major Plays of Chikamatsu, tr. Donald Keene   1961

Four Major Plays of Chikamatsu, tr. Donald Keene. Paperback text edition   1961

Records of the Grand Historian of China, translated from the Shih chi of Ssu-ma Ch'ien, tr. Burton Watson, 2 vols.   1961

Instructions for Practical Living and Other Neo-Confucian Writings by Wang Yang-ming, tr. Wing-tsit Chan   1963

Chuang Tzu: Basic Writings, tr. Burton Watson, paperback ed. only   1964

The Mahābhārata, tr. Chakravarthi V. Narasimhan. Also in paperback ed.   1965

The Manyōshū, Nippon Gakujutsu Shinkōkai edition   1965

Su Tung-p'o: Selections from a Sung Dynasty Poet, tr. Burton Watson. Also in paperback ed.   1965

Bhartrihari: Poems, tr. Barbara Stoler Miller. Also in paperback ed.   1967

Basic Writings of Mo Tzu, Hsün Tzu, and Han Fei Tzu, tr. Burton Watson. Also in separate paperback eds.   1967

The Awakening of Faith, Attributed to Aśvaghosha, tr. Yoshito S. Hakeda. Also in paperback ed.   1967

Reflections on Things at Hand: The Neo-Confucian Anthology, comp. Chu Hsi and Lü Tsu-ch'ien, tr. Wing-tsit Chan   1967

The Platform Sutra of the Sixth Patriarch, tr. Philip B. Yampolsky. Also in paperback ed.   1967

Essays in Idleness: The Tsurezuregusa of Kenkō, tr. Donald Keene. Also in paperback ed.   1967

The Pillow Book of Sei Shōnagon, tr. Ivan Morris, 2 vols.   1967

Two Plays of Ancient India: The Little Clay Cart and the Minister's Seal, tr. J. A. B. van Buitenen   1968

The Complete Works of Chuang Tzu, tr. Burton Watson   1968

The Romance of the Western Chamber (Hsi Hsiang chi), tr. S. I. Hsiung. Also in
  paperback ed.   1968
The Manyōshū, Nippon Gakujutsu Shinkōkai edition. Paperback text
  edition.   1969
Records of the Historian: Chapters from the Shih chi of Ssu-ma Ch'ien. Paperback
  text edition, tr. Burton Watson.   1969
Cold Mountain: 100 Poems by the T'ang Poet Han-shan, tr. Burton Watson.
  Also in paperback ed.   1970
Twenty Plays of the Nō Theatre, ed. Donald Keene. Also in paperback ed.   1970
Chūshingura: The Treasury of Loyal Retainers, tr. Donald Keene. Also in
  paperback ed.   1971
The Zen Master Hakuin: Selected Writings, tr. Philip B. Yampolsky   1971
*Chinese Rhyme-Prose: Poems in the Fu Form from the Han and Six Dynasties
  Periods*, tr. Burton Watson. Also in paperback ed.   1971
Kūkai: Major Works, tr. Yoshito S. Hakeda. Also in paperback ed.   1972
*The Old Man Who Does as He Pleases: Selections from the Poetry and Prose of Lu
  Yu*, tr. Burton Watson   1973
The Lion's Roar of Queen Śrīmālā, tr. Alex and Hideko Wayman   1974
*Courtier and Commoner in Ancient China: Selections from the History of the Former
  Han by Pan Ku*, tr. Burton Watson. Also in paperback ed.   1974
*Japanese Literature in Chinese, vol. 1: Poetry and Prose in Chinese by Japanese
  Writers of the Early Period*, tr. Burton Watson   1975
*Japanese Literature in Chinese, vol. 2; Poetry and Prose in Chinese by Japanese
  Writers of the Later Period*, tr. Burton Watson   1976
Scripture of the Lotus Blossom of the Fine Dharma, tr. Leon Hurvitz. Also in
  paperback ed.   1976
Love Song of the Dark Lord: Jayadeva's Gītagovinda, tr. Barbara Stoler
  Miller. Also in paperback ed. Cloth ed. includes critical text of the
  Sanskrit.   1977
Ryōkan: Zen Monk-Poet of Japan, tr. Burton Watson   1977
*Calming the Mind and Discerning the Real: From the Lam rim chen mo of Tsòn-
  kha-pa*, tr. Alex Wayman   1978
The Hermit and the Love-Thief: Sanskirt Poems of Bhartrihari and Bilhaṇa, tr.
  Barbara Stoler Miller   1978
The Lute: Kao Ming's P'i-p'a chi, tr. Jean Mulligan. Also in paperback ed.   1980
A Chronicle of Gods and Sovereigns: Jinnō Shōtōki of Kitabatake Chikafusa, tr. H.
  Paul Varley   1980
Among the Flowers: The Hua-chien chi, tr. Lois Fusek   1982
Grass Hill: Poems and Prose by the Japanese Monk Gensi, tr. Burton Watson   1983
Doctors, Diviners, and Magicians of Ancient China: Biographies of Fang-shih, tr.
  Kenneth J. DeWoskin. Also in Paperback ed.   1983
Theater of Memory: The Plays of Kālidāsa, ed. Barbara Stoler Miller. Also in
  paper ed.   1984

The Columbia Book of Chinese Poetry: From Early Times to the Thirteenth Century,
ed. and tr. Burton Watson. Also in paperback ed.   1984
Poems of Love and War: From the Eight Anthologies and the Ten Songs of Classical Tamil, tr. A. K. Ramanujan. Also in paperback ed.   1985
The Columbia Book of Later Chinese Poetry, ed. and tr. Jonathan Chaves. Also in paperback ed.   1986
The Tso Chuan: Selections from China's Oldest Narrative History, tr. Burton Watson   1989
Selected Writings of Nichiren, ed. Philip B. Yampolsky   1990
Saigyō, Poems of a Mountain Home, tr. Burton Watson   1990
The Cilappatikāram of Ilaṅkō Aṭikaḷ, tr. R. Parthasarthy   1993
The Lotus Sutra, tr. Burton Watson   1993
Beyond Spring: T'zu Poems of the Sung Dynasty, tr. Julie Landau   1994

Studies in Asian Culture

1. *The Ōnin War: History of Its Origins and Background, with a Selective Translation of the Chronicle of Ōnim,* by H. Paul Varley   1967
2. *Chinese Government in Ming Times: Seven Studies,* ed. Charles O. Hucker 1969
3. *The Actors' Analects (Yakusha Rongo),* ed. and tr. by Charles J. Dunn and Bungó Torigoe   1969
4. *Self and Society in Ming Thought,* by Wm. Theodore de Bary and the Conference on Ming Thought. Also in paperback ed.   1970
5. *A History of Islamic Philosophy,* by Majid Fakhry, 2d ed.   1983
6. *Phantasies of a Love Thief: The Caurapañcāśikā Attributed to Bilhana,* by Barbara Stoler Miller   1971
7. *Iqbal: Poet-Philosopher of Pakistan,* ed. Hafeez Malik   1971
8. *The Golden Tradition: An Anthology of Urdu Poetry,* ed. and tr. Ahmed Ali. Also in paperback ed.   1973
9. *Conquerors and Confucians: Aspects of Political Change in Late Yüan China,* by John W. Dardess   1973
10. *The Unfolding of Neo-Confucianism,* by Wm. Theodore de Bary and the Conference on Seventeenth-Century Chinese Thought. Also in paperback ed.   1975
11. *To Acquire Wisdom: The Way of Wang Yang-ming,* by Julia Ching   1976
12. *Gods, Priests, and Warriors: The Bhargus of the Mahābhārata,* by Robert P. Goldman   1977
13. *Mei Yao-ch'en and the Development of Early Sung Poetry,* by Jonathan Chaves   1976
14. *The Legend of Semimaru, Blind Musician of Japan,* by Susan Matisoff   1977
15. *Sir Sayyid Ahmad Khan and Muslim Modernization in India and Pakistan,* by Hafeez Malik   1980
16. *The Khilafat Movement: Religious Symbolism and Political Mobilization in India,* by Gail Minault   1982

17. *The World of K'ung Shang-jen: A Man of Letters in Early Ch'ing China*, by Richard Strassberg 1983
18. *The Lotus Boat: The Origins of Chinese Tz'u Poetry in Tang Popular Culture*, by Marsha L. Wagner 1984
19. *Expressions of Self in Chinese Literature*, ed. Robert E. Hegel and Richard C. Hessney 1985
20. *Songs for the Bride: Women's Voices and Wedding Rites of Rural India*, by W. G. Archer, ed., Barbara Stoler Miller and Mildred Archer 1986
21. *A Heritage of Kings: One Man's Monarchy in the Confucian World*, by JaHyun Kim Haboush 1988

Companions to Asian Studies

Approaches to the Oriental Classics, ed. Wm. Theodore de Bary 1959
Early Chinese Literature, by Burton Watson. Also in paperback ed. 1962
Approaches to Asian Civilizations, ed. Wm. Theodore de Bary and Ainslie T. Embree 1964
The Classic Chinese Novel: A Critical Introduction by C. T. Hsia. Also in paperback ed. 1968
Chinese Lyricism: Shih Poetry from the Second to the Twelfth Century, tr. Burton Watson. Also in paperback ed. 1971
A Syllabus of Indian Civilization, by Leonard A. Gordon and Barbara Stoler Miller 1971
Twentieth-Century Chinese Stories, ed. C. T. Hsia and Joseph S. M. Lau. Also in paperback ed. 1971
A Syllabus of Chinese Civilization, by J. Mason Gentzler, 2d ed. 1972
A Syllabus of Japanese Civilization, by H. Paul Varley, 2d ed. 1972
An Introduction to Chinese Civilization, ed. John Meskill, with the assistance of J. Mason Gentzler 1973
An Introduction to Japanese Civilization, ed. Arthur E. Tiedemann 1974
Ukifune: Love in the Tale of Genji, ed. Andrew Pekarik 1982
The Pleasures of Japanese Literature, by Donald Keene 1988
A Guide to Oriental Classics, ed. Wm. Theodore de Bary and Ainslie T. Embree; third edition ed. Amy Vladek Heinrich, 2 vols. 1989

Introduction to Asian Civilizations

Wm. Theodore de Bary, Editor
Sources of Japanese Tradition, 1958; paperback ed., 2 vols., 1964
Sources of Indian Tradition, 1958; paperback ed., 2 vols., 1964; 2d ed., 1988
Sources of Indian Tradition, 1988; 2d ed., 2 vols.
Sources of Chinese Tradition, 1960; paperback ed., 2 vols., 1964

Neo-Confucian Studies

Instructions for Practical Living and Other Neo-Confucian Writings by Wang Yang-ming, tr. Wing-tsit China 1963

Reflections on Things at Hand: The Neo-Confucian Anthology, comp. Chu Hsi
   and Lü Tsu-ch'ien, tr. Wing-tsit Chan   1967
Self and Society in Ming Thought, by Wm. Theodore de Bary and the
   Conference on Ming Thought: Also in paperback ed.   1970
The Unfolding of Neo-Confucianism, by Wm. Theodore de Bary and the
   Conference on Seventeenth-Century Chinese Thought. Also in
   paperback ed.   1975
Principle and Practicality: Essays in Neo-Confucianism and Practical Learning, ed.
   Wm. Theodore de Bary and Irene Bloom. Also in paperback ed.   1979
The Syncretic Religion of Lin Chao-en, by Judith A. Berling   1980
The Renewal of Buddhism in China: Chu-hung and the Late Ming Synthesis, by
   Chün-fang Yü   1981
Neo-Confucian Orthodoxy and the Learning of the Mind-and-Heart, by
   Wm. Theodore de Bary   1981
Yüan Thought: Chinese Thought and Religion Under the Mongols, ed. Hok-lam
   Chan and Wm. Theodore de Bary   1982
The Liberal Tradition in China, by Wm. Theodore de Bary   1983
The Development and Decline of Chinese Cosmology, by John B. Henderson   1984
The Rise of Neo-Confucianism in Korea, by Wm. Theodore de Bary and
   JaHyun Kim Habouch   1985
Chiao Hung and the Restructuring of Neo-Confucianism in Late Ming, by Edward
   T. Ch'ien   1985
Neo-Confucian Terms Explained: Pei-hsi tzu-i, by Ch'en Ch'un, ed. and trans.
   Wing-tsit Chan   1986
Knowledge Painfully Acquired: K'un-chih chi, by Lo Ch'in-shun, ed. and trans.
   Irene Bloom   1987
To Become a Sage: The Ten Diagrams on Sage Learning, by Yi T'oegye, ed. and
   trans. Michael C. Kalton   1988
The Message of the Mind in Neo-Confucian Thought, by Wm. Theodore de Bary 1989

Modern Asian Literature Series

Modern Japanese Drama: An Anthology, ed. and tr. Ted Takaya. Also in
   paperback ed.   1979
Mask and Sword: Two Plays for the Contemporary Japanese Theater, Yamazaki
   Masakazu, tr. J. Thomas Rimer   1980
Yokomitsu Riichi, Modernist, Dennis Keene   1980
Nepali Visions, Nepali Dreams: The Poetry of Laxmiprasad Devkota, tr. David
   Rubin   1980
Literature of the Hundred Flowers, vol. 1: *Criticism and Polemics,* ed. Hualing
   Nieh   1981
Literature of the Hundred Flowers, vol. 2: *Poetry and Fiction,* ed. Hualing Nieh   1981
Modern Chinese Stories and Novellas, 1919–1949, ed. Joseph S. M. Lau, C. T.
   Hsia, and Leo Ou-fan Lee. Also in paperback ed.   1984

A View of the Sea, by Yasuoka Shōtarō, tr. Kären Wigen Lewis   1984
Other Worlds, Arishima Takeo and the Bounds of Modern Japanese Fiction, by Paul
    Anderer   1984
Selected Poems of Sō Chōngju, tr. with intro. by David R. McCann   1989
The Sting of Life: Four Contemporary Japanese Novelists, by Van C. Gessel   1989
Stories of Osaka Life, by Oda Sakunosuke, tr. Burton Watson   1990
The Bodhisattva, or Samantabhadra, by Ishikawa Jun, tr. with intro. by
    William Jefferson Tyler   1990

Designer: Linda Secondari
Text: 11.5 / 13 Perpetua
Compositor: The Composing Room of Michigan, Inc.
Printer: Edward Brothers
Binder: Edward Brothers